ROUTLEDGE LIBRARY EDITIONS:
SOVIET SOCIETY

Volume 4

DE-STALINIZATION AND
THE HOUSE OF CULTURE

DE-STALINIZATION AND THE HOUSE OF CULTURE

Declining State Control over Leisure in the USSR, Poland and Hungary, 1953–89

ANNE WHITE

Routledge
Taylor & Francis Group

LONDON AND NEW YORK

First published in 1990 by Routledge

This edition first published in 2025
by Routledge
4 Park Square, Milton Park, Abingdon, Oxon OX14 4RN

and by Routledge
605 Third Avenue, New York, NY 10158

Routledge is an imprint of the Taylor & Francis Group, an informa business

British Library Cataloguing in Publication Data
A catalogue record for this book is available from the British Library

ISBN: 978-1-032-86028-2 (Set)
ISBN: 978-1-032-88538-4 (Volume 4) (hbk)
ISBN: 978-1-032-88541-4 (Volume 4) (pbk)
ISBN: 978-1-003-53832-5 (Volume 4) (ebk)

DOI: 10.4324/9781003538325

Publisher's Note
The publisher has gone to great lengths to ensure the quality of this reprint but
points out that some imperfections in the original copies may be apparent.

Disclaimer
The publisher has made every effort to trace copyright holders and would
welcome correspondence from those they have been unable to trace.

De-Stalinization and the House of Culture

Declining state control over leisure in the USSR, Poland and Hungary, 1953–89

Anne White

London and New York

First published 1990
by Routledge
11 New Fetter Lane, London EC4P 4EE

Simultaneously published in the USA and Canada
by Routledge
a division of Routledge, Chapman and Hall, Inc.
29 West 35th Street, New York, NY 10001

© 1990 Anne White

Typeset by LaserScript Limited, Mitcham, Surrey

Printed and bound in Great Britain by
Mackays of Chatham PLC, Chatham, Kent

British Library Cataloguing in Publication Data

White, Anne
    De-Stalinization and the House of Culture : declining
    state control over leisure in the USSR, Poland and Hungary, 1953–1989.
    1. USSR. Political Socialisation. Ideology. Public opinion. Policies of
government.
    I. Title
    306'.48'0947

ISBN 0-415-04244-5

Library of Congress Cataloging in Publication Data

White, Anne, 1959–
De-Stalinization and the house of culture : declining state control over leisure
in the USSR, Poland, and Hungary, 1953–1989 / Anne White.
    p.   cm.
Includes bibliographical references.
ISBN 0-415-04244-5
1. Recreation and state—Soviet Union. 2. Recreation and state—Poland.
3. Recreation and state—Hungary. 4. Soviet Union—Cultural policy.
5. Poland—Cultural policy. 6. Hungary—Cultural policy. I. Title.
GV93.W47 1990
306.4'8—dc20   89–10974
                                                                      CIP

Contents

List of tables		vi
Acknowledgements		vii
List of abbreviations and administrative divisions		ix
Introduction		1
1	De-Stalinization, ideology and leisure policy	9
2	A brief history of cultural enlightenment	31
3	Changing content – changing goals?	69
4	Policy and practice 1: party and state	96
5	Policy and practice 2: house of culture staff and the public	114
6	The effectiveness of cultural enlightenment	131
7	Conclusions: the death of Communist cultural enlightenment?	151
	Notes	160
	Bibliography	178
	Index	190

Tables

1 Russian and Polish repertoire material 1986–7.   75
2 Party membership among Soviet club workers, cultural
  officials and Institute of Culture students and staff.   99
3 'How, in your opinion, is the profession of cultural worker
  regarded in society?' The status of cultural-enlightenment
  workers in the USSR.   121
4 Attendance of 992 Kashubians at houses of culture, clubs and
  swietlice, 1970–1, by socio-professional status and place of
  residence.   142
5 Hungarian house of culture users, by education.   143
6 'Why do you visit the house of culture?' The responses of
  8,170 Hungarian house of culture users.   146

Acknowledgements

The visits to houses of culture which form the basis for much of this book were always entertaining, whether they involved listening to ancient bagpipes in Poznań or an atheist lecture in a remote Russian village, watching *The Good Soldier Švejk* on stage in Budapest or singing 'The whole world knows our [wooden] spoons' in Leningrad. I should like to begin by thanking the many performers and house of culture employees who participated in these events.

I am also very grateful to those cultural-enlightenment workers whom I interviewed in 1985–8 in Leningrad, Moscow, Voronezh, Poznań, Warsaw, Debrecen, Hajdúböszörmény, Budapest and London. I should like to thank too the specialists whom I interviewed in the following institutions: Leningrad Institute of Culture; Poznań University Institutes of Cultural Studies and Education; Cultural-Enlightenment Institute, Budapest; Leningrad, Moscow, RSFSR and Voronezh *oblast'* methodological centres for popular creativity and cultural enlightenment; Higher Trade Union School of Culture, Leningrad; All-Union Society for Blind People, Leningrad branch; Culture Research Institute of the RSFSR ministry of culture and Academy of Sciences; Philosophy Institute, USSR Academy of Sciences; Institute of Culture of the ministry of culture and art and Central Cultural Diffusion Methodological Centre, Warsaw; Debrecen Literary Museum; Budapest Cultural Centre. József Kargul and Garbriele Gorzka generously sent me copies of their books on Polish cultural enlightenment and Soviet workers' clubs after 1917. I am also indebted to Irina Olegina in the History Department of Leningrad University who supervised my Ph.D. research in 1987.

I am grateful for help and (in Eastern Europe) tea and cake from librarians at: the British Library of Political and Economic Science and the School of Slavonic and East European Studies (University of London); the British Library; Bath University Library; the Academy of Sciences and Saltykov–Shchedrin Libraries and Shelgunov Palace of Culture in Leningrad; the Lenin Library and Culture Research Institute,

Moscow; Institute of Culture, Warsaw; Institute of Cultural Studies and University Library, Poznań; Cultural-Enlightenment Institute, Budapest; Déri Museum, Debrecen.

The Economic and Social Research Council funded the Ph.D. (for the Government and Sociology Departments of the London School of Economics and Political Science) on which this book is based. The British Council arranged research visits to the USSR in 1987 and 1988 (as well as an undergraduate scholarship in 1981–82, which also furnished material for the book) and visits to Hungary in 1983 and 1987.

Finally, I should like to thank my Ph.D. supervisors George Schöpflin, Peter Reddaway and Elizabeth Weinberg, and my husband Howard, for all their criticisms, suggestions and support.

Anne White

Abbreviations

CC	Central Committee
CRZZ	Centralna Rada Związków Zawodowych (Central Trade Union Council)
DK	Dom kultury/kul'tury (house of culture)
GOK	Gminny Ośrodek Kultury (Commune Cultural Centre)
gorkom	town/city party committee
HNF	Hazafias Népfront (Patriotic People's Front)
KISZ	Kommunista Ifjúság Szövetsége (Communist Youth Union)
KPSS	Kommunisticheskaia Partiia Sovetskogo Soiuza (Communist Party of the Soviet Union)
MSZMP	Magyar Szocialista Munkáspárt (Hungarian Socialist Workers' Party)
NI	Népmüvészeti/Népmüvelési Intézet (Popular Art/Cultural-Enlightenment Institute, from 1987 the National Cultural-Enlightenment Centre (Országos Közmüvelödési Központ))
obkom	*oblast'* party committee
ONT/OKT	Országos Népmüvelési/Közmüvelödési Tanács (National Cultural-Enlightenment Council)
partkom	party committee
PZPR	Polska Zjednoczona Partia Robotnicza (Poland United Workers' Party)
raikom	raion party committee
SK	Sovetskaia Kul'tura
SZOT	Szakszervezetek Országos Tanácsa (National Trade Union Council)
TIT	Tudományos Ismeretterjesztö Társulat (Society for the Dissemination of Knowledge)
TWP	Towarzystwo Wiedzy Powszechnej (Popular Knowledge Society)

VTsSPS	Vsesoiuzny Tsentralny Sovet Professional'nykh Soiuzov (All-Union Central Trade Union Council)
Znanie	Obshchestvo 'Znanie' (Knowledge Society)
ZSL	Zjednoczone Stronnictwo Ludowe (United Peasant Party)

Administrative divisions

USSR

oblast'	province
krai	region, of mixed ethnic composition
raion	district, county, borough

Poland

województwo	province
powiat (to 1972)	district, county
gmina (from 1972)	smaller district, commune

Hungary

| *county (megye)* | largest administrative unit |
| *járás* | district |

Introduction

What is there in common between breakdancing in Leningrad, astrology in Poznań and sex counselling in Budapest? Probably the only possible answer is that they all take place in official 'houses of culture' and huddle under the motley and somewhat tattered umbrella of 'cultural enlightenment'. In the early 1950s, this umbrella covered far fewer but, at the same time, more intensely political activities: folk dancing and choral odes to Stalin everywhere from Khabarovsk to Kaposvár, with the odd dancing bear poking his nose in by mistake. The umbrella of cultural enlightenment also served to protect citizens from undesirable Western or 'bourgeois' cultural influences, a function which it now performs very imperfectly indeed.

How and why has change in this one area of official socialization policy taken place? This study analyses the fate of cultural enlightenment in an endeavour to shed light on broader political and social developments in the Soviet Union and two East-Central European countries since the Stalinist era. In other words, developments in cultural-enlightenment policy are studied as an aid towards understanding and comparing de-Stalinization in three Soviet-type systems. De-Stalinization is understood as an uneven and incomplete process lasting from 1953 to the present day.

As an activity organized by the regime in Soviet-type systems, cultural enlightenment is an area of ideological work. It involves the socialization of adults and children in their spare time through participation in non-professional arts and other cultural activities. It supplements the work of the formal education system and the mass media as a method of socialization, inculcating values and mobilizing the population over particular issues. Its three basic principles are belief in the need to equalize access to culture, belief that such access can change human behaviour, and belief that the party can and must control the nature of the culture which is created or provided.

Cultural enlightenment usually takes place in a collective setting. It is the central activity in clubs, in houses and palaces of culture and in

1

adult education organizations such as 'free' or 'people's' universities and 'societies for the dissemination of knowledge'. Houses of culture and clubs may be run either directly by the state administration, or else by trade unions and enterprises, collective farms, housing co-operatives, or cultural and other organizations.

Cultural enlightenment is not a Communist Party creation: it has a long history in all three countries as well as approximate equivalents in other, pluralist systems. Cultural enlightenment in this sense is more amorphous than the official Communist variety. It shares the principles of equalizing access to culture and faith in the power of art and education, but not that of Communist Party guidance. This type of cultural enlightenment has re-emerged in all three countries in periods of rapid de-Stalinization, and has been conducted by autonomous or 'informal' organizations, which have often been critical of the existing system. This study is primarily concerned with 'official' cultural-enlightenment policy, but unofficial culture cannot be ignored. After all, official policy reacts to unofficial cultural developments. Moreover, unofficial cultural enlightenment is often more successful than its official counterpart for reasons which shed light on why the official system fails.

The core activities organized officially by houses of culture and similar institutions from 1953 to 1989 consisted of amateur theatricals, music-making and dance; non-school education in the form of courses and lectures; entertainments such as films, dances and performances by visiting professional and local amateur groups; and new socialist rites and festivals. Since the 1960s and particularly in recent years there has also been an expansion of small clubs and associations where people can pursue specialist interests within a house of culture or under the auspices of another official institution like a university or ministry.

The more traditional activities have often been designed to slot into one or other of the categories of official socialization. A model house of culture might, for example, organize a concert on a patriotic theme on Friday, a lecture on the international political situation on Saturday and an amateur play about family problems on Sunday, meanwhile devoting its foyer space to an exhibition of photographs of outstanding local workers. The themes of cultural-enlightenment activities have often reflected those of current political campaigns, particularly in Gierek's Poland and in the Soviet Union. Today, however, it is only in the Soviet Union that houses of culture seriously attempt to emulate the model just described, and as will be shown, even there they often do so only by stretching definitions. To some extent, especially in Poland and Hungary, entertainment has been recognized as a valid additional or even alternative objective to socialization, although it would be simplistic to see a clear-cut dichotomy of entertainment versus ideology.

2

Cultural enlightenment has many other potential functions, cultural, educational and social, which do not necessarily fit into the schematic strait-jacket of the Stalinist period, and it is these which have largely found expression in the new small clubs and associations which have mushroomed since the 1960s.

By making participation in the arts and non-school education available to everyone, cultural-enlightenment institutions are supposed to improve the quality of life and diminish social inequalities. The main objectives of cultural policy in all three countries are to provide equal access to culture for all members of society and to 'raise the level of culture' in society by state patronage of 'socialist' culture. Cultural enlightenment is actively concerned with both objectives, whereas participation in or even attendance at exhibitions or performances by professionals is more elitist in character and presupposes the attainment of a certain level of education or training. Cultural enlightenment can provide an introduction to professional arts. It is socialization 'through culture' but also 'for culture'.[1]

Moreover, cultural enlightenment has a preventative and supervisory role: it is intended to ward off social problems. It is supposed to guide young people into officially accepted leisure pursuits, prevent the formation of alternative or counter-cultures and contribute to the elimination of social evils such as crime, drunkenness and drug addiction in favour of more 'cultured' leisure activities. In addition, by these and other measures it should attempt to strengthen family and other approved group loyalties. Further goals – more commonly expressed in East European than in Soviet sources – include community development, and the integration of immigrants into new environments and of disabled people, ex-prisoners and other disadvantaged groups into society.

These are ambitious goals, and many institutions and organizations share some responsibility for cultural enlightenment, even though this is only one part of their activities. Particularly involved in this partial sense are libraries, museums, theatres and cinemas – acting in a specifically educational capacity – and the Main Political Administrations of the armed forces.

Cultural enlightenment is often described in Soviet and East European sources as 'an integral component of ideological work'.[2] The central question examined in this book is: how far has this been true over the period 1953–89, and is it true today? The answer to this question should contribute to our understanding of some wider issues connected with de-Stalinization and the relationship between ideology and culture. The first is the extent to which the Communist Party has attempted to maintain control over leisure time as a whole, and how far such control is possible. The second, related issue concerns policy making: the role of society in the formation of cultural policy as opposed to Moscow, the local party/state apparatus, established doctrine or bureaucratic inertia. How flexible has cultural policy in each of the countries proved to be, and how much room for adaptability can there be in a Soviet-type system? What are the parameters of reform? Finally, there is the issue of the effectiveness of official policy. How successfully has cultural enlightenment helped to realize social goals in the sphere of culture? Why do people participate in cultural enlightenment – or not?

The main conclusions of the book may be presented as answers to the issues raised in the previous paragraph. Briefly, and in the same order, they are as follows.

Social changes – notably widespread disillusionment with, and rejection of, Stalinism and Stalinist cultural institutions, the spread of television and individual flat ownership, higher educational levels, the emergence of organized dissent and the greater exposure of ordinary citizens to Western culture – had led to a situation by the 1980s in which the leading role of the party in determining how leisure time was spent was becoming seriously eroded.

After the Stalinist period most citizens could choose how to spend their leisure time and reacted against the type of collective, socializing leisure activities into which they had previously been forced. They either opted not to spend their free time in official cultural institutions or else attempted to use houses of culture for the activities which *they* preferred. The regimes made concessions to society in order to gain at least a modicum of legitimacy, and abandoned their more Utopian aspirations.

The three countries made this transition at different speeds and have gone to different lengths in permitting the de-ideologization of cultural enlightenment. (Initially Poland was the most flexible and liberal, but it was overtaken by Hungary in the 1970s.) This transition has relevance not only to the abandonment, to whatever extent, of Stalinist forms of political socialization, but correspondingly also to the development of what began to replace it in periods of intense de-Stalinization and social renewal: *glasnost'* and democratization, the acceptance of a diversity of political opinion and the creation of independent cultural/political organizations which could to some extent play the role of, or ultimately possibly be transformed into, political parties. (Such independent organizations have often begun their lives in connection with cultural-enlightenment activities, frequently using the premises of a house of culture, or as intellectual discussion clubs. Examples include the Petofi Club in 1956 with its strong interest in 'people's colleges', Polish Catholic Intellectuals' Clubs in the 1970s, or the 'unofficial club movement' in the Soviet Union today.) The boundary between acceptability and its opposite lies where the party perceives its leading role to be in danger, rather than where cultural enlightenment ceases to perform the function of political socialization (which often occurs at a much earlier stage).

The success of the regimes' social policies for cultural enlightenment can really only be judged in any quantitative fashion for the 1970s and 1980s. There is little survey evidence available before this period, so our main sources must be official statistics, policy statements and descriptions in newspapers and journals, many of which are concerned with 'propaganda of success'. Surveys, when they appear, also vary in quality, and must be treated with care, but in the best cases they have contributed to undermining the 'propaganda of success'. The information available suggests that cultural enlightenment has contributed to widening access to culture, although participants are still on average better-educated and contain a higher proportion of members of the intelligentsia than the population at large. Cultural enlightenment has been notably more successful among children than among adults.

Cultural enlightenment can be a success when participants feel interested and genuinely involved. Much depends on resources, material and human. However, even when an individual institution enjoys local success and acquires 'authenticity', its visitors do not necessarily conclude that the official cultural system as a whole is legitimate: exceptions sometimes seem to be viewed as proving the rule.

Often success is also dependent on the non-political nature of the activities organized. Occasionally, there is even an element of opposition to official policies and cultural enlightenment functions as an umbrella for pressure groups or shelters alternative cultural pursuits. This reflects the original role of cultural enlightenment before the Communist takeovers (for instance in keeping alive Polish culture under the partitions), but is diametrically opposed to the function of Stalinist cultural enlightenment. In such cases, official cultural enlightenment becomes dysfunctional.

Cultural enlightenment has been very neglected in English- language scholarship. In fact it is probably true that modern cultural enlighten-ment has not been studied in depth, as an entire system, at all. (There are many valuable studies of aspects of the early Soviet period.)[3] One of the strange features of cultural enlightenment is that the term means nothing to many Western scholars of the USSR and East-Central Europe, while being crystal clear to any Soviet or East European person. The first conceptual problem of my research was therefore to establish the nature of cultural enlightenment. There were two possible approaches to this problem.

The first was to set cultural enlightenment within the context of Western political science and sociology. The most appropriate context proved to be that of socialization. A secondary aspect of cultural enlightenment is that it provides opportunities for political participation. However, the main function of cultural enlightenment has traditionally been described in Russian, Polish and Hungarian as *vospitanie, wychowanie* or *nevelés*. These words literally mean 'bringing up' or 'education', but can more accurately be translated as 'socialization' since the process does not concern only children, nor it is only about the acquisition of information and skills. Instead, it implies learning accepted values and ways of behaviour by people of all ages. Since cultural enlightenment is a form of socialization, it can be placed in the context of Western literature on ideology, political culture and the effectiveness of propaganda work in the USSR and East-Central Europe. The first part of Chapter One therefore surveys some of this literature and its relevance to cultural enlightenment, and vice versa. However, cultural enlightenment can only be properly understood within the context of Soviet and East European assumptions about culture, the nature of political culture and the use of leisure time. The middle part of Chapter One examines these areas. This is a particularly difficult topic since, although official Soviet definitions are reasonably clear, it is harder to determine the real (but often unstated) positions of many Hungarians and Poles – and even of some of the Soviet specialists. These positions often seem to be closer to Western definitions. After exploring these two approaches, it is possible to understand cultural enlightenment more exactly. The third and final section of Chapter One therefore discusses in greater depth the concept of cultural enlightenment (of the officially-approved variety).

The absence of previous analysis was in itself perhaps sufficient reason for undertaking the research, since cultural enlightenment is worthy of study in its own right. It is a ubiquitous feature of East European Communist systems. It is interesting historically since it is a mix of three very different elements, originating from the special political culture of the region, from socialist aspirations towards equality of opportunity for education and self-expression, and from the Leninist identification of culture with political education. The three elements have combined in different proportions on the levels of both theory and practical policy.

Chapter Two provides a historical analysis, sketching out developments which are discussed more thoroughly in later chapters and describing the similar pre-Stalinist and almost identical Stalinist heritage of cultural enlightenment in all three countries, and the very similar problems which cultural enlightenment has encountered since 1953. A working assumption of the book is that Stalinist cultural enlightenment was essentially the same in all three countries, being imposed by the Soviet Union. It was an essential element of the 'Soviet-type system' in its Stalinist form. As part of the process of de-

Stalinization, cultural enlightenment underwent transformation, and the nature of this transformation differed in each of the countries examined. The process reflected (in a distorting mirror) differing social and political developments after 1953. An examination of these transformations in cultural enlightenment can contribute to our analysis of the changing nature of Soviet-type systems and their potential (or lack of the same) for change in general.

The assumption of similarity under Stalin is accurate in so far as concerns the intentions of the policy-makers: cultural enlightenment was supposed to be the same everywhere. In the implementation of policy, this was not quite the case, as Chapters Two and Three suggest. Stalinism was too ambitious a system to be wholly effective, especially in rural areas: hence the wandering bears and wizards who substituted for enlightenment. Moreover, success was hampered in Poland and Hungary by the fact that the people who spread cultural enlightenment, the 'cultural workers', were often either young Communists unskilled in cultural work or else creative artists and teachers untrained and uninterested in – or even opposed to – turning cultural enlightenment into agitation. The latter might not even be aware of important spheres of socialization.[4]

To a certain extent my findings confirm the suggestions of revisionist historians of Stalinism who question the effectiveness of 'totalitarianism' and emphasize the gap between word and deed and the inefficient and haphazard way in which Stalinist policies were implemented. However, my major source of evidence for inadequate work is press reports of the period, which should perhaps be treated with caution. They may have been exaggerated to suggest wrecking in the house of culture and to create an alarmist atmosphere. Moreover, despite inefficiencies in implementation, the evidence on the whole suggests that cultural enlightenment was highly standardized and was very largely forced to be part of the prevailing 'front-line climate'.[5]

Chapters 3 to 5 show how since 1953 the party has found it increasingly difficult to maintain political socialization and social control as the chief functions of the house of culture, and how to a certain extent the latter has become the home of activities which many members of the public and cultural workers consider to be more useful to both the individual and the community. Chapter Three examines how the content of cultural enlightenment has changed and discusses the party's response. Chapters Four and Five adopt a different perspective, investigating where cultural-enlightenment policy is made and how it is implemented. Finally, Chapter Six addresses the question of how far cultural enlightenment is successful in achieving its aims.

The three countries studied were chosen on the grounds that, first, the USSR as the founder of Communist cultural enlightenment was the natural focus of attention. Developments since the research was begun (before Gorbachev's accession) further justify such attention, since in its new innovative phase the USSR may be influential in creating conditions for real change everywhere. Conversely, the USSR is now much readier to borrow from East European experience, and from Hungary and Poland in particular.

Second, Poland and Hungary were chosen as the countries in East–Central Europe where the system has undergone the most substantial de-Stalinization. Moreover, both countries experienced dramatic crises as they struggled with the implications of de-Stalinization, crises which were largely about legitimacy, ideology and culture, and which highlighted the strained points in the cultural-enlightenment system and forced its modification.

The book devotes more attention to the USSR than to either Poland or Hungary; the latter are given approximately equal treatment. In some sections the evidence available was inadequate to permit an equally thorough discussion of all three countries.

Chapter one

De-Stalinization, ideology and leisure policy

Cultural enlightenment and ideology

By analysing cultural enlightenment, the book addresses problems which have relevance for ideological work as a whole, since cultural enlightenment is a vehicle for most such kinds of work. Does the leadership really care any longer whether or not this elaborate system of institutions is used successfully for ideological work? What is its real purpose?

A number of scholars have suggested that the whole socialization effort is not taken seriously any more as a means of legitimation, having been replaced by material guarantees such as job security and a reasonable standard of living as major legitimating factors.[1] If this were true, the implication would be that in the post-Stalinist period cultural enlightenment lost its previous *raison d'être*. However, the traditional system of ideological work is still extant, including houses of culture and all their trappings. Either they do still perform a useful legitimating function or else there are powerful other reasons why they should be kept. It has already been suggested that cultural enlightenment has lost a great deal of legitimacy.[2] Although individual citizens may approve of their local house of culture, they frequently do not approve of the cultural-enlightenment system *as a whole*, because of its associations with Stalinism or with the provision of a primitive cultural 'service'. Cultural enlightenment as a system does not perform a legitimating function. It is therefore worth exploring other possible reasons for the longevity of cultural enlightenment. Some of these reasons became evident in the course of the research, others are hypotheses based on the suggestions of Western scholars about the functions of ideology in general.

It may be that the system remains standing only because of inertia and conservatism, and the 'sacred cow' quality of institutions which are seen as part of the revolutionary tradition and also of the 'way of life' of an advanced socialist society. This is certainly a part of the explanation.

It may also be, as Stephen White has suggested, because there is an 'ideological establishment' with a vested interest in keeping the ideological system going.[3] This too is a convincing partial explanation.

Ideology has important proscriptive functions. Its closed language precludes the formulation and communication of alternative points of view.[4] This affects cultural enlightenment as well as the work of the mass media, literature, art or music. Where cultural enlightenment in particular is concerned, the provision of officially-sanctioned leisure activities frequently coexists with the assumption that what is not officially sponsored is prohibited. Amateur arts and adult education outside the walls of the house of culture or other official institutions is (in theory) always suspect, if not illegal.

Symbol is often more important than substance. It may not be necessary for participants to believe in the ideology, but it remains important for them to go through the motions by publicly participating in cultural enlightenment. This is particularly true in the case of the more ceremonial functions of cultural enlightenment, the new rites and festivals. Finally, cultural enlightenment serves the purpose of reminding the population of power realities. This is most notoriously true in the case of the Warsaw Palace of Culture, Stalin's 'present to Poland', a grotesque skyscraper in a central location on the site of the former Russian Orthodox cathedral (the tsars' present to Poland).

Such negative and symbolic functions undoubtedly form part of the picture, but do not exclude the possibility of other more positive functions for ideology and especially for cultural enlightenment. As has been suggested, cultural enlightenment in particular is principally concerned with socialization. It is perceived as necessary because permanent *adult* socialization is felt to be necessary in Soviet-type systems. This contrasts with the West where socialization – a considerably more spontaneous process – is generally considered to take place during childhood and adolescence. Soviet, Polish and Hungarian children are obviously not considered to be so effectively socialized that no more is necessary, despite the fact that they are the targets of so much conscious and highly-directed socialization in school and youth organizations.

One reason commonly advanced for the existence of large-scale, directed adult socialization is the insecurity of the regime about the efficacy of official childhood socialization, when parents may be inculcating their children with values quite different from those of the regime. The attention paid in all three countries to joint cultural-enlightenment activities for parents and children supports this suggestion. Gayle Hollander emphasizes in addition the importance attached to life-long activism. 'Although people may be successfully socialized to the political order, it is necessary to continually reinforce earlier learning in order to keep them from slipping into apathy.' This prevalent attitude supposes the existence of 'original sin' which has to be constantly expunged.[5]

Another explanation is connected with the *changing* nature of some aspects of the ideology closely connected with particular policies. This requires adults to be informed about the latest policy zigzags. The process of continuous and sometimes contradictory socialization need not necessarily be confusing. If the adult has as a child been successfully socialized into loyalty to a political party or state, he or she may experience no difficulty in adapting to changes in its operative ideology.[6] The sociologist Shlapentokh suggests a 'bi-level concept of Soviet mentality', according to which in addition to stable, private values, citizens have a superficial 'adaptive' layer of mentality which can cope with being required to profess a series of changing and often contradictory beliefs.[7]

However, although cultural enlightenment is in theory intended for both adults and children, in practice it has often become largely concerned with children and young people, indicating a diminishing intention or possibility of using it for adult political socialization. Once again, we are back to the problem of accounting for its continued existence.

In discussing the positive functions of ideology, we need to be clear about exactly what people conceive the ideology and the functions and goals of cultural enlightenment to be. Given the nature of the subject, however, exactitude and clarity are elusive qualities. It is vital to distinguish between the different components or layers of the official ideology. In particular, it is useful to separate the doctrine – consisting of a more or less fixed body of Marxist-Leninist ideas, and accompanying methodology – from the operative or practical ideology, which Ray Taras has defined as 'explanations and justifications of policy formulated'.[8] In addition, the operative ideology can provide a form of legitimation acceptable to a specific society or audience, as in the case of the slogan 'the Soviet way of life' of the 1970s.[9]

Obviously the distinction is a crucial one to consider when addressing the question of whether ideology is taken seriously, and if so by whom. In each context, does 'ideology' mean doctrine or operative ideology? For example: it was possible to be a convinced Marxist but cynical about the cult of Stalin; alternatively, for most people it was probably easier to believe in Stalin, not fully understanding Marxist philosophy. Cultural enlightenment is taken seriously on the levels of both doctrine and operative ideology, but often by different people.

In the case of cultural enlightenment, I understand the *doctrine* to include the humanist and egalitarian ideals of socialist cultural policy, faith in 'creative activity' and belief in the perfectability of individuals and society. I refer to people who believe in some or all of these aspects of the ideology as 'enthusiasts'. George Lukács is perhaps their outstanding representative. Through art, Lukács believed, the individual could experience unity with the species, temporarily attain true consciousness and from such artistic experience develop the rounded personality of Marx's vision. Aesthetic education and access to art must therefore be provided for everyone.[10]

The *operative ideology*, i.e. the ideas and beliefs justifying and supporting current policies, is reflected in first, the everyday process of socialization into the values and forms of behaviour necessary for the building and maintenance of the regime and second, campaigns specifically concerned with the furtherance of short-term policies. Those who see cultural enlightenment's functions as lying in this field I call 'manipulators'. Examples of such manipulation are, for example, the saturation of East European amateur arts with Soviet culture or Soviet songs about the wonders of maize or the dangers of 'Star Wars'. Equally manipulative are socialist rites of passage like the simultaneous glorification of labour and temperance in the celebration of young Siberian tractor drivers' first harvest with the ceremonious presentation of a flask of mint tea ('the Siberian's favourite drink').[11]

Frequently, activities which seem to be perfectly in tune with the doctrine may also be examples of open or covert manipulation. For example, equalizing access to culture and developing individual creativity for its own sake may be hard to distinguish from the homogenization of society for the avoidance of conflict and the encouragement of initiative (such as technological inventiveness) which can be channelled by the regime for its own purposes. Both these ambiguities are found within the concept of developed socialism.

On the whole, the evidence suggests that cultural enlightenment has become de-politicized to a large extent, although, in the area and period studied, this was most true for Hungary and for Poland pre- and post-Gierek.[12] Cultural enlightenment has been able to partially escape from the clutches of the operative ideology and either become wholly non-ideological or else recover some of the values of the doctrine (which largely coincided with pre-revolutionary values). This marked a failure on the part of the manipulators. However, this did not mean that there has been a happy ending. The process is not yet complete and until late 1988/early 1989 it was difficult to imagine the party, especially in the USSR, willingly relinquishing its power to dictate over leisure spending, for example, by allowing the continued existence of unregistered clubs and associations. However, it may now have accepted that the latter situation is unavoidable. If the manipulators among the leadership decide to wash their hands of cultural enlightenment then they will be very unlikely to continue to support it financially – a disengagement which has already begun, and which must lead to either a collapse of a considerable part of the system or, as is already happening, much greater commercialization. This is incompatible with the goals of the 'enthusiasts'.

Who exactly are these manipulators and enthusiasts? The top leadership has generally fallen into the category of 'manipulators'. Apart from Khrushchev and Imre Nagy none of the post-Stalin leaders can probably be seen as an idealistic Marxist-Leninist, although Gorbachev is more of an enthusiast than a manipulator. According to the testimony of Zdeněk Mlynář, as a student Gorbachev was critical of propaganda which projected a false view of reality, but believed both in the fundamental doctrine and in its relevance for helping to meet people's real needs.[13] This seems likely to be an accurate description of how Gorbachev thinks today. However, the political leadership and middle-ranking bureaucrats in general seem to have viewed 'cultural enlightenment' (in their very impoverished understanding of the concept) as a means of manipulation (even if they have decreasingly considered it to be very effective), and in this they have been supported by conservatives at all levels.

The Polish cultural-enlightenment specialist Józef Kargul writes, for example, about the

> instrumental use of the [Polish] house of culture: instrumental in the sense that it has been and in some cases remains today a tool in the hands of local politicians and the organizers of community affairs, who with manipulative reasoning and argument oblige the houses of culture to pursue short-term and secondary goals which are out of line with local expectations.[14]

However, the fact that cultural enlightenment has over the period become decreasingly manipulative and increasingly abandoned to the enthusiasts suggests that the top leadership does not really view it as an effective tool. They continue to list it among the 'weapons in the arsenal of socialization work', but this may be out of force of habit or from a need to believe that, if they have a 'whole arsenal' of unreliable weapons at their disposal, then at least some of the weapons may go off some of the time.

Cultural enlightenment is also dismissed as irrelevant and manipulative by cynical members of the public who are themselves uninvolved in cultural enlightenment. This phenomenon has clearly traceable historical roots, since traditionally in all three countries before the Stalinist period there was considerable public faith in the importance of cultural enlightenment. If we think of 'decline' in the ideology in terms of the decline of intellectual respectability of Marxism-Leninism which took place under Stalin, and, as a consequence, the decline in popular acceptance of official socialization, then this process is very clearly illustrated by the history of cultural enlightenment. The process of disillusionment was described in the Hungarian journal *Népmüvelés* in 1985:

> Houses of culture, when they were established in the 1950s, were not without precedent. For hundreds of years various social classes and strata had created their own forms and frameworks for cultural and communal activity. Houses of culture tried to substitute for those among the rainbow of traditional activities which were judged 'progressive'. But today we can see that this 'nationalization' turned the system grey. The population's attitude to houses of culture is usually a passive one, and rarely do these institutions become the scene for lively and path-breaking work.[15]

József Kargul, describing the same phenomenon, points out that 'myths and stereotypes [dating from the Stalinist era] are passed on from generation to generation, and it is very difficult or even quite impossible to dispel them... and for the house of culture to acquire authority'.[16]

As a result of this loss of credibility, official cultural enlightenment lost much of its inspirational Utopian character. In so far as its brief remained political, it partly acquired a negative, containing and excluding role. By extension, cultural- enlightenment policy in Poland and Hungary became very largely reactive to the threats posed by unofficial cultural currents and by political crises which usually contained a strong cultural element.

However, this does not mean that the entire population rejects cultural enlightenment as 'inauthentic' (a favourite Polish term). On the contrary, where cultural enlightenment has largely escaped from operative ideology in practice, people who happen to become involved in cultural enlightenment are often enthusiastic participants of one individual section of cultural enlightenment, even if they feel antagonistic towards the cultural-enlightenment system as a whole. It is not only Communists who attend houses of culture, despite the fact that houses of culture as a species are strongly identified with the regime or even with Stalinism, and are regarded as part of what the Hungarian sociologist Hankiss terms the 'first society': formal institutions and values which are remote from citizens' real concerns.[17]

My research suggests that the extreme views of some Western scholars, that no one even in the USSR believes in the ideology, are really not tenable, at least in the area of cultural enlightenment. Some people have taken, and do take, cultural enlightenment seriously and at face value, and these people have been important and numerous. Their attitudes may reflect a conscious identification with the humanist and egalitarian aspects of the official ideology, and awareness (especially in

Hungary and Poland) of the possibilities of using cultural enlightenment to spread traditional, pre-Communist culture and values, or else may simply be based on ignorance or ignoral of the ideological aspects of cultural enlightenment. To elaborate on the last point: it is possible for consumers to enjoy educational and artistic activity and ignore any fictional ideological gloss. Thus, for example, both choirmaster and participants in a house of culture Russian folk choir in which I sang in 1987 seemed to be entirely interested in voice training and singing for its own sake. However, at a concert in which the choir participated, every song was prefaced with some lines of patriotic verse or sentimental prose. This apparently artificial device presumably allowed the choir's contribution to be put down in the appropriate report as providing 'patriotic education': a function which was never mentioned to me by the choir members themselves.

Throughout this period many of the people professionally involved in cultural enlightenment have been enthusiasts and not manipulators. Many administrators, scholars and cultural workers have genuinely believed in the cause of making culture accessible to the whole population and helping people to develop their creative abilities. Contrary to frequently expressed opinion, specialists in ideology and cultural administrators are not all hacks, and those I interviewed and met in all three countries were, on the whole, committed, intelligent and serious people who were trying to provide an effective service often in the face of great financial and other difficulties. The same was true of many of the people working in houses of culture and clubs. Many cultural-enlightenment workers grow disillusioned and cynical with time; but then they often leave and are replaced by a new cohort of enthusiasts (as often seems to happen in British arts centres and is no doubt a universal pattern where art is underfunded and working hours are long and inconvenient).

Political culture and the effectiveness of ideological work

To discover how the ordinary public perceives cultural enlightenment we need to examine its effectiveness, which is also an important subject in its own right. Of course, the question of effectiveness is irrelevant to those who deny ideology a positive role. If the main function of ideology was as a legitimating factor, and if the population now recognizes the legitimacy of the regime thanks instead to the fact that it enjoys a reasonable standard of living, then the socialization system does not have to be efficient. I have argued that on the contrary ideological work – of some types – is taken seriously, by some people. Even if it is not a legitimating factor, it is still seen as useful (by enthusiasts) for satisfying cultural 'needs', and (by manipulators) for averting or eliminating social problems. If this is so, then the question of effectiveness must be of issue. Of British and American scholars, Stephen White and Ellen Mickiewicz have been particularly interested in the effectiveness of propaganda. In general they doubt whether it is very successful.[18] Victor Zaslavsky, on the other hand, demonstrates the effectiveness of socialization in the army, as shown by the responses to an unofficial survey of attitudes towards the invasion of Czechoslovakia. Overall, however, he suggests that socialization work is not very effective.[19] This book arrives at the same conclusion, although with the qualifications made in the previous paragraph.

Lack of evidence and the complicated character of causation are among the more formidable of the 'brambles at the foot of the mountain' among which, according to Mary McAuley, scholars writing about political culture are currently struggling in their attempt to assess how successfully Communist regimes have been able to change the traditional political culture and replace it with 'socialist' values.[20] Socialization work is an essential component of this effort. If effectiveness is defined as the successful changing of the pre-revolutionary political culture then socialization policy can be seen as a kind of struggle waged against 'vestiges of past': a straightforward and even Soviet approach. The complexities arise because the process is in reality not one of replacing one set of ideas and values ('bourgeois') with a totally different set ('socialist') (as Lenin, for example, realized); instead there is substantial overlap. So, Stephen White and others argue, the continuing existence of certain values desired by or supportive of the regime reflects the survival of the pre-revolutionary political culture, rather than successful indoctrination by the regime, whose official socialization efforts have had little success where they have been in conflict with the pre-Communist political culture. Moreover, the new political culture is fed by the old, which provides ideas and symbols which are adapted by the new regime for its own purposes.[21]

This would seem to be exactly what has occurred in cultural enlightenment in Poland and Hungary, and possibly also in the Soviet Union, wherever the manipulative and over-formalistic approaches typical of the Stalinist period have been overcome, and cultural enlightenment has recovered a more spontaneous and small-scale character. However, it would be unwise to attribute too much weight to the effect of pre-revolutionary political culture in the USSR. It is now so long since 1917 and Soviet attitudes towards the Tsarist period are so contradictory, compared to those of Poles and Hungarians towards the pre-revolutionary period, that it is hard to believe that the old political culture is very influential in cultural enlightenment in the USSR today. Rather, in the USSR as in all three countries traditional attitudes towards cultural enlightenment have been strengthened and also developed by ideas about how to solve the particular problems of contemporary society. Often (especially in Poland and Hungary) these ideas have been Western in origin and applicable equally to East and West.

Culture and political culture: Soviet, Polish and Hungarian concepts

Fortunately it is not the purpose of this book to define 'culture'. However, some brief discussion of how the word is used, and of the functions attributed to culture, is necessary in order to understand the nature of cultural enlightenment. In English, 'culture' may be used in a narrower or a broader sense. The narrower, more colloquial usage refers to 'artistic and intellectual life'.[22] The broader, anthropological usage refers to a way of life and civilization. The distinction is fairly clear-cut. Contemporary Polish and Hungarian writers recognize the same distinction although they sometimes describe it as insubstantial, because culture in the narrower sense cannot be disassociated from its social context.[23] Even Soviet authors may mention the two meanings of culture although they insist that it is incorrect to use 'culture' in the narrower sense: 'spiritual (that is, non-material) culture' is more correct.[24] In the opinion of these more conventional Marxist-Leninists, it is a bourgeois fallacy to separate the sphere of culture from that of social and economic life.

Marxist writers – even those who are not theorists or sociologists of culture – cannot make a tidy distinction after the manner of everyday English usage. 'Culture' cannot be separated off from political institutions and political and social behaviour, class consciousness, the social structure, and ultimately the relations of production. This leads to extremely broad definitions of culture, which is understood to include material production and social relations as well as intellectual and artistic creation and its products.[25]

Marx himself 'never developed a systematic *theory* of culture'. Sometimes Marx seems to view culture as something higher than ordinary production, which can only be created after basic productive needs are satisfied, and only achieve its full development in a Communist society. At other times, he sees all productive activity as part of culture.[26] Culture is an elusive concept which does not fit neatly into either the base or the superstructure. Iván Vitányi believes that Marx, Engels and Lenin all understood that instead culture could be considered to belong to both, and that the relationship was one of mutual influence, upwards and downwards.[27] Hence Lenin's insistence on the need to preserve the best of Russia's cultural heritage and use it to build a more cultured society. Stalin's understanding was simpler: culture was part of the superstructure. Even when in 1950 he turned against Marrism in linguistics and asserted that *language* was part of the base, he still denied that this was true of culture as a whole.[28] However, many commentators have pointed out that this was the logical extension of his argument, since language can hardly be separated from culture.

Lenin believed that art could and should be used for propaganda, and that cultural enlightenment – primarily the literacy campaign – was a vehicle for political socialization and the extension of bolshevik power. However, he did not equate art with propaganda. Creative artists were not forced to become apologists for the regime. This was a Stalinist phenomenon; although, as Sheila Fitzpatrick and others have shown, the 'cultural revolution' of the first five year plan cannot be attributed to Stalin alone: it had a wider base of support.[29] Stalin, however, was personally responsible for the post-war doctrine that the principles of Pavlovian animal psychology held for humans, and that people were merely objects ready to respond to the signals of propaganda.[30]

The cruder strains of Stalinism were abandoned after 1953, but an instrumental approach to culture, equating indoctrination and cultural policy, persisted among the political leadership and party/state apparatus. For example, Brezhnev stated in November 1964: 'The creation of good cultural and general everyday living conditions is a mighty lever for raising productivity on collective and state farms.'[31] As ideological attack evolved into system maintenance and consumerist policies, culture was often reduced to being merely a 'service'.

De-Stalinization created the conditions for philosophers and sociologists to re-examine the nature of culture, taking a fresh look at the classics of Marxism-Leninism. East European scholars also discussed the ideas of their Western colleagues and participated in international intellectual movements and debates, while Soviet cultural specialists remained insular by comparison.[32] Vitányi, Kloskowska, Kmita and many others created within Hungary and Poland independent and flourishing new disciplines of cultural theory and sociology. Simultaneously or slightly lagging behind these developments, cultural enlightenment began to find its feet as an academic discipline – very much within the context of this wider theoretical activity. (Another stimulus was the practical need to train more specialized and highly-educated cultural-enlightenment workers.) A 1980 Hungarian survey of recent work in cultural studies identified the effectiveness of cultural enlightenment as one of the three major areas of current research in the theory and sociology of culture.[33]

Since Marxist theory is historical, culture is naturally viewed within a historical framework. There is a tendency to refer to the 'level of culture' which bears some (not always corresponding) relation to the level of social and political development and which in a socialist society moving towards Communism is constantly being 'raised' and 'perfected'. Culture is a necessary precondition of progress. Hence Lenin's conviction of the necessity of cultural revolution during NEP; hence Gorbachev's emphasis on 'new thinking' and insistence that 'we still lack political culture'.[34] The propaganda of success of Brezhnev and Gierek, on the other hand, proclaimed a society which was both politically and culturally mature. For example, the announcement of the successful achievement of the basic aims of the socialist cultural revolution in Poland in 1974 was a statement of political achievement.[35]

In practice, in all three languages culture is usually used in the normal English sense to refer to artistic and intellectual life or, by bureaucrats and cultural workers, even more narrowly to mean officially organized cultural activities. Thus there is a ministry of 'culture' which is responsible for the arts, houses of 'culture', etc. However, although culture is used in this narrow sense, it is assumed that 'cultural' *achievements* will have wider implications. In other words, a Soviet worker who plays the balalaika is not only a performing artist, but (to theorists, if not to him- or herself) someone who is enriching his or her spiritual life, a responsible and healthy citizen who is building socialism by contributing to the overall level of culture of the working class and of society and to his or her own rounded development.

In ordinary Polish and Russian speech, *'kulturalny'* or *'kul'turny'* is an adjective which has positive connotations. A 'cultured' person is often described as such merely because of his or her polite behaviour, although it may also be because he or she is well-informed about cultural life. In political life, a cultured person is someone with a high degree of political consciousness (which subsumes both courtesy and patriotism): this is the context of Gorbachev's lament that 'we still lack political culture'. However, ordinary members of the public do not necessarily equate 'cultured' with 'ideologically sound' or 'party-minded'. This was strikingly illustrated by the results of a 1989 *Moscow News* poll about the qualities Soviet voters most wished to find in their deputies to the Congress of People's Deputies. 'A high level of inner culture' was the second most popular response, while 'ideological conviction, loyalty to ideals of socialism' came eleventh and last. In other words, the respondents (about 1,500 people, largely male Russian or Ukrainian professionals) did not equate general culture with 'political culture'.[36]

'Political culture' in Soviet usage is just one aspect of culture. It differs from common Western usage in that it is always *dynamic* and has the same positive connotations as does culture in general. It is something which grows together with the level of political development and which has to be constantly raised. It also differs from some Western definitions in that it definitely includes *behaviour* (a point that should in theory make the effectiveness of ideological work easier to measure). 'Political culture' – after Lenin – seems to have entered Soviet political science vocabulary in the late 1960s and early 1970s.[37] Fedor Burlatsky defined it in Leninist terms in 1970 as the 'level of consciousness, education and political activeness achieved, which permit different sections of the population to genuinely participate in the governing of the state and in *kontrol'* [supervision]'.[38] This is the sense in which 'political culture' is normally used in Soviet, Polish or Hungarian official language, although some scholars and journalists use it more loosely, with some or all of its Western flavour, and others use it entirely in its Western sense.

Raising political culture is in practice closely linked to an improved work ethic and technological knowledge and skills. In theory, of course, material production is part of culture. So it is not totally nonsensical for a house of culture to be decorated with graphs showing the cotton harvest or for house of culture premises to be used for the manufacture of snow ploughs.

I shall often be using the word 'culture' in the commonest official sense, to mean those activities which take place in institutions under the aegis of the ministries of culture. Thus the production of a kitchen table *in a house of culture* (not a factory) is as 'cultural' as the writing of a novel. I decided to do this despite the fact that I dislike naming things for the ministry which organizes them and, more seriously, despite the fact that the word 'culture', used in this fashion in English, often sounds ugly and imprecise. In Soviet and East European usage, on the other hand, the imprecision and all-embracing quality of the term is often a virtue, allowing for a multitude of ambiguities. These would be lost if in reproducing Soviet arguments and theories 'culture' was translated by some more specific English expression.

Leisure time and culture

Marx suggested that the measure of wealth in Communist society would be the quantity of leisure time: time which people would be able to spend on the 'harmonious development of their personalities'. According to official doctrine, as Communism approaches, so the working day should be shortened and more time made available to workers for cultural activity. This ambition was an important element in Khrushchev's programme. In May 1959 he predicted a three to four hour or shorter working day under Communism and from 1956–60 workers were transferred onto 7 and 6 hour work days. The working week fell from an average of 47.8 to an average of 41.6 hours.[39] An article by A. Kharchev in *Kommunist*, no. 7, 1960 asserted that 'In consequence [of the shortened working week] the forms of using free time will be perfected also and the life of the family will be ever more closely connected with the work of clubs, sporting organizations, creative art collectives'.[40] The newspaper *Sovetskaia kul'tura* claimed that the measure had indeed opened new possibilities for cultural enlightenment.[41] This was surely true, although the flowering of cultural enlightenment at the time also had other causes.

A shorter basic working week did not however always result in more free time for members of the public. Instead, planners often encouraged overtime work, or part-time employment for housewives and pensioners. William Moskoff argues that 'there is a fundamental conflict between Soviet planners who want to increase the labour input into the economy and Soviet households who supply labour' and whose desire for extra income is mitigated by their desire for greater leisure.[42]

Few would question Moskoff's assertion of the primacy attached by 'planners' to the economic sphere over that of leisure and culture. This is the so-called 'residual principle' or 'principle of least priority' (*ostatochny printsip* in Russian, *maradék-elv* in Hungarian) which is lamented in every conceivable context by anyone with anything to do with providing culture or leisure facilities.[43]

The following section therefore discusses the accuracy of Moskoff's second assertion, which is that 'planners would like to control the way in which individuals divide their life between work and leisure and they would like to control the leisure activities people select.'[44] Moskoff suggests that they do have the power to limit choice of leisure pursuits, by allocating insufficient funds, but that they can no longer control leisure in the way they could under Stalin. This second suggestion is certainly true. However, do they still wish to control leisure and if so, why? How far do they realize their ambitions?

The absorption of free time

One aspect of the control of leisure activities is regime monopolization of free time. Under Stalinism, collective 'leisure' pursuits, especially those designed to declare support for the regime, were often in effect compulsory. This was one aspect of totalitarianism. After the Stalinist period, cultural enlightenment lost much of its compulsory character, except for certain groups like children and soldiers. It seems to have been only in the USSR that totalist aspirations to 'absorb' the population's time continued to be seriously discussed. Under Khrushchev, theorists argued that 'the private domain must be transformed into the public domain – controlled, supervised and dominated by the Communist Party'.[45] Both political and cultural enlightenment could be used to force citizens into the public domain.[46]

Soviet books on the subjects of culture and leisure published between 1971 and 1982 had a tendency to quote Brezhnev's warning given at the 15th Trade Union Congress that free time was not time free from responsibility towards society. The rise of organized dissent, the increased number of individual flats and the increasingly private pattern of leisure spending, together with the alarming influx of ideologically unsound Western leisure pursuits may have been among the reasons for the occasionally almost hysterical character of the officials' reaction to their loss of control over leisure. This was particularly marked in the early 1980s during the 'second cold war'. For example:

> Urban society is fragmented into a multitude of 'microenvironments'... Moreover, there is no single social institution which fully controls the activity of the individual. As a result he may fall into a particular kind of 'vacuum', free of social control and regulation. This is precisely what happens when socialization work is devoid of system...[In addition, imperialist propagandists hope that] the increased quantity of free time ... will create a certain leisure 'vacuum', which they hope to fill with their own products.[47]

At the June 1983 Central Committee plenum on ideology, Chernenko claimed that socialization work 'achieves lasting results ... when it encompasses all aspects of the person's life and work including their daily lives, their leisure and their family relations....It is important that every person, not only at work but also in his spare time, sense concern for his well-being.'[48] Some Soviet scholars in the 1970s and 1980s, particularly economists, attempted to measure the amount of free time absorbed by cultural institutions and to establish a desirable norm which would make possible more precise planning. S. I. Abalkin commented at a conference in Tomsk in March 1978:

> We consider that indices of absorbed free time may be widely employed on various levels of management, including in the planning of cultural provision for the population...the final result of the functioning of this branch of the economy may be measured according to the quantity of free time absorbed from the local population.[49]

The present state of knowledge about rational time budgets, Abalkin continued, allowed planners to work out how much of his free time each member of society should spend in organized non-professional cultural activity, with the ultimate goal of achieving the Communist ideal of the harmoniously developed personality.

A project conducted by the ministry of culture of the RSFSR and described at the Tomsk conference 'proved' the method's viability. The average amount of absorbed time per person was calculated for a given area, based on data for the total number and duration of cultural events and total attendance figure. The survey found that 'the free time of the population of the Russian Republic absorbed by various agencies in 1974 was more than twenty milliard hours, of which trade unions absorbed more than five, the state cinema committee more than three and the ministry of culture more than eleven milliard.' Since most of the ministry of culture institutions were to be found in rural areas, it was concluded that the rural population must spend more time at officially organized cultural events.[50]

At the same conference the sociologist L. N. Kogan seems to have been in disagreement with some of the normative attitudes expressed and asked, 'who can say how many times a month a person should ...visit the cinema, the theatre, concerts...' pointing out the unreliability of quantitative indicators. In his opinion, the discerning cinema-goer was *more* 'cultured' than someone who went to everything irrespective of quality.[51] Boris Grushin in 1967 was the first sociologist to investigate the qualitative as well as the quantitative aspect of the leisure pursuits surveyed. In his works in the 1960s Grushin also discussed the important point which seems to have been realized only later by other scholars that there is no direct correlation between a shorter working week and greater participation in cultural activities.[52] It is rather non-working time which needs to be restructured; otherwise any extra time made available would be eaten up by more housework, cardplaying or other activities which are not considered to be 'cultural'. Soviet scholars, who are sceptical about the importance of more time as a factor in promoting greater cultural activity suggest that other, more important, factors are, first, people's inability to organize their leisure time and, second, shortcomings in what cultural institutions are able to offer.

This tendency to play down the significance of the time factor would appear to be common today. However, one exception is that authors writing about the position of married women do still stress that they have not even the minimum time necessary for participation in cultural enlightenment. Moreover, totalist aspirations to absorb the greatest possible quantity of the population's free time in supervized or rational leisure pursuits were still voiced even as late as the early Gorbachev period. An article in *Sovetskaia kul'tura* on 7 February 1985 praised the Latvian Republic for absorbing an especially high percentage of the population's free time in cultural pursuits.

Although such totalist aspirations seem to be absent in both Poland and Hungary, specialists in both countries are also worried about the fact that citizens do not spend their increased leisure time in cultural pursuits. For example, a Hungarian journal in 1984 included a survey of press articles on the effects of introducing a five-day week. Only the intelligentsia had used the opportunity 'well'. Most of the population, being 'home-centred', simply watched more television.[53]

Rationality and ideological struggle

Abalkin was quoted at the Tomsk conference in 1978 as referring to 'rational time budgets'. What is a rational time budget? 'Rational' is a favourite adjective of writers about cultural enlightenment, not only of sociologists concerned with time budgets. It seems to be as natural for them to think in terms of 'rational' ways of spending time as it does for environmentalists to describe the 'rational use of nature'.[54] A Marxist approach must, it is assumed, be rational. Ultimately of course the party decides what is rational, whether in environmental or in cultural policy. This thesis argues that the party's definition of rational has substantially widened over the period in question. Ideology is creative, and rationality is an elastic concept.

If some leisure pursuits are rational, then others are irrational. These irrational leisure pursuits may be largely identified with so-called 'vestiges of the past' – church-going, for example, or heavy drinking – although it is increasingly recognized that such 'negative phenomena' may stem from tensions in the existing society.[55] Rational leisure pursuits can be used in the battle against irrational. Hence 'the contemporary almost general hope that varied leisure pursuits are a panacea against drunkenness'.[56] It is not just a question of stealing time from irrational pursuits, but also of creating a more rational population which should have a better understanding of how to spend its leisure time in a 'rational' way, and recognize the party's definition of 'rational'.

Moreover, it has become necessary to define attitudes towards new foreign fashions of dubious ideological content (for example, discos, martial arts, yoga) as well as new cultural technology (for example, videos, computer games) with potentially dangerous applications. Which is rational and which irrational? The usual official response has been to screech 'irrational!' but then to attempt to co-opt and 'rationalize' in the face of widespread and ineradicable public interest in these new activities. This need for a sharp defining of boundaries is connected with the wider philosophical assumption of an ideological struggle between socialism and capitalism.

The development of socialist culture is seen in the context of this struggle. When Khrushchev reintroduced the doctrine of the possibility and necessity of peaceful coexistence in the sphere of international relations, the concept of ideological struggle was not abandoned. Rather the reverse: it was now the main area of battle. As the 1961 party programme noted, 'Peaceful coexistence of states with different social systems does not mean a slackening of the ideological struggle.'[57]

At different periods over the last thirty years the global ideological struggle has received varying degrees of attention. It has never disappeared from the propaganda entirely. Will the focus on ideological struggle continue? It seems to have been at least partially dropped from the 'new thinking' about international affairs which is associated with *perestroika*. Here, it is accepted that capitalist countries may have legitimate national interests which are not detracted from because of the fact that their policies are controlled by capitalists.[58]

However, even by 1987 there was less evidence of 'new thinking' along similar lines in the area of culture, although some had begun to surface by 1988. Culture in bourgeois societies was said to be still controlled by capitalists and manipulated in their interests, with an elite culture for themselves and a mass culture to pacify and atomize the workers. Lenin's 'two cultures theory' – asserting the existence of two cultures in capitalist society, bourgeois and proletarian, was said to be ever relevant. The ideological struggle continued, as the imperialists sought to export their 'culture' in order to disorientate socialist citizens.[59] However, with the new openness of access to Western information and culture it seems hard to believe that this position can be seriously maintained for much longer.

Culture and ideology in the building of socialism

Common sense would suggest that once a high degree of culture had been achieved among the population the party would not need to devote so many of its energies to the ideological struggle, and that its role in directing culture would become less important, because people would be better able to organize their own creative pursuits. However, this is not the traditional doctrine, which is that the party's role grows greater in culture as socialist transformation progresses. This is logical in terms of the assumption that the party's influence over all areas of society is bound to increase. Logical, but not true: in practice the party's role in culture has, as common sense would suggest, actually decreased and political socialization and cultural policy have become to a great extent disentangled.

While *ideological* work has always been unquestionably the role of the party, *culture*, or certain areas of culture, have at many times during this period been granted considerable independence of party control. This is largely because since Stalin's death it has been realized that creative work cannot be totally dictated and that this is a fruitless and unpopular endeavour. Independent culture has also been sponsored at various times to allow rein for the expression of approved values which cannot be officially spelled out (like nationalist sentiments in Soviet literature).

As has already been mentioned, cultural enlightenment has, like certain other areas of culture, managed to increasingly escape away from its old role of providing socialization according to the operative ideology. This is despite the fact that according to official definitions it is an area of ideological work. But before tracing the long and uneven course of the escape, it will be helpful to look in more detail at the particular characteristics, goals and functions of cultural enlightenment.

Cultural enlightenment

Cultural enlightenment is supposed to complement the work of other agencies of socialization such as the mass media, schools and tertiary educational institutions, professional theatre, and the party educational system (known in Russian as 'political enlightenment'). It is similar to the mass media but different from some of the other socialization agencies in that it is 'accessible to everyone'. Its catchment should include the entire population. This used in the Stalinist period to mean that it was pitched at the most primitive of intellectual levels, suitable perhaps for illiterate Soviet peasants of the 1920s, but hardly suitable for the 1950s. Old habits and associations die hard and journalists and scholars in all three countries frequently complain even in the 1980s of the outdated nature of cultural enlightenment, with its emphasis on the masses rather than the individual.

In addition to accessibility, other special features of cultural enlightenment include: (1) the fact that activities are usually *collective*; (2) its largely *voluntary* nature (since Stalin's death); (3) the emphasis on the desirability of *active participation* rather than passive spectating. For example, participation in amateur theatricals is more truly a part of cultural enlightenment than organized theatre visits. Thus the June 1985 KPSS Central Committee resolution on cultural enlightenment finds it a matter for complaint that clubs and sports institutions 'as a general rule orient their work only towards spectator events'.[60] Collective, voluntary, active participation in both creative activities and club administration is regarded as a particularly effective means of socialization if the participants themselves socialize others. Intellectuals are socialized by co-option into the cultural enlightenment system to give lectures and, in the case of writers and performing artists, to meet with the public and answer their questions.

During the Stalinist period the terminology of cultural enlightenment was practically identical in the USSR, Hungary and Poland, and in all cases 'house' of culture had the double meaning 'home' of culture. Since Stalin, there has been a partial and in the Hungarian case almost total rejection of the Stalinist terminology. The 'Stalinist' Hungarian word *népmüvelés* could be translated as 'cultural work for and among the people' and is identical to the common Soviet term *kul'turno-massovaia rabota*. *Népmüvelés* lives on in popular (often contemptuous) usage, but in the 1970s it was officially replaced by the word *közmüvelödés*, which means public (not popular) participation in culture and is an intransitive and reflexive noun: suggesting that cultural enlightenment is voluntary, not imposed, and that the system is a democratic one.[61] Moreover, this word is often used to mean all of education and the arts, fuzzing the distinctiveness of cultural enlightenment as a concept and a system. Partly because *közmüvelödés* is such a general term, though also because of the decentralized nature of the system and the relatively low concern with ideology, there is an enormous variety of opinion about what it is and should do.

In Poland during the 1970s 'cultural enlightenment' was frequently replaced by other terms. Favourite substitutes were 'participation in culture' and 'work in the cultural sphere'. More often, however, scholars and leaders used the term 'cultural diffusion'. This phrase had a long heritage and has been used throughout the postwar period as an alternative to cultural enlightenment. It has the advantage of stressing egalitarian objectives and not necessarily implying any political element. 'Cultural diffusion' was the phrase used in the title of an important law about cultural enlightenment which was passed in April 1984. The emphasis on participation and spreading access to culture mirrors the goals of British cultural enlightenment, in so far as it makes sense to think of the existence of such a phenomenon, as expressed for example in the Beaford Declaration of 1974.[62] This egalitarian objective is of course partly political, and an intrinsic element of any socialist cultural policy, but it is not political in the usual Soviet sense of equating culture with indoctrination. The one feature all Polish definitions of the 1960s and 1970s had in common, however, was their agreement on the central role of socialization and therefore of propaganda. However, during the 1980s Polish scholars moved away from this view, 'growing out of their pedagogical corset' and becoming more interested in functions connected with encouraging creativity or forms of amateur arts with local historical traditions.[63]

Some Soviet scholars themselves have during the 1970s and 1980s expressed discomfort with the expression 'cultural enlightenment'. They dislike the word 'enlightenment', and point out that houses of culture no longer have a communicative function now that television is almost ubiquitous. But 'cultural-enlightenment work' remains the normal expression, although in narrower cases the expressions 'club work' or 'the work of club institutions' is often used.

Soviet writers are less prone than their Polish and Hungarian colleagues to debate the goals and functions of cultural enlightenment, as opposed to merely listing them as given. Moreover, pre-1988 Soviet definitions of cultural enlightenment, unlike their Polish and hungarian equivalents, always mention that it is a type of socialization. As one would expect, Soviet specialists have in print deviated much less from the definitions given in party resolutions and other official documents than have their Polish and Hungarian colleagues. In interviews, however, they often expressed views more similar to those of their East–Central European colleagues.

As an example of a typical pre-*perestroika* official definition, the 'Model statute for club institutions in the ministry of culture network' (2 February 1983), paragraph 9, states that:

> Club institutions are state ideological institutions which, under the guidance of party and soviet organs, conduct Communist socialization, the organization of amateur creative work and leisure activities. They support the mass-political and cultural-enlightenment work of party, soviet, trade union and Komsomol organs and organizations.[64]

In the 1988 draft statute, however, references to ideology and Communist socialization had been dropped.[65]

Houses of culture in all countries are supposed to liaise with all appropriate local organizations. Together they organize the leisure of the local population from every possible quarter. In addition, the post-Stalinist period has been marked in all three countries by the adoption of a 'differentiated' approach towards different social groups. This is supposed to go hand in hand with a more coherent, 'comprehensive' or 'multi-faceted' approach towards providing each citizen with the full range of different components of socialization: political socialization, moral education, atheist education, labour training, internationalist and patriotic education, etc. There are also wider political and social functions and goals, such as the control of leisure time and the integration of all sections of the population into a single society.

One of the main conclusions of this book is that at present it is only on the level of an ideal type (as portrayed, for example, in the 1983 Model Statute) that cultural enlightenment can be considered as a directed and unified system based on a coherent theory. In practice, it is a mosaic of forms and intentions, directives fulfilled and unfulfilled, grassroots initiatives realized and unrealized. Cultural enlightenment, like some Russian novels in Henry James's description, is a 'loose and baggy monster'. Scholars dream of finding in it some sort of conceptual tidiness while bureaucrats and the public continue to stuff it with ever new activities, from cactus-growing to boat-building. As one director of a Khar'kov Palace of Culture exclaimed: 'But club institutions do not have rubber walls. It is quite wrong to go on stuffing and stuffing them with every new type of leisure pursuit, when these should be given some accommodation of their own.'[66]

The area of responding to, or creating, cultural needs and demands in a culturally-advanced socialist society is riddled with tensions. Cultural enlightenment has to reconcile two separate objectives: it has to consider the population both as it is today and as it should ideally be in the future. As a service, partially commercialized, it takes into account people's present needs as consumers. As an official socializing agency, it has to instil in them the 'spiritual needs' of the developing new socialist person – in the words of the June 1985 KPSS Central Committee resolution, 'developing cultural needs that would further their spiritual growth'. There is always a tension between what people want now, what will attract them into the house of culture, and what they should ideally want. Most cultural enlightenment has in the past been aimed at the latter objective, 'dictating over needs', but this has partially changed.[67]

During recent years cultural-enlightenment experts have considered various approaches to the problem of combining these often contradictory objectives. The orthodox Soviet position in the 1980s is that cultural workers should not slavishly satisfy the demands of the population, but should guide and socialize: however, this has to be done subtly and tactfully.[68] Hungarian writers develop the idea, also expressed by at least one Soviet scholar, that cultural enlightenment should respond to spontaneous cultural developments in society itself, with the house of culture abandoning its image as a 'patronising' institution and instead providing a setting for whatever activities members of the public want to undertake.[69] Iván Vitányi asserts that 'official means cannot be used to direct cultural enlightenment....An office – any office – cannot direct it in the sense that was imagined at one point both here and elsewhere'. (Presumably by 'elsewhere' Vitányi has in mind the USSR.) The only sense in which cultural enlightenment is directable today is from below, that is, it should respond to initiatives spontaneously arising from the public. It cannot ignore *unanticipated* social developments which affect its work. Hungarian society has developed otherwise than Communists intended or expected, since they were too idealistic in expecting a great interest in high culture to manifest itself almost immediately, and, later, in supposing that participation in culture could develop satisfactorily in an economic situation where participation in the second economy was a much more attractive occupation than cultural activity.[70]

Conclusion

During the period 1953–89 cultural enlightenment became increasingly diversified, to a large extent shedding totalist aspirations and attempts to socialize the population into the operative ideology. It partly returned instead to the often overlapping ideals of socialism and, in East–Central

29

Europe, of the pre-revolutionary political culture – in so far as these seemed appropriate to modern society – while also borrowing many ideas from Western experience. Changes in political leadership and de-Stalinization provided the essential backdrop for such developments, but social pressures were more important in shaping cultural enlightenment. Thus, even in the conservative atmosphere of the 1970s in the USSR, patterns of leisure spending continued to change, independently of party control. The trend was towards more private and small-scale or local activities.

However, official aspirations to manipulate cultural enlightenment are still strong, and since cultural enlightenment cannot exist entirely without state funding, official pressures are difficult to resist. Moreover, the 'enthusiasts' are beset by dilemmas: the problems of simultaneously staving off state control *and* commercialization, of studying and responding to popular needs, and of efficient co-ordination. After all, like the neo-Stalinists, the enthusiasts see culture as an instrument of progress as well as its goal.

Chapter two

A brief history of cultural enlightenment

Introduction

This chapter describes briefly the history of cultural enlightenment in the USSR, Poland and Hungary, taking each country in turn. It is intended to provide only the essential background for the chapters that follow. Each country section discusses the extent of continuity between pre-Communist and Communist cultural enlightenment, the nature of the Stalinist experience, and the process of de-Stalinization, with particular focus on the issues which are to be explored later in the book: the changing content of cultural enlightenment in response to public pressure, the decentralization of policy-making, and concern about the ineffectiveness of official policies. A concluding section draws out some comparisons between the three countries.

The Russian Empire and the USSR

Interest in popular education among the intelligentsia, common all over Europe in the nineteenth century, was intensified in the Russian Empire because of the frequent absence of such interest, or the hostility, of the tsarist regime. Moreover, interest in popular education reflected the guilty feelings of the intelligentsia about the huge educational gap between themselves and the mass of the population: feelings which easily became politicized and oppositional.[1] Painters and, particularly, writers, were viewed as having a social responsibility to make statements about the plight of the common people, in the absence of political forums and under conditions of censorship. The intelligentsia's enthusiasm for voluntary educational work was demonstrated by the brief flourishing of the Sunday school movement and other social initiatives in the first years of the reign of Alexander II.[2] It was continued by the Lavrovrians among the Russian populists, with their strong belief in the importance of raising the consciousness of the peasant masses through education. When they 'went to the people' in the 1870s they often took with them to the villages simple propaganda such as brochures written in the accessible form of fairy-tales: a type of easy, fictional introduction to political ideas which was in essence little different from much Soviet cultural enlightenment.[3] Perhaps the most outstanding and influential individual to be involved in cultural enlightenment was Lev Tolstoy, who not only set up his own school for peasant children, but also turned his literary talents to producing literature which was accessible and meaningful to the common people.

Despite the enormous impact of earlier endeavours upon the educated public, particularly upon the revolutionaries themselves, it was only in the latter part of the nineteenth century and the beginning of the twentieth that popular educational work began to make a sizeable impact among its recipients, the ordinary people. This was largely thanks to the educational work of the *zemstvo* (local council) activists, among the peasants, and, to a more limited extent, of the revolutionaries, among the new working class. Nadezhda Krupskaia was to become the best-known of the Marxist educationalists. Education was essential both from the point of view of consciousness-raising and also as preparation for the assumption of political power.

However, cultural enlightenment was not only the province of the *zemstvo* 'third element', the revolutionaries and others among the progressive intelligentsia. Church and state provided their own equivalents. For example, the ministry of finance ran an 'anti-alcohol campaign' in which the masses were offered sermons, dances and other entertainments. The Assembly of Russian Factory Workers (famous for the 'Bloody Sunday' procession which sparked off the 1905 revolution) was, among other things, a state-sponsored cultural-enlightenment organization. According to its charter, it purpose was to provide 'sober and rational leisure pursuits' and appropriate socialization.[4]

Factory owners provided cheap entertainments for their workers in the form of 'people's theatre', both professional and amateur, and 'people's houses', (*narodnye doma*). The latter were the precursors of Soviet houses of culture. The first of them were set up in the 1880s in Tver', Iaroslavl' and Perm'.[5] In the following decades, the initiative was followed by both the state and private individuals. The first state institution was established in the capital in 1900, with a staff of clergymen, and organized both lectures and popular entertainment.[6]

The most famous of all the people's houses was set up by Countess Panina, the future deputy minister of education in the Provisional Government, in St Petersburg in 1903.[7] The activities of the people's house included courses for workers, a literary and art club, theatre, visits to museums and exhibitions of paintings by the *peredvizhniki* (known for their unglamourized depictions of Russian reality). In other words, the institution functioned very like a large modern house of culture. The lecturers were careful not to be too overtly political but the people's house did have radical connections. Its most glorious moment (in Soviet historiography) arrived in May 1906, when Lenin visited it to make a speech on Bolshevik policy towards the duma.[8]

Workers' clubs mushroomed during the 1905–6 revolution and they and the people's houses were frequently used for political meetings. Lenin saw the political potential of a workers' club movement.[9] After the revolution, when trade unions were allowed to operate, amateur arts as well as adult education began to develop in trade union clubs.[10] Indeed, given the limitations imposed on their more important functions, it was natural that the unions should pay cultural enlightenment special attention, particularly since it could be used as a front for political activities. The liberal intelligentsia also continued their cultural-enlightenment work, particularly through literacy societies.[11]

Any conclusions about the pre-revolutionary history of cultural enlightenment must stress the connections made from the very beginning between popular education and politics. Even when the organizers of popular education were actually not engaging in political activity, the state often assumed that this connection existed and proceeded accordingly. The perceived connection was only bolstered by the writings of Belinsky and his followers stressing the service role of art. This identification between cultural enlightenment and political socialization was, therefore, the most important heritage of Soviet cultural enlightenment from the pre-revolutionary period.

Two further features were the role played by the state and the commitment of the intelligentsia as a whole to cultural enlightenment. However, the significance of these should not be exaggerated for Soviet history. On the one hand, the role of the state was far smaller than it was to become in the Soviet period: cultural enlightenment was largely conducted by independent organizations, and it was the competition between them, and between them and the state, which lent cultural enlightenment much of its vitality in the late Tsarist period. As for the intelligentsia, the argument that its service mentality continued far into the Soviet period seems to me to be unconvincing. The new Soviet intelligentsia which emerged under Stalin and his successors has imitated its nineteenth century equivalent in many ways, but less so in this respect. The post-Stalinist intelligentsia has not always shown interest in making culture accessible to the people. Moreover, where a service mentality is displayed, this may equally well be thanks to the influence of the official Soviet political culture.[12]

A final point concerns two secondary elements of pre-revolutionary cultural enlightenment – scale and rhetoric. In both the huge size of many cultural-enlightenment enterprises and in the rhetoric of 'rational leisure pursuits', Soviet practice has obviously inherited some of its most characteristic features from the Russian Empire.

1917–53

During 1917, many of the clubs operating in people's houses and similar institutions evolved into politicized youth organizations. In the October takeover, many workers' clubs were used as headquarters for military units, party district committees and trade unions.[13] After 1917, new workers' clubs were founded in considerable numbers, on the initiative of local factory committees or by the commissariat of enlightenment (education ministry), Proletarian Culture movement, trade unions or youth organizations.[14] These clubs were intended to be social as well as educational and cultural centres. In the countryside, cottage reading rooms were established as centres for literacy teaching and simultaneously for establishing Communist Party influence.[15] Between 1917 and 1920 the number of cultural-enlightenment institutions is said to have risen from 13,316 to 94,745.[16] However, the cultural-enlightenment network in the countryside was much weaker than it was in the towns.

Lenin now considered the literacy campaign to be of prime importance. He identified political socialization with the liquidation of cultural backwardness, partly because 'the illiterate person stands outside politics' and partly because the educational campaign could be used to establish Bolshevik power in the countryside and disseminate Bolshevik propaganda. The government's literacy decree of December 1919 began: 'For the purpose of allowing the entire population of the Republic to participate consciously in the political life of the country, the Council of People's Commissars decrees...'[17]

Lunacharsky, commissar of enlightenment from 1918–29, stressed the political importance of cultural enlightenment for the *intelligentsia*. The old, pre-revolutionary intelligentsia could best be won over to the ideals of the new regime by participating in active cultural enlightenment among the masses and helping to build up a new, socialist intelligentsia.[18] Lunacharsky hoped that the pre-revolutionary intelligentsia tradition of social service could be maintained, but with more positive results in regard to the drawing together of intellectuals and the people. The ultimate goal was of course the creation of a classless society. Both Lenin and Lunacharsky recognized that participation in socialization was the best means of socializing oneself. All classes of society were therefore to be both the recipients and the purveyors of socialization.

Direction from the centre was initially confused, as numerous different institutions and organizations concerned with education and propaganda struggled for power. At the local level, party organizations were often uninterested: they did not consider education and ideological work to be priorities, since they had more immediate practical problems (such as war and famine) with which to contend.[19] Although the initial literacy and propaganda campaign of 1917–20 made important achievements, it was nowhere near as comprehensive as the leadership had intended.

During the period of the New Economic Policy (from 1921 to approximately 1929) the literacy campaign slackened off. Cultural enlightenment became the responsibility of local authorities, who often neglected their duties, and sometimes charged fees for clubs and libraries or closed them because of lack of funds.[20] The 1926 census revealed that illiteracy had actually increased.

However, although the mass propaganda offensive slackened, targeted groups of potential political educators – such as the trade unions and young Communists – remained heavily engaged in cultural enlightenment.[21] The trade union network was developed and the first houses of culture were opened in Leningrad in 1927. However, the Stalinist features of cultural enlightenment were not yet established and the trade union leadership, and Tomsky in particular, were forced to admit that the trade union clubs had been too much concerned with arts and sports and too little with politics and education. In April 1929 a Central Committee resolution 'On trade union cultural enlightenment' defined the major function of cultural enlightenment as the socialization of the masses and spoke of the need to root out remaining elements of 'apoliticism'.[22] Cultural enlightenment then suffered the same fate as did other branches of the arts and education, becoming highly standardized and politicized.

In 1930 the Council of People's Commissars passed a resolution 'On the beginning of the mass construction of clubs for the population'. According to the reminiscences of a cultural worker writing in 1986, 'clubs were built throughout the country – by means of citizen construction projects, to the music of brass bands, and with genuine enthusiasm. This was the beginning of a new system – cultural-enlightenment.'[23] Training courses were set up for cultural workers and a professional journal, *Klub*, was founded in 1932. Mass amateur artistic events were organized and propaganda work became identified with productivity drives, thus establishing what were to be the main characteristics of Stalinist cultural enlightenment.

Cultural enlightenment in the countryside only really became effective with collectivization and the simultaneous massive literacy campaign (launched in May 1929), when thousands of agitators poured into the villages. 'Effective', that is, in terms of the imposition of conformity, quantity of agitprop produced plus superficial knowledge imparted; the acquisition of real education and culture in the sense that they were understood by Lenin, Krupskaia or Lunacharsky was indefinitely postponed.

During the 1930s and 1940s this type of cultural enlightenment prevailed. The purpose was to use adult education and collective amateur arts to mobilize the population to industrialize and fight the war. A network of 'enlightenment' institutions was also necessary, according to Stalin, to integrate underdeveloped areas inhabited by national minorities into Soviet life.[24] Between 1922 and 1939 the number of club institutions grew 4.3 times, to reach the figure of 103,983.[25]

During the Second World War, 44,000 clubs, palaces of culture and libraries were destroyed. However, as the Nazis retreated the institutions were resurrected to conduct socialization and re-socialization in the liberated areas. Lecturers and amateur arts groups helped to enthuse the population to rebuild the factories after the war and fought religion, 'cosmopolitanism' and other 'harmful influences', guided by the 1944 Central Committee resolution 'On the immediate tasks of the Communist Party organizations of Belorussia in the sphere of mass-political and cultural-enlightenment work among the population'.[26]

In the specialist press, clubs were constantly nagged to improve the quality of their work, not always to much effect. For instance, in Kiev in 1951 'many club institutions had not restructured (*perestroili*) their work'. Complaints concerned the poor quality of cultural-enlightenment workers, the non-political character of much cultural enlightenment (for example, the infrequency of lectures on political topics, or plays on 'production themes') and the performance of frivolous plays and music.[27]

1953–64

The death of Stalin was followed by modification of Stalinist cultural-enlightenment policies and, from the late 1950s, by a blossoming of organized 'popular initiative' and new forms of cultural enlightenment. These were aimed at mobilizing the whole population by giving it the opportunity to truly participate in creative cultural activity, rather than being totally directed from above. But popular initiatives were naturally considerably less spontaneous than in Poland or Hungary, partly because there was no possibility in the Soviet Union of a return to traditional forms of cultural-enlightenment work interrupted by Stalinism. Unlike in East-Central Europe, the abandoning of Stalinist policies in cultural enlightenment did not make room for the return of popular pre-revolutionary or even pre-Stalinist artistic and social movements. Moreover, the whole tone of the period was not of returning to the Russian past, but of looking towards the future, building the new Soviet person in the house of culture. It was claimed that everyone was equally capable of becoming a great artist[28] and Marx was often cited on the diverse activities of the future Communist worker/intellectual/artist.

Despite their Utopian rhetoric, cultural officials were also worried by the unintended influx of contemporary Western cultural fashions, for example in jazz and dance. Leading ideologists responded by claiming that 'there was no peaceful coexistence in the realm of ideology'; instead 'there is acute, worldwide conflict of two irreconcilable ideologies – socialist and bourgeois'.[29] Houses of culture were encouraged to participate in the struggle, for instance by demonstrating the superiority of realist over abstract art. One recommended method was to organize exhibitions containing both. It was assumed that the viewers would instinctively ridicule and reject the Western paintings.

The usual official attitude was to condemn non-political entertainment: all spare time should be exploited for socialization. Houses of culture which confined their work to showing films and holding dances were strongly criticized. In practice there was only limited control over the content of cultural enlightenment in the countryside. *Oblast'* and *raion* houses of culture had no administrative authority over institutions in outlying villages. Magicians, dwarves, giants and performing bears roamed the countryside, as did other artistic *shabashniki* (illegal workers). Possibly this had also been the case in the Stalinist period, given the complaints in those days as well about lack of control over cultural enlightenment. Now, too, the press carried complaints about worthless, non-ideological and even 'anti-artistic' plays, with intriguing names like *The C Major Lady*.[30]

The limited, unintended 'thaw' in the area of cultural enlightenment was accompanied by official attempts to use all the new forms of cultural enlightenment in the attack on cultural and psychological 'vestiges of the past', particularly religion. The major forms of cultural enlightenment employed during the period were:

1. lectures given by members of the All-Russian Society for the Diffusion of Political and Scientific Knowledge, after 1963 the Knowledge Society (*Znanie*);
2. people's universities and universities of culture;
3. participation in 'amateur artistic activity', supposedly on a more spontaneous and enthusiastic basis than had previously been the case;
4. film, television and radio sessions in the house of culture;
5. new Soviet rites and festivals;
6. 'persuasive work' with individuals (especially believers).

Khrushchev encouraged the expansion of the underdeveloped rural cultural-enlightenment network in his attempt to increase agricultural yields. This was a consistent concern from at least 1956, to which he devoted a paragraph in the Central Committee report to the 20th party congress:

> One of the important tasks is to improve cultural-educational work in the countryside....Often cultural institutions function in estrangement from the practical tasks of building Communism. The culture centres, clubs, libraries and Red Corners must become the basis of the Party organizations' mass political and cultural-educational work. These institutions, helping to publicize and spread advanced experience and study of agro-technical methods, should play an important role in carrying out the program of further advance in agriculture.[31]

After the launch of the Virgin Lands programme, resources were diverted to cultural development in the area, to attract, reward and keep new inhabitants. Khrushchev insisted that 'they need libraries, clubs, amateur arts, they need to create cultured conditions'.[32]

However, despite the intentions expressed in the 1956 plan, the overall number of cultural-enlightenment institutions actually decreased between 1959 and 1963. This was partly because of lack of funds for investment but probably also because of the amalgamation of smaller collective farms and consequent abandonment of some small rural settlements with clubs.[33]

Other attempts to expand cultural enlightenment included the transfer of state clubs to trade unions in keeping with Khrushchev's wider policy, developed in 1955–7, of developing the social organizations in order to encourage public responsibility and participation (without any intention of relinquishing party control or sanctioning ideological diversity). Also encouraged were the election of public management committees, supposedly consisting of unpaid activists, to the houses of culture and clubs; the encouragement of members of the urban intelligentsia, including both professional creative artists and anyone else with specialist knowledge, to spread culture in the countryside; the involvement of village professionals like teachers and agronomists as permanent voluntary workers in the houses of culture; greater involvement of workers and peasants in house of culture activities; and finally, the use of public vigilantes to supervise leisure pursuits and prevent card-playing and drunkenness.[34] New emphasis was laid on penetration by propaganda of the *entire* population. The most important formulation of this was in the CC resolution on propaganda of 1960. Whereas previously propaganda work had been conducted almost exclusively at the workplace or in attached cultural-enlightenment institutions, from 1959 onwards CC resolutions called for political socialization work also at places of residence.[35] Buses were used to bring cultural enlightenment to isolated areas.

Enthusiasm was supposed to substitute for investment, but could obviously do so only partially. Moreover, there was much shamming of statistics to conceal the shortage of volunteers. (Professional cultural workers even passed themselves off as 'simple kolkhoz girls'.) The scheme for transferring clubs to trade unions – from one bureaucracy to another – had few positive results.[36] In addition, the philosophy was obviously questionable – and was accordingly rejected by the Brezhnev regime. Voluntary work, however politically formative for the individual volunteer, was not necessarily an effective method of getting things done on a mass scale.

The Brezhnev years

The Brezhnev regime, as part of the process of restoring power to the ministries, abandoned the practice of transferring cultural-enlightenment institutions out of ministry of culture control. However, almost all the new forms of cultural enlightenment which had been introduced under Khrushchev were continued. The difference was in a pronounced change of emphasis: a more professional approach to cultural enlightenment, as to ideological work in general. More attention was paid to professionalism in methodology and training, and an academic cultural-enlightenment establishment was created.

In addition, more money was invested in selected areas, chiefly in the countryside. The number of cultural-enlightenment institutions increased fairly steadily from 1963 onwards. This reflected Brezhnev's use of village cultural amenities as a carrot to keep people on the collective farms. There is no evidence that this was successful on a significant scale (and certainly migration from the countryside in general continued).

One very important development which took place during the 1960s and 1970s was that many families were able for the first time to acquire their own self-contained flat. This, combined with the spread of television and tape recorders, resulted in a significant change in the pattern of leisure. There was now little incentive to go out to the house of culture. Moreover, there was increasing public interest in small-scale, often experimental art forms. Studio theatre, chamber choirs and pop groups began to proliferate. In many cases, especially that of pop music, there was no point in seeking advice from the house of culture, since there were no Soviet prototypes to copy.[37]

At first the official 'propaganda of success' policy which encouraged mendacious statistics, together with the almost complete absence of sociological research, concealed the deleterious effect which this new tendency towards privatization of leisure was having on house of culture activities.

At the 1971 and 1976 party congresses two new themes emerged. The first was to rationalize and centralize the cultural-enlightenment system by creating houses of culture in all *raion* centres, to co-ordinate work within the district. Ultimately, all cultural institutions in one area were to be organized into a 'centralized club system' or 'culture and sports complex'. This ambition was not realized during the 1970s except in certain areas of northern Russia and western Siberia. The second theme was the development of new industrial areas in Siberia and the Far East: this included the development of their cultural amenities. After the 1976 party congress a campaign was launched called 'Let's transform Siberia into a highly cultured land'.

The 1970s saw the production of literally dozens of Central Committee resolutions on ideological matters, including several of direct relevance to cultural enlightenment.[38] The ministry of culture and the trade unions also produced many new regulations on subjects as diverse or as similar as atheist propaganda and discos. It is hard to escape the impression that this splurge of regulation (for example not just one but several rulings on discos alone) was an alarmed response to an increasingly uncontrollable situation with regard to patterns of public leisure spending, particularly since it was in the 1970s that sociological surveys began to show up a serious problem of non-attendance at official cultural institutions.

In addition to all the old problems of lack of resources in cultural enlightenment, there were also new difficulties which were similar to those experienced in East-Central Europe, connected with social and technological progress. The rise in educational levels, competition from television and influx of Western culture all created a demand for more sophisticated cultural provision than the house of culture could usually provide. In addition, despite rhetoric about the need for a 'more differentiated approach' answering the needs of the population, there was often confusion about what to do if particular conceivably dangerous fashions became popular 'needs', as in the case of collectors' clubs or of discos.

However, despite these problems, many of the initiatives of the Khrushchev era were substantially developed. These included the creation of new Soviet rites and festivals on a mass scale to replace religious ones. Adult education in people's universities expanded rapidly. The 1960s and 1970s were a period of fast expansion in secondary education and heavy emphasis on the need for professional qualifications, without a concomitant expansion of tertiary educational opportunities. Adult education therefore became a necessary substitute, not least because of its social control function of 'cooling off' the frustrated ambitions of would-be university students. Following on developments of the Khrushchev period, there was increased emphasis on work organized around blocks of flats and, in particular, the creation of youth clubs to keep so-called 'difficult teenagers' off the streets.

Succession struggle and cold war, 1980–5

The end of detente, the Polish crisis and the consequent intensification of concern about proper political socialization led to much ideological debate, with important conferences in Moscow in 1981 and 1984 and Tallinn and Riga in 1982, and a Central Committee plenum devoted to ideology in June 1983. The concern with staving off harmful cultural influences naturally involved cultural enlightenment, although apart from general recommendations that it be improved little specific was suggested (at least in the published records of these events). In fact, little was actually done of a positive nature until Gorbachev became leader: presumably because the uncertain and changing political climate was not favourable to the introduction of reform.

The emphasis during this rather repressive period was on party control over people's leisure time, to an extent reminiscent of the Khrushchev era. A typical statement was that by Chernenko in 1983, which was quoted in Chapter One: socialization was only effective when it was all-encompassing. A resolution of July 1982 'On creative links between literary and art journals and the practice of communist construction' stressed the responsibility of the intelligentsia to undertake voluntary cultural work among workers, peasants and members of the armed forces.[39] The Komsomol was told to become more active in combating the lack of interest in ideology among young people and warning them of the dangers of Western cultural fashions. All pop groups in the RSFSR were called before review boards in the course of 1984.

The early 1980s were a period of much interesting research. For example, in 1981–2 a massive nationwide survey was organized by a group of institutions involved in arts research, which found that amateur arts activities were everywhere much more widespread in the home than in the club. The response to this discovery was to try to organize this so-called 'unorganized independent activity', to persuade it to participate in the All-Union Review of Amateur Arts in 1983–5 and, more generally, to entice such unorganized art into official institutions. However, scholars writing about the subject were aware that in order to do this successfully, compromises had to be made, and non-traditional forms of work to be tolerated. In their opinion, what was needed was a *'perestroika'*. Gorbachev's accession was well timed.

Perestroika, 1985–9

Soon after Gorbachev became general secretary, a comprehensive and very critical Central Committee resolution appeared on the subject of cultural enlightenment and sports facilities. The June 1985 resolution was prompted by recognition of the disturbing trends in patterns of leisure spending; a further incentive to reform the work of houses of culture was that they were to play a large role in the anti-alcohol campaign, which was launched the same spring. Cultural enlightenment came in for criticism at the twenty-seventh party congress and several more resolutions on cultural enlightenment appeared within a short space of time, showing that their plight was being taken seriously (although no more seriously than that of other areas of culture: this was a period marked by resolutions on all subjects). In March 1986 the Politburo discussed cultural enlightenment and the Central Committee passed a resolution 'On measures for expanding the building and strengthening the material and technological base of *raion* houses of culture and village clubs'. In May 1986 a ministry of culture regulation appeared regulating the work of hobby clubs and amateur associations (*kluby po interesam, liubitel'skiie ob''edineniia*).[40] This last regulation had important implications for the new 'informal' clubs and societies which began to mushroom in the climate of *glasnost'*.

The period 1985–9 has been a time of intense activity in the cultural and ideological spheres. New men were put in all the 'top' jobs: first Ligachev and Iakovlev, then Medvedev became the secretaries responsible for ideology; Voronov and Skliarov became CC department heads for culture and propaganda; and Zakharov replaced Demichev as minister of culture. The ministry itself was also purged (there is evidence to suggest that the cultural-enlightenment department was included in this) and restructured.[41] The Soviet Cultural Fund was established with a brief which included sponsoring amateur cultural activity. In 1988, as part of the reorganization of the Central Committee apparatus, an ideological commission was created which included cultural enlightenment among its responsibilities. Since 1985, a long list of resolutions and statutes have been passed on various aspects of 'cultural development'.

A number of new ways of improving cultural enlightenment are being attempted in addition to the more vigorous pursuit of traditional approaches like institutional reorganization, providing more resources and attempting to force managers and party bosses to concern themselves with the subject – all of which may be more successful now than before. For example, houses of culture are changing and increasingly becoming (as in Poland and Hungary) places where people can engage in do-it-yourself or craftwork and sell the products. In 1986 a decision was announced to set up 'youth centres' in every town or *raion* by the end of the year. By the end of the century there are also to be 1,000 self-financing 'leisure centres', run by *Rossattraktsion*, outside the cultural-enlightenment network and apparently not engaged in political socialization (but educational in the sense that they are to possess computer clubs).[42] Thus, there seems to be a more realistic approach to non-political individual leisure activities – a willingness to let them exist in peace without trying to force them into an ideological strait-jacket. Almost any harmless (by today's definition) spare time activity may be dubbed 'cultural'. Such an approach is dictated not only by realism but also by a desire to energize the 'human factor', to encourage involvement and responsibility within the state cultural sector.

In view of the now admitted sharp decline in attendance, cultural enlightenment has to find an acceptable compromise between what people want to do in their leisure time and what it is trying to make them want, i.e. find a new solution to the vexed question of what constitutes 'social need'. Under Gorbachev, much greater priority than before is assigned to what the public really wants, significantly changing the nature of the house of culture as an institution, while some leisure activities have been removed from the sphere of cultural enlightenment altogether (as in the case of leisure centres). Indeed, some specialists by March 1989 were forecasting that there would be no such thing as a standard cultural-enlightenment institution in the near future.[43]

However, this does not mean that traditional methods and assumptions about the usefulness of art for socialization have been abandoned, and many party officials retain their aspiration to control collective leisure pursuits. Types of artistic activity regarded as suspicious are still closely monitored, as are 'clubs of social initiatives' and other independent social, cultural and political organizations. The May 1986 regulations on hobby clubs and the wide press given to such clubs has encouraged them to come out and let themselves be counted, without its being made clear exactly where the limits of acceptability are to be found. In the words of Vladimir Iakovlev, writing in *Ogonek*:

> Social organizations have come out of the darkness of their formerly hidden, underground and fragmented existence. They have come out of the darkness, but not yet quite into the light. They have remained in a kind of intermediate state, in a twilit condition, as if awaiting the further development of events. The state organizations also bide their time, not hastening too quickly to raise the old, but soundly constructed barrier.[44]

Conclusion: Soviet Union

What is the implication of the emergence of all this informal cultural activity? Will we see a total collapse of the Stalinist model of cultural enlightenment in the near future? It would be unwise to make such a prediction, but one indication that the 'problem' of informal cultural activities is permanent and serious is that contrary to what is often suggested in the Western press today – its emergence is not a sudden phenomenon of the Gorbachev era.[45] Nor should the new groups be associated too exclusively with pre-1985 dissident activities. The emergence into the open of the informal organizations was made possible by *glasnost'*, but their creation often pre-dated Gorbachev and the way for an unofficial but open club movement had been paved by the steady decline in official control over the content of public leisure time and, over the last decade, the willingness of some cultural authorities to tolerate non-ideological leisure pursuits in the houses of culture.

This section on cultural enlightenment in the USSR has described the privatization of leisure which began to occur under Khrushchev and Brezhnev and the opening of possibilities for individuals to engage in unorganized, non-collective cultural activity. The regime's response to this was first, under Brezhnev, to seek to contain new aspirations by providing a more rationally organized network of institutions and also to a certain extent by providing the opportunity for people to engage in new and fashionable leisure activities. It wished to involve as many of the population as possible in organized leisure and accepted unreliable statistics which 'showed' involvement to be increasing, while refusing to admit that most of the population was actually avoiding cultural enlightenment. Under Gorbachev, sociological research which showed the latter to be the case was acknowledged to be accurate. The attempted solutions were to rationalize the collection of sociological data, to allow a wider range of depoliticized activities to occur in the houses of culture, to let small clubs organize their own affairs, to provide commercial incentives for participation and to some extent to turn a blind eye to the presence of clubs existing 'informally' outside official institutions – while trying as far as possible to persuade them that under conditions of *perestroika* they could feel at home in the cultural-enlightenment network. It was natural, given the tensions which such a situation created and the conservatism of many ideological officials, that clubs which had existed informally before 1985 often joined houses of culture only briefly and then left finding that little had really changed, or else remained suspicious and kept outside the houses of culture altogether. However, despite the fact that informal groups pre-date 1985, and that *perestroika* has not yet reached many houses of culture, the psychological impact of *perestroika* cannot be underestimated. The comparable Polish experience of 1980–1 had profound and lasting effects on culture.

Poland

> We are dealing with three facts, like the three sides of a triangle. Society needs mass culture. Mass culture is under the control of the Communist authorities. The Communist authorities do not enjoy society's trust....This triangle is the origin of the basic paradox of mass culture in a state like the Polish People's Republic, the basic contradictions between the functions it performs. Mass culture is like a horse which is trying to pull two carts ... social demands [and]...the demands of authority....The problem is that the carts are set to go in opposite directions, and one horse cannot pull both of them at once.[46]

Cultural enlightenment before the Second World War

Most authors trace the origins of Polish cultural enlightenment to the late eighteenth century, to the 'community house' (*dom spofeczny*) created by the social reformer P. K. Brzostowski for the peasants on his estate in the Vilna area. His initiative was followed between 1816 and 1831 by the educationalist Stanisław Staszic.[47] In the course of the nineteenth century cultural enlightenment developed a new character. It had been the initiative of a few gentry reformers. It now became a key part of the nationalist movement: of the 'organic work', or small-scale, gradualist activity among the Polish population through which nationalists increased popular awareness of the Polish identity and culture. In the late nineteenth century a number of community houses were founded: in 1877 there were three; in 1900, 145; in 1918, 185. They were concentrated in the Austrian and Russian sections of Poland; in Prussian Poland, church reading rooms and parish halls performed the same functions.[48] In addition, many scholarly and educational societies were established during the nineteenth century which kept Polish culture alive.[49] In 1916–17, a new institution emerged, the *świetlica*, a type of social club.

The inter-war period was a time of dynamic growth, particularly in the years immediately preceding the Second World War. Trade unions, workers' circles, co-operative societies, political parties, educational and cultural associations, the leisure organization Sokol, the Association of Polish Youth, the fire brigade and the Church were all active in cultural enlightenment, as were the national minorities (particularly the Ukrainians through their nationalist cultural association *Prosvita*). Community houses organized adult education, amateur arts, entertainment, tourism and often provided other local services, such as chemist shops and cafés without alcohol. Although the government became increasingly interested in managing and controlling such activity, it was only in 1938 that it began to encourage local government authorities to build their own cultural houses.[50] *Swietlice* grew in great numbers, and were often centres of political activity as well as social and arts clubs.[51] They were to become intensely politicized after the Communist takeover.

Traditions established before the Second World War strongly influenced developments later. Just as in Russia (within which, of course, much of Poland had been included), the aspirations of traditional Polish cultural enlightenment were clearly political, although nationalism was obviously a more important element of this politicization among Poles than it was among Russians. Nationalist cultural aspirations remained (hidden) throughout the Stalinist period, but the strength of their existence was shown by their emergence in full force after 1956.

1944–56

Until about 1949–50 spontaneous and variegated local cultural-enlightenment work continued with even greater energy than before. Many groups and individuals participated, with the Church in particular playing an active role. In the brief period of relative freedom for individual initiative, hope and enthusiasm for rebuilding the country and integrating the new territories abounded, old cultural-enlightenment institutions were rebuilt, new ones founded and various measures were taken to resurrect Polish culture and make it accessible to the whole population. The movement has often been described as a 'going to the people' – in other words, compared to the action of the Russian populists of the 1870s. The difference seems to be that the actions of the Polish enthusiasts found widespread popular acceptance.[52] A campaign against illiteracy was mounted. Historic cities destroyed in the war were rebuilt with public help and participation. The classics of Polish literature were published cheaply in large numbers. One could classify almost all cultural activity in this period as cultural enlightenment, since its intention was either to popularize the Polish cultural heritage or else to inculcate knowledge of Marxism-Leninism and the party programme. This latter aspiration was particularly clearly displayed when the Communist Party (PPR) used non-professional performers to enhance the emotional impact of Communist propaganda during the 1947 elections, following the pattern of Soviet agitation work during election campaigns.[53]

The Communists had been putting out general statements of intent about culture ever since the PPR's first manifesto of March 1943. The 'Ideological Manifesto' of the Polish United Workers' Party (PZPR) at its Unification Congress in 1948 spoke of the active participation of the masses in the building of a new culture and the need to reform the traditional concept of patriotism (that is, to stand it on its head by making its main element friendly feelings towards Russia).[54]

Non-Communist cultural campaigns were easily taken over by the new Communist government and independent cultural organizations were liquidated. Resolutions of the fifth plenum of the PZPR Central Committee and fifth plenum of the Central Trade Union Council in 1949 centralized all cultural activity.[55] Cultural enlightenment was placed firmly in the hands of a Main Commission for Cultural Affairs, headed by prime minister Cyrankiewicz, which had been founded the previous year. The high stature of the politicians who sat on the Commission is said to have been reflected in the large investments made during this period into cultural enlightenment. The funds were channelled through the trade unions and the Peasant Self-Help organization. The Commission's brief was to professionalize and ideologically purify cultural enlightenment.[56]

The monopoly of the state and its 'transmission belts' was not quite total. For example, the last sixty-seven people's colleges (*uniwersytety powszechne*) managed to keep going until 1953.[57] Moreover, individual artistic ensembles survived from before the war, and despite their necessarily changed repertoires remained a reminder of pre-Communist cultural life. For instance, the 'Harmonia' choir at Nowe Miasto Lubawskie in Pomerania, founded in 1898, managed to survive the Stalin years with the help of long-standing members, despite apparent attempts by the local Communist Party organization to dissolve it. Some house of culture regulations remained in existence from before the Second World War, or even the First World War (and in some cases are still in force today). Even more significantly, amateur choirs and orchestras dating from before the war were able to preserve their traditions of genuine self-management, traditions never successfully established in post-war amateur groups.[58] There was thus, in contrast to Hungary and in very marked contrast to the USSR, at least an element of continuity between pre- and post-Stalinist Poland; the shortness of the Stalinist period made it possible to revive pre-Stalinist traditions fairly easily, although some of them emerged in a distorted form.

It took several years for the Main Commission for Cultural Affairs to establish a unified network of cultural-enlightenment institutions for the general public. One reason for this slowness was the refusal of many former cultural workers to participate in the new institutions and the dismissal of many more on grounds of suspected political unreliability. Their places were taken by inexperienced members of the Communist youth movement. (Compare the part played by the Komsomol in the Soviet cultural revolution of the late 1920s–early 1930s.)[59] There were various other impediments to the speedy creation of a new network: 'many reorganizations, searches for appropriate models, and polemics and discussions which sometimes even raised the issue of liquidation'. Since from the Soviet point of view the appropriate model was ready and waiting for export, one can only suppose that these polemics reflected divisions between the Muscovite and national factions of the party leadership.[60]

The content of cultural enlightenment in the Stalinist period was set by the need to copy Soviet policy, to spread knowledge of Russian culture and to socialize the population and inspire it to take part in the drive for industrialization and collectivization. In 1951 Ochab, future leader of the party and at that time responsible for propaganda, made a speech at the opening of the party school for cultural-enlightenment workers (the mere existence of which well indicates the degree of politicization) which underlined the ideological and political character of cultural-enlightenment work. Its task was indoctrination and encouraging the fulfilment of productivity quotas.[61]

Stalinist cultural enlightenment did achieve some successes, in continuing the initiatives of the immediate post-war years (for example, the mass printing of Polish classics) and in integrating settlers in new areas in both town and countryside. However, Polish scholars of the 1980s unite in criticizing Stalinist cultural-enlightenment policy, chiefly because of its manipulative attitude to 'culture' and its suppression of Polish traditions. The only positive factor was that it was so short-lived.

In the final analysis the Stalinist attempt must be seen as counterproductive. This is not to deny that numerous people – especially during the Stalinist period itself – were successfully indoctrinated, as Milosz describes so vividly in *The Captive Mind*. But on the whole and in the long term, attempts to force repeated declarations of loyalty to the regime and to the Soviet Union through mass amateur artistic events were worse than useless. Like the grandiose new houses of culture, they alienated the population and distracted money and attention away from specific, real local needs. The whole cultural-enlightenment system in these years was discredited and has never fully recovered a reasonable image among the Polish public.[62] Thus, a too blatant use of cultural enlightenment for political purposes was dysfunctional. It failed to build a base for mass socialization work and instead helped to ensure that ideological work would lack effectiveness in future years.

1956–70

Cultural enlightenment was profoundly influenced by the events of

1956, when a divided party leadership thrashed out its response to de-Stalinization under pressure from above (Khrushchev's secret speech) and below (notably the Poznań demonstrations of June 1956). In October Wacław Gomułka was selected as first secretary of the party against the will of the Kremlin leadership and a short period of genuine liberalization was won. In the first years after 1956 professional creative artists and journalists enjoyed extensive freedoms. These, like other gains of 1956 such as the workers' councils, were gradually eroded as party control was reasserted in all areas of Polish life. Cultural enlightenment, as an area of ideological policy, was always in theory more closely controlled than were professional literature or art: there was no suggestion that it should be less concerned with socialization than it had been under Stalin. Official policy statements were in most respects identical to those expressed by contemporary Soviet leaders.[63]

In the years 1956–8 extensive debate on the past and future of cultural enlightenment was however permitted among specialists. There were even suggestions that the whole cultural-enlightenment system was redundant in the era of mass media, and discussion as to what should replace it.[64] The number of general knowledge lectures fell sharply, although their quality is said to have improved. Many newspaper articles appeared with titles such as 'Abolish *świetlice!*'[65] and after 1956 most were spontaneously liquidated 'because institutions which did not try to introduce new, attractive forms of work were not attended'.[66] This was total de-Stalinization, of a type which neither the Polish authorities nor of course Khrushchev had envisaged. The spontaneity and extreme quality of the Polish events found no parallel in either the USSR or Hungary then or since. Debate over the future of cultural enlightenment was closed at a national conference of cultural-enlightenment workers in December 1958 and by its accompanying resolution.[67] The main speech was made by Politburo member and Central Committee secretary J. Morawski. He strongly criticized the overcentralization of the preceding era and its narrowly instrumental approach to cultural enlightenment. Official cultural enlightenment had to be more effective, since it was under competition from trivial entertainments – including popularized theatrical versions of lives of the saints – and from the renewed 'so-called' cultural enlightenment being vigorously conducted by the Catholic Church. The 1958 resolution promised extensive freedom to operate for a diversity of institutions – as long as the cultural activities they organized were socialist in content. Local people's councils acquired greater freedom over the shaping of their own cultural-enlightenment policy.[68]

Some *świetlice* were restored, although many had gone for ever.[69] On the other hand, cultural-enlightenment institutions not associated with Stalinism flourished, especially during the first half of the 1960s, before lack of money, an ebbing of enthusiasm and the rise of television led to a certain trailing off of activity. Thousands of clubs and café-clubs were set up in the countryside, often on the initiative of local teachers or activists in the Rural Youth Union.

Khrushchev should have been delighted at this manifestation of public initiative, which seems to have been far more genuine than the contemporary (also partly genuine) flourishing of public participation in the USSR. However, success in Poland was only achievable because of significant differences, in terms of motivation and content of work, between Polish and Soviet cultural enlightenment. In Poland, party control was diminished rather than increased. This was de-Stalinization as understood by the population, rather than de-Stalinization as understood by the Soviet Communist Party.

Why did the Poles show such initiative in cultural enlightenment in the years after 1956? The looser party control over culture was an enabling factor, but there were also more positive reasons. One important factor was the increasing influence of the city on the Polish village and the aspirations of many, especially young, rural inhabitants for more urban-style leisure pursuits. Polish villages, being in general not collectivized, had more interest in and scope for individual small-scale initiative (though this meant that money was more limited than it was in theory on a Soviet farm). The club was primarily a place for socializing, Western types of entertainment (for example, jazz) and watching television, rather than amateur arts: in this it differed sharply from the *świetlica*. Since the club was often the only place in the village to possess a television set, it had a strong attraction.[70] Moreover, the club movement benefited from the fact that many villages already had a rudimentary, pre-Communist tradition of organized cultural life, often based on voluntary work and using the premises of the firemen's association.

Many of the pre-Stalinist social and cultural societies were resurrected and new ones were founded along the same lines. They included regional cultural societies, clubs of friends of libraries, committees for building cultural-enlightenment institutions and various amateur artistic ensembles.[71] The new societies worked with and often within the house of culture, which resumed something of the function of a 'community house'. Thus in post-1956 Poland cultural activists had no need to search for an alternative to Stalinist policies: they returned to tradition, both of local patriotism and of participation in European cultural trends. However, it was not always easy to overcome the doubts of Stalinist-minded local authorities.[72]

The year 1966, the millennium of Poland and of Polish Christianity, was used as a focus for ideological campaigns and amateur arts from 1955 onwards. This was done largely in order to compete with the celebrations being organized simultaneously by the church.[73] People's councils held cultural conferences and the activity culminated in a congress of Polish culture. However, cultural enlightenment often eluded party control. Ministry officials during this period lamented the absence of 'enlightenment' in cultural enlightenment. One official complained in 1964 that a spot check in the Wrocław *województwo* showed that none of the village *świetlice* were concerning themselves with publicizing agricultural techniques and that in all her own travels she had never come across such a club.[74] Another official noted in January 1968 that much amateur arts work was totally devoid of ideological content.[75]

The problem (as the ministry perceived it) was lack of central control caused by the extreme decentralization of the system, the shortage of well-qualified cultural workers and dependence on voluntary work. Moreover, the state did not have many purse-strings to pull. In 1964, the ministry of culture had claimed that 'the national economic situation does not permit the systematic development of a network of houses of culture and *świetlice* in the countryside'.[76] Less money was invested in culture as a whole in the second half of the 1960s and 'economic goals were given almost exclusive preference, and the budgetary obligations of the state towards culture were diminished, as a non-productive area which had no obvious links with the economy'.[77] The lack of state support sapped public initiative in cultural diffusion and destroyed the fragile trust in official cultural policy which had been established immediately after 1956. In January 1968, a senior ministry of culture official admitted that the public had a poor opinion of houses of culture. He also complained that they were insufficiently supervised by the cultural departments of the people's councils.[78]

In 1968 government policy took a sharp turn, possibly in response to these internal problems of cultural enlightenment but also in response to the 1968 political protests and anti-semitic campaign. Cultural-enlightenment activists do not appear to have been directly involved in protest against the official cultural policy, but they were directly affected by the backlash. This was a return to a much more controlled and campaign-oriented cultural-enlightenment policy (1968–80). At the same time, public feelings about official cultural enlightenment became still more bitter.

In keeping with official response to the events of March 1968, statements by official cultural-enlightenment agencies became full of demands to improve the teaching of patriotism and the political socialization of young people. New statutes were drawn up for houses of culture in 1968–9 which emphasized that they must adhere to the ministry's directives and state cultural policy.[79]

The Gierek years, 1970–80

Gierek as PZPR leader from December 1970, initially pursued a fairly liberal cultural policy. His minister of culture was reported as declaring that 'the party has realized that the arts cannot be ordered about'.[80] As an important gesture of concern for the Polish cultural heritage, it was decided to rebuild the royal castle in Warsaw – a kind of nationalist counter-symbol to the Stalinist Palace of Culture. However, liberalism in the arts was accompanied by a sustained ideological attack on young people. For example, the Central Committee recommended that young people be more involved in planning the programmes of houses of culture.[81]

More money was invested in cultural-enlightenment institutions in the first years of the Gierek regime.[82] However, priority was assigned to what were considered to be the more important areas of film, radio and television: because of shortage of funds, houses of culture, theatres and other institutions were to be improved more gradually.[83]

Cultural enlightenment was centralized in the course of the general administrative reorganizations which occurred during the mid-1970s. This benefited only the new *województwo* centres. The new, smaller *województwa* had fewer resources to spend on culture and preferred to spend what they had on new central houses of culture to enhance the prestige of the new regional centres and their governments. Cultural centres in the communes were built much more slowly, and village clubs received little attention. The inadequacy of village cultural enlightenment caused some concern to the propaganda department of the PZPR Central Committee.[84] Party worries about village cultural enlightenment may be seen in the context of Gierek's policy of bringing private farms into the state sector and attempting to increase the integration of the peasantry into socialist society.[85]

The nature and content of cultural-enlightenment work was exactly defined by yearly directives issued by the ministry of culture to the *województwo* houses of culture and used by them to plan local work. The 1977–8 directives, for example, reveal great attention to Soviet-Russian friendship (for example, by celebrating the 100th anniversary of Dzerzhinsky's birth), the inculcation of 'socialist values' and respect for national symbols.[86] Work was organized around anniversaries (sometimes preposterously obscure, by Polish if not Soviet standards) 'witnessing to a total lack of sense of reality'.[87]

The depths of primitiveness to which cultural enlightenment occasionally sank are well-illustrated by two rhyming slogans, which were recommended as decoration for club walls:

It's sad at home, but the club's full of fun,
With laughter and jokes for everyone.

Of knowledge and culture we can always do with more:
Here in our club you'll find out what they are.[88]

It was hard to see any sustained cultural policy in the constant hurry from one campaign to another. The Polish specialist Kargul claims that serious cultural enlightenment was deliberately neglected, in favour of television (very much Gierek's favourite propaganda instrument) and frivolous light entertainment imitating Western trends, all of which atomized the population and sapped its creative energy.[89] The poet Barañzcak suggests that popular culture in the later 1970s had a 'compensatory' function: it aimed to persuade Poles that things were not as bad as they thought they were.[90] This policy backfired, since people were simply irritated and became more antagonistic towards the regime.

Ever since its demise, the Gierek regime has been depicted as cynical and manipulative in cultural enlightenment: to the extent that one suspects such criticism is positively encouraged by the Jaruzelski government in order to highlight its own opposite qualities. Perhaps the picture is somewhat overstated. For example, the party had intended to define cultural policy and generous investment limits at a Central Committee plenum, but this never occurred. The expenses caused by administrative reorganization at national and local levels meant that extra funds had to be found from somewhere – and this led to the postponement of the proposed discussion on cultural policy.[91]

The creation of new planning and research institutions in 1973–4 testified to government concern about cultural enlightenment. Another manifestation of interest was the commissioning of the Prognosis for Cultural Development (1973), which stressed the importance of making culture accessible to the whole population – and which was subsequently frequently quoted against the government, since it signally failed to do so. The Experience and the Future discussion group found that one of the chief grievances of its respondents was 'the disadvantage of broad segments of society as regards access to culture' ('in no other area has the departure from the ideals of socialism emerged in such a statistically demonstrable manner'). In particular, the group registered complaints about the lack of cultural opportunities open to young people in rural areas; a complaint also expressed in other opinion surveys.[92]

The flourishing of the underground publishing movement in the late 1970s caused an important psychological breakthrough among those who had become alienated from participating in cultural activity inside state cultural institutions: they now realized that they could get away with organizing cultural events totally outside the state network.[93] The dynamic growth of non-official culture over the past decade has formed the context for and a major influence upon official cultural policy.

1980–1

In June 1980 the culture and arts commission of the *sejm* (parliament) met to assess the previous 'difficult' year. They heard of the drop in the number of visitors to theatres, art galleries and village libraries in 1979. A member of the commission pointed out that 'it has to be said that the public's lack of use of and interest in these possibilities is a problem of fundamental political and social importance'. A ministry official confirmed that the number of events organized by houses of culture and the number of people attending them had fallen. The effective boycott of official cultural institutions by many Poles is thus not only a response to the crushing of the 1980–1 revolution, but also a phenomenon stretching back to the latter part of the Gierek era.[94]

The party was soon forced by public actions in 1980–1 to realize that culture was in a state of crisis. As in so many other respects, the events of 1980–1 in Poland made the regime recognize facts with an honesty which was only paralleled in the USSR under Gorbachev (when the authorities finally publicly admitted that lack of public attendance at official cultural institutions gave grave cause for concern). However, the problem in Poland in 1980 was more acute. Not only was there extreme resentment at recent manipulative policies (representing re-Stalinization, including particularly abhorrent sovietization of Polish cultural life) but also, as was mentioned above, there was considerable resentment at the regime's failure to live up to its socialist promises of equality of access to culture. However, cultural diffusion was the main issue of complaint about cultural enlightenment during 1980–1.

Within the party, this issue was critically discussed in the 'Theses on party and state cultural policy' produced by the Kuznica group of party intellectuals and cultural figures.[95] The promises made in the programme produced by the ninth party congress in June 1981 were less far-reaching, but promised tolerance, the 'non-instrumental' treatment of creative work and the levelling of the 'drastic disproportions in meeting cultural needs'.[96]

Many house of culture workers were active in Solidarity, especially in their local committees.[97] The Solidarity programme adopted at its September–October 1981 congress included as 'Thesis 28' that 'Culture and education must be available for everyone' and as 'Thesis 29' 'The union will support and protect all independent measures aimed at self-government in culture and education'. The Pope was quoted to the effect that Poland had 'survived and preserved its identity not because of physical strength, but exclusively because of its own culture'. Solidarity pledged its 'support for all initiatives aimed at promoting active participation in culture and at making culture available for the most neglected communities'. Thesis 29 criticized the state monopoly in culture. Instead, the government should provide resources for society to 'become the master of its own culture and education'. Solidarity promised to support independent cultural initiatives, including cultural centres, and to set up its own centres.[98]

There was little time to set up independent cultural-enlightenment institutions. However, people's colleges did start up, sponsored by the reestablished Rural Youth Union.[99] The old trade union houses of culture found themselves in a helpless position. Solidarity had taken on responsibility for culture but had not yet worked out what this was to mean in practical, including financial, terms. Meanwhile the former trade unions had suddenly lost much of that part of their income which came from subscriptions. They could not afford to keep their houses of culture afloat.[100] Many houses of culture shut down, although sometimes their public management committees were able to help them survive.[101]

1981–8

After the events of 1980–1, the liquidation of many cultural-enlightenment institutions and the demise of old trade unions and the Central Trade Union Council, CRZZ, itself, the situation became very confused. In early 1987 CRZZ's successor was still only at the stage of making progress towards establishing itself in CRZZ's place in cultural enlightenment. Since December 1981, official policy has been both repressive and highly permissive. Houses of culture have been purged of unsubmissive arts groups.[102] The law on artistic institutions of December 1984 subjected all artistic groups, including amateur ensembles, to closer control by the people's councils.[103] At the same time, the regime's commitment to reform in the area of cultural diffusion was expressed by a new law on the subject in 1984 and new statutes for houses of culture in 1983. The latter made houses of culture's programmes and financing entirely the responsibility of local government. A National Cultural Council and Fund for Cultural Development have been established and have responsibilities for sponsoring cultural diffusion, although the new money available for culture does not seem to have been spread fairly or evenly and in the Fund's budget for 1985–6 the Polish–Soviet Friendship Society received by far the largest allocation of any single institution.[104] Moreover, several heavy industry ministries were released from the obligation to contribute to the Fund in 1986. The conclusion of the confidential 'Report on the state of culture' prepared for the National Cultural Council in 1985 also suggested that the situation had not improved, and pointed out that state investment had declined.

Cultural enlightenment has been extensively decentralized, presumably partly because of the shortage of central funds, but also in a bid for legitimacy, reversing the 1970s centralization and lack of egalitarianism. In addition, this trend may be a manifestation of the same sense of impotence which prompts the regime to largely tolerate the existence of unofficial cultural activities, providing they do not take place in official institutions. Although in theory ministry of culture yearly guidelines are to be observed, in fact they are interpreted very loosely. The type of campaigning and Chinese-style mass parades which characterized the 1970s have disappeared.[105] The head of the house of culture department of the ministry of culture acknowledged the depoliticization of official leisure activities when he wrote in 1986 that in the *1950s* houses of culture had conducted ideological work as well as cultural enlightenment.[106]

The post-1981 period in Poland bears a certain resemblance to the extreme de-Stalinization obtaining temporarily after 1956. Not only is there depoliticization, but also some houses of culture have closed, although since statistics are no longer published, it is impossible to tell how many. However, there remains the obvious difference between the two periods that whereas in 1956 there was still a residue of trust in the regime, Poles in the 1980s trusted only in themselves. The 1970s boycott of the houses of culture continued, combined with a flourishing unofficial culture.

Conclusions: Poland

Most Polish scholars seem to agree about the periodization of the history of cultural enlightenment. They adopt political watersheds, since each political turning point involved an evaluation and partial rejection of the cultural policy of the preceding period. This was almost inevitable, since no political crisis in Poland can occur without intense consideration of cultural matters: Polish culture is such an essential element of Polish nationalism and Polish nationalism is such a fundamental constituent of all Polish crises. Moreover, cultural policy is strongly reactive. Gomulka reacted to the situation in 1956 by almost entirely relinquishing control over culture for several years; Gomulka reacted to the events of 1968 and Gierek to those of 1970 by increasing control; Jaruzelski has zigzagged from one extreme to the other. Official attempts to depict Polish cultural history since 1944 as a steadily progressing cultural revolution ring hollow. It is true that in the area of access to cultural institutions and participation in organized cultural activity there has been progress since the death of Stalin (though with important social and geographical inequalities). There has, however, been no cultural revolution in Polish people's attitudes and behaviour: they have not acquired appropriate 'political culture' in the Soviet use of the term and many refuse to take advantage of increased cultural facilities precisely because they do not wish to be socialized by the regime.

Hungary

In September 1974, Hungary's leading spokesperson on culture, György Aczél, stressed the importance of cultural enlightenment's ideological role. He warned that it faced a dual danger. On the one hand stood populism, on the other, the West.[107] Whereas in the USSR Western cultural trends have been the main competitors to Stalinist cultural enlightenment, in Hungary and Poland the erosion of Stalinist forms of cultural enlightenment has been caused by the adoption of both Western models and those drawn from the national cultural heritage. The remainder of this chapter will take as its touchstones regime and public attitudes towards these two phenomena.

Cultural enlightenment before 1945

The first adult education societies and clubs were established in Hungary in the early nineteenth century.[108] The most important was the Hungarian Society for Natural History (1841). This was the first national society concerned with 'diffusion of knowledge' (*ismeret-térjesztö munka*) – voluntary educational work, chiefly in the form of lectures given by intellectuals for the benefit of the less well-educated. Diffusion of knowledge became one of the main components of the Hungarian cultural-enlightenment tradition. After the Compromise of 1867 cultural-enlightenment activity increased, with some participation by the state. The Budapest Association for Public Education provided state aid for literacy teaching and the establishment of public libraries.[109] 'Education outside the school' and popular cultural activities were also sponsored by the churches and the Trade Union Council, after its formation in 1899. Sunday schools, evening courses and workers' choirs became widespread.[110]

In rural areas, especially on the Great Hungarian Plain, the most common institutions were the 'reading clubs', which often had connections with political groups. From the 1880s these were frequently clerical and nationalist associations, while in the twentieth century some clubs had ties with social democrats.[111] In 1906 the Society for Social Sciences established a Free University of Social Sciences with the aim of educating the working classes as a precondition for socialism. Members of the intelligentsia volunteered to lecture at the free university, which had a student membership of around three thousand workers. The Galileo Circle, a radical student organization founded in

Budapest in 1908, also participated in adult education programmes together with the trade unions.[112]

In 1907, the first national co-ordinating body, the Hungarian National Congress for Education Outside the School, was set up.[113] However, until 1919 cultural enlightenment mostly remained the concern of individuals and non-state organizations. In 1919 the Republic of Councils made cultural enlightenment one of its major responsibilities, and pursued it energetically. For example, theatres were nationalized on the second day of the Republic's existence.[114] Government decrees on adult general and political education were issued in March and April. Four-month literacy courses were supposed to be established alongside every school for children. In Budapest 6,525 people attended workers' universities and evening courses. Leading cultural figures, including Babits, Moricz, Bártok and Kodály participated in the movement to make the arts accessible to the ordinary public.[115]

With the suppression of the Republic, many of the initiatives of 1919 were liquidated or disappeared, but some continued. The state retained an interest in adult education and made considerable progress in attacking illiteracy. However, cultural-enlightenment work was also, as in the pre-1919 period, undertaken by a very wide range of other organizations. It continued during most of the Second World War, during which it was partially mobilized by the government for war propaganda, but also continued to exist independently. Club work was an especially significant element in cultural enlightenment between the wars. Surveys conducted in 1921 and 1937 indicated that there existed reading or farmers' clubs in every second community. (However, these were unevenly distributed within the country, being more concentrated on the Great Hungarian Plain). The clubs were supported by various organizations, including the government, churches and political parties. Although in all cases the ostensible aim was to improve the agricultural and general knowledge of the peasants, in fact the creation of a political constituency and recruitment of activists were often important considerations. This was reflected in the nature of books read and plays performed. The Communists operated covertly (for example by spreading anti-militarist propaganda) through the clubs of the Social Democratic Hungarian Farm Labourers' Union. The clubs were normally run by local librarians or teachers and were also supported by writers, especially the populists.[116]

Thus the principles of post-1945 cultural enlightenment, already sketched out before the First World War, were firmly established. As in Russia and Poland, these were that adult education and the arts could legitimately be used to extend political influence and that the intelligentsia would regard as a duty co-operation in the democratization of culture (often regarded as equivalent to political socialization). *Clubs* were to become the core institutions of Communist cultural enlightenment.

Other institutions of the inter-war period were not destined to survive the Communist takeover. These included a wide range of cultural associations, the people's colleges and sociographical camps. They were either too hard for the post-war Communists to assimilate or too much associated with the churches or the populists to be acceptable. However, they are of significance, since the awareness that they constituted part of the national tradition was not lost. Interest in them was expressed again in 1953–5 and 1956, and from the late 1960s they began to be resuscitated.

The 'people's college' (*népföiskola*) was a nineteenth-century Danish institution, an adult education institute which offered courses – usually residential, and of several months' duration – to young people from peasant families. The object was for them to return to their villages and impart what they had learned in the way of agricultural and general knowledge and Christian morality. The ex-students also maintained strong ties with their colleges. The colleges aroused interest all over East–Central Europe as being suited to the special needs of under-developed rural areas. After some abortive experiments in the mid-1920s, many people's colleges were founded during the later 1930s and early 1940s. Most were run by the protestant churches, others by right-wing and nationalist organizations. Left-wing groups also ran colleges, some of which had connections with the populist writers and some of which the Communists were able to infiltrate. The colleges trained many future Communist politicians and administrators. The colleges encouraged the maintenance of contacts between ex-students and since many of the latter were to play a prominent role in public life after 1945, such informal links became significant, particularly in 1956.[117]

Another type of cultural enlightenment was the sociographical or village study camp. Although sociography, a combination of sociological and geographical fieldwork and fiction, was a genre normally practised by one individual writer or journalist, in the years before the Second World War sociographical camps were organized for scouts, young church members, university students and student teachers. Their purpose was primarily to educate the young town-dwellers about the life and culture of the peasantry, but they were also meant to bring benefit to the communities under study.[118]

1945–53

The years immediately after the war were, as in Poland, a time of intense cultural-enlightenment activity by many different organizations and individuals.[119] The 'free adult education' (*szabadmüvelödés*) movement declared itself an independent non-party organization of 'semi-official' nature. At the village level, about 70 per cent of the chairmen of the free adult education councils were priests. From 1946 the National Board for Free Education attempted to co-ordinate the work of the mass organizations, political parties and churches. However, the ministry of religion and culture was also heavily involved, and for example set up its own people's colleges. The Communists also used the people's colleges – which were sponsored by two members of the top party leadership, Révai and Rajk[120] – and organized a wide range of rural cultural-enlightenment or propaganda activities.

During the final stages of the Communist takeover, in 1947–8, the National Board for Free Education and all non-Communist cultural societies and institutions were abolished, as were people's colleges as a genre (1948). The fact that the Communists had successfully infiltrated the cultural-enlightenment movement of the immediate post-war years gave them a base upon which to build a Soviet-type cultural-enlightenment system. Yet the fact that they had destroyed so many popular and 'authentic' institutions was to be a serious handicap.

In 1949 a cultural-enlightenment ministry (*Népmüvelési Minisz-térium*) was established and became responsible for cultural enlightenment, as its name suggests. However, it was also in charge of education and culture in general, indicating the primacy of political socialization among its tasks. Révai, one of the most prominent members of the Stalinist leadership, was minister until 4 July 1953. Despite Révai's power and his commitment to the imposition of Stalinist policies, the introduction of the Soviet model was far from smooth and was to some extent resisted by the very bureaucrats responsible for executing the policy.[121] In particular, there are said to have been constant arguments with the Folk Culture Institute (*Népmüvészeti Intézet*: hereafter NI), which was set up in 1951 and was supposed to carry out 'cultural-agitational work' jointly with the ministry.[122] The NI also functioned as a replacement for the liquidated Hungarian cultural organizations and some of the latters' personnel (such as former members of the Bártok Society) were co-opted to work in the Institute. It emerged in 1953–6 that many of the staff still had populist sympathies.[123] However, in the Stalinist period the institute and ministry did generally co-operate, in manufacturing new mass 'folk' dances and songs which addressed specific contemporary political and production issues – or sponsoring their spurious 'discovery' – and in spreading Russian culture.[124]

Cultural enlightenment was imposed through a new network of houses of culture and clubs: 'we copied the Soviet Union exactly in every point'.[125] The houses of culture were regulated by law in 1951 and in the same year their purpose was defined to be agitation and mass political socialization.[126]

The houses of culture were required to involve as many as possible of the population in their activities. Thousands of amateur groups were created, although many were shortlived. In practice, although the central organs aspired to absolute control, they had only limited influence over what really went on. When a house of culture was built and there was thus a large hall at public disposal the area was often soon made use of for arts events and light entertainment unconnected with socialization.[127] The Stalinist era saw some real achievements in opening access to culture among the mass of the population.[128] But policy also backfired since, as in Poland, much of the population was alienated from the official ideology and all things Soviet, and retreated whenever possible into frivolous apolitical leisure activities.

1953–6

After Stalin's death differences of opinion about cultural policy emerged in the Hungarian leadership. Révai was dismissed and replaced by József Darvas, former populist and national peasant party authority on cultural enlightenment.[129] For a while it seemed that real reform might be possible within cultural enlightenment as a whole. The June 1953 Central Committee resolution, which initiated the de-Stalinization process in Hungary, created the climate for such a reform, especially with its reference to the need to cherish national traditions.[130] More space for local initiative was promised to cultural-enlightenment workers and they were given the opportunity to air their views.[131] A conference of culture house directors was held in December 1953 and addressed the problem of public antipathy towards the institutions. The cause was said to be their use as agitpoints (in respect of which a certain peasant was quoted as saying 'there's agitation indoors, there's agitation outdoors, but all we want to do is read'). A return to more traditional Hungarian activities was advocated.[132] Another forum was provided by the journal *Népmüvelés (Cultural Enlightenment)*, which first appeared in January 1954.

However, reform attempts were soon frustrated by party interference. Just as in many other areas Rákosi, as party leader, used the party machine to undermine reform undertaken by the state apparatus (headed by Imre Nagy). It was not Darvas, the minister, who was in control of cultural policy, but the party's academic and culture department.[133] Many reform proposals were written within the ministry, but only for the drawer or the waste-paper basket.[134]

The nineteenth-century Natural History Society was recreated in 1953 as the Society for Propagating Natural and Social Sciences (TTIT, later TIT) and soon became a debating house for radical reformers.[135] The chief initial forum for opposition to Rákosi's Stalinist policies in 1956, the Petőfi Club, was also concerned about cultural enlightenment, especially about the closure of the people's colleges. Several leaders of the Petőfi Club were former people's college directors or students.[136] In September 1956, as a concession to opposition demands, the Politburo passed a resolution re-establishing the people's college movement. The extent to which the culture of the people's colleges had made its mark was evidenced by the fact that on the march which began the uprising on 23 October the crowd sang a people's college song, 'Tomorrow we shall change the world'.[137] The dangers of bringing together workers and unreliable intellectuals for the purpose of adult education was demonstrated during the uprising when Miskolc students infected local workers with their dissent.[138]

After 23 October reform proposals for cultural enlightenment were put forward within the ministry and NI.[139] However, among the wider public, the issue of specific national cultural traditions seems to have been important rather in the run-up to the uprising than during the uprising itself – although the wider issue of autonomy from the Soviet Union necessarily contained cultural implications. The Writers' Union supported the Budapest workers' council, an action which led to the effective liquidation of all arts and intelligentsia associations in the months after the uprising.[140] The journal *Népművelés*, normally a useful source of information on cultural enlightenment, was not published from November 1956 to August 1957 (which in itself indicates how long it took to re-establish a 'normal' situation). The September 1957 issue's leading article acknowledged that 'during these months written directives from the central bodies have been very lacking' and spoke of the fact that although the main wave of opposition had occurred in professional arts organizations, this had created a smaller, but more lingering, wave of opposition in cultural enlightenment.[141]

The early Kádár years: 1957–68

The first five years after the uprising were a period of intensive consideration of ideology.[142] The most important directive on culture was the 1958 Central Committee Cultural policy directives, which emphasized the role of art in the construction of socialism and which have remained, in theory, the framework within which all subsequent cultural policy has operated. The directives largely decentralized cultural administration to county level. As in Poland, where there was a similar reaction against, and decentralization of, the Stalinist cultural-enlightenment system, the role of houses of culture came under extensive discussion. The Politburo discussed houses of culture in 1959 and passed a resolution emphasizing their particular responsibilities for encouraging peasants to collectivize and for work among young people.

Administrative reorganization and new regulations aimed at making cultural enlightenment more efficient and co-ordinated in numerous ways were not very effective. Local party committees were not in general very interested in making them so. Houses of culture were also dogged by all the other usual problems of cultural enlightenment, such as shortage of material resources and of trained staff, despite improvements in both areas. As in Khrushchev's Soviet Union, much was made of the need for propaganda to reach every corner of society. Stress was laid on the voluntary and active participation of the public in cultural life, for example by contributing lectures or helping to build a new house of culture. No mention, however, was made in official pronouncements of positive public work conducted in the pre-Stalinist period. The people's college issue, for example, seemed to be dead. This was in tune with Kádár's wider policy of suppressing manifestations of Hungarian nationalism in the aftermath of 1956, at a time when other East–Central European leaders were adopting a more permissive or encouraging stance towards rediscovery of the pre-Stalinist cultural heritage. One important and relatively spontaneous new initiative was the founding of many new clubs, especially youth clubs, both inside and outside the house of culture network. This was similar to contemporary developments in Poland, but without the Poles' strong rural emphasis.

Kádár's 'alliance policy', launched in 1962, of wooing the support and participation in public life of non-Communists had inevitable implications for cultural enlightenment. It became more concerned with general persuasion and the spreading of culture, and less with forcing people to participate in campaigns. However, despite the considerable liberalization of literary life, cultural enlightenment did not enjoy the same freedom and seems to have been more tightly controlled by the leadership than its Polish equivalent, although it was also realized that houses of culture could only be effective if they took account of local requirements. In practice, they may have often ignored ideological requirements. For instance, a spot check of sixteen houses of culture on international women's day 1967 revealed that only two of them were celebrating this least 'ideological' of official festivals. Six were closed (although one had earlier housed a co-operative farm meeting); in the others, people were watching television or films, rehearsing, and in one case drinking beer in advance of a performance by a popular entertainer.[143]

The years preceding a major reclassification of houses of culture in 1968 witnessed a wide-ranging debate on the future of cultural enlightenment, in the course of which it became respectable again to refer to the achievements of the 1930s. This was also the time when the

1930s genre of sociographical journalism was recovering respect-ability.[144] If attitudes towards national cultural traditions are one of our touchstones for change in official policy, then 1968 can be seen as an important year. Internal developments and recognitions of inadequacies within cultural enlightenment were undoubtedly a major cause of reappraisal. But the external climate of reform also provided a more favourable attitude to pre-revolutionary traditions.

1968–88

The New Economic Mechanism (NEM) introduced in 1968, did not apply to the field of cultural enlightenment, where there was supposed to be no relinquishing of state funding and control to market forces. The ongoing reforms in cultural enlightenment were specifically discon-nected from the economic reform. They were said to be in response to social change and more sophisticated cultural requirements. The leading party cultural officials took pains to make this clear and criticized people who had expressed hope that there would be reform equivalent to that in the economic sphere. They also, at first, tried to allay fears that greater freedom for market forces would damage high culture, that enterprises would be able to get away with spending less on culture and that state subsidies would also be reduced.[145] But after the invasion of Czechoslovakia and as opponents of NEM regained influence in Hungary, 'harmful' effects of NEM were admitted. These were said to include rising book prices, a decreasing number of high-quality films and plays, decreasing political content of repertoires and an influx of Western popular culture.[146]

The introduction of NEM and subsequent economic reforms did in fact in the long term have a profound and unintended effect on cultural enlightenment: attendance at houses of culture became even worse, since the new possibilities for working in one's spare time often appeared a more attractive pursuit than cultural enlightenment. Moreover, since the beginning of the present economic difficulties in the late 1970s, a second job has often become an imperative for many people, further reducing the time they can spend on cultural activities. However, this effect only became noticeable in the second half of the decade. Indeed between the falling attendance figures of the late 1960s and the later 1970s there was a crest of increased participation. This was largely caused by a surge of public interest in spontaneous and collective cultural activity and the enormous popularity of youth clubs in this period.

Clubs began to be built at the end of the 1950s and the Communist youth organization, KISZ, sponsored their expansion in the following decade. However, the authorities became increasingly worried about the ideological content of the clubs' activities and the strength of their attraction for young people. Their fears were aroused, as in the USSR and Poland, by the popularity and influence of the Western youth movement and its music. Another, particularly Hungarian, cause for concern was that enthusiasm for Western culture was complemented by a wave of enthusiasm for Hungarian folk culture, of which the chief manifestation was the *táncház* (dancing house) movement, in which thousands of young people learned traditional Hungarian dances. Up to a point this was acceptable, but much of the activity could be branded nationalist and some was certainly anti-Soviet.

The regime responded by attempting to improve the effectiveness of political socialization for young people and continuing the debate on the crisis in cultural enlightenment in general. A Central Committee resolution in March 1974, 'On the position of cultural enlightenment and tasks for its development' was only the most authoritative of a series of new resolutions and regulations leading up to a comprehensive law on the subject in 1976. This guaranteed the right of every citizen to cultural enlightenment and also established participation in this as a *duty*. The law was presented as a significant development in the democratization of culture.[147]

The law on cultural enlightenment was conceived in the optimistic atmosphere of the mid-1970s, but the social and economic difficulties of ensuing years, as was mentioned above, contributed towards a decrease in participation in cultural enlightenment in many areas. However, despite often unfavourable conditions, including obstruction from some semi-Stalinist county authorities, since the 1970s radical cultural-enlightenment specialists within the NI, HNF, universities, individual council administrations and county cultural centres have developed their knowledge of 1930s–1940s Hungarian work and modern Western developments in adult education and social care and then applied these on a small-scale, sometimes experimental basis. In particular, work has been conducted in large Budapest cultural centres and also at the village level (bypassing county administrations). There is populist influence in the sociographical village research camps (functioning since the late 1960s) and the recent attempts to set up people's colleges.[148] These have been viewed with suspicion by the authorities, because of their association with nationalism and clericalism. Some of their Hungarian supporters were interested in the achievements of the Polish people's colleges set up during the Solidarity era.[149]

Since about 1980 cultural enlightenment has been increasingly used as an instrument for attempting to solve specific social problems, although initiatives in many problem areas began in the 1970s on an individual basis. The main experiments in the 1970s were the 'open house' cultural centres, where the public helped themselves to the activities on offer, and 'family clubs' to provide support for families under stress. Counselling and self-help groups for, among others, divorced people and alcoholics, began to take place in houses of culture in the mid-1970s. Another development has been the establishment of cultural associations, which were regulated by law in 1982. In June 1985 their members were said to number nearly 20,000. Some of these associations have been set up as alternatives to official cultural institutions in recognition of the unpopularity of houses of culture.[150]

However, the widest, if not politically significant, development in recent years has been the growth of interest in purely practical activities. The 1987 plan of the Debrecen Cultural Centre, for instance, described it as the major trend in recent cultural enlightenment. The centre had been involved in organizing various exhibitions, for example of medical and fashion products from local and foreign factories, which had drawn tens of thousands of visitors.[151]

The 1982 law on the formation of associations finally opens cultural enlightenment to market forces, since it permits the establishment of competition from the private sector, for example, in language tuition, at present one of the principle sources of income for large houses of culture. In 1983 houses of culture were reorganized according to a new three-tier system, by which the lowest category has no economic independence, but in the other two, 'partly-independent' and 'independent' institutions, the staff possess greater freedom in handling the house of culture's income and can share in its profits. This benefits the big houses of culture, but places small institutions in the villages and housing estates in a still more unequal position.[152]

In 1984 a national conference discussed the situation of cultural enlightenment.[153] The chairman of the National Cultural Council, who opened the conference, suggested that its main themes should be the democratization of culture, the connection between culture and the economy and the declining interest in amateur arts, accompanied by increased interest in amateur technical activity.[154] Pozsgay pointed out that the activization of culture which had been so important a concern in 1974 was still a highly relevant issue and pleaded for 'state and other organs' to put more faith in people's ability to organize their own cultural activities. Other speakers expressed the same idea. Democratization was also discussed in terms of widening access to culture for lower income groups. The secretary of the National Trade Union Council, SZOT, mentioned, for example, large families and young people with low incomes. He criticized sharply the decline in state spending on culture: it was a fallacy to think that investments in culture could safely be allowed to decline without causing any serious damage to the long-term interests of society.[155]

The connection between culture and the economy was widely

discussed, with different speakers attaching differing degrees of importance to the reduction of state aid. The minister of culture, Köpeczi, said that it was possible to exaggerate the harmful effect of the New Economic Mechanism on cultural spending, which he presented as something of an intelligentsia myth. At present a satisfactory 27.1 per cent of spending on culture overall came from the state, 3.7 per cent from enterprises and co-operatives and 62.9 per cent from the public. (A handbook published in 1984 stated that 'more than half' of house of culture running and personnel costs were covered by the state, the remainder being met by enterprises, co-operatives, etc. and by the public.)[156] Köpeczi said that priorities for cultural-enlightenment policy were to:

1 combat the spread of pseudo-science, such as astrology and mystical Christianity;
2 combat scepticism about and distortions of the official ideology;
3 provide more state aid for popularly accessible art, and less for experimental;
4 learn from East European, especially Soviet cultural life; assist national minority culture in Hungary;
5 not tolerate low class entertainment;
6 aid amateur arts;
7 develop the culture of everyday life;
8 widen access to culture, for example, for retired people;
9 develop self-management in small cultural groups; encourage KISZ, the trade unions and the HNF to co-operate, not compete in organizing cultural life;
10 improve production and use of new technology, such as videos, so as to stem the import of Western horror and pornographic films.[157]

In 1986–7, houses of culture in Budapest, Debrecen and Hajdúböszörmény seemed to concentrate to a great extent on Hungarian folk art (dance, music and embroidery) and on computers, Western videos and foreign language teaching. Political elements were largely confined to participating with local party/state authorities in celebrating official or socialist holidays (for example, Lenin's birthday) and to helping organize workers' socialist brigades. The mushrooming of cultural associations was mentioned above; as in the USSR and Poland, the later 1980s have witnessed a blossoming of independent cultural/social/political organizations outside the official network.

Conclusions: Hungary

It is hard to draw conclusions about the state of Hungarian cultural enlightenment today, particularly in view of its extreme decentralization. Most of cultural enlightenment has become almost devoid of political content and in many respects is comparable to British adult education (from which it has borrowed). The intense concern of many cultural specialists with social problems gives some recent Hungarian cultural enlightenment a relevancy to real issues which Polish and Soviet cultural enlightenment rarely matches. In this one can observe a return to the genuine traditions of cultural enlightenment, although the social issues themselves are often different from those of the pre-Communist period (in many cases being by-products of the economic reform). Hungarian cultural enlightenment is thus quite the opposite of Stalinist cultural enlightenment, which addressed political rather than social tasks.

Conclusions: general

Returning to the imagery with which the section on Poland began, one can see a pattern in all three countries (most clearly in Hungary and least clearly in the USSR) of the house of cultural enlightenment pulling increasingly away from Stalinist forms of *political* socialization and highly politicized leisure, towards new forms of cultural enlightenment which use the arts and adult education to tackle *social* problems. These 'new' forms are often based either on traditional national types of cultural enlightenment (like the people's college) or on new Western ideas; they are described in the next chapter.

At the same time as dedicated cultural-enlightenment specialists have attempted to de-Stalinize in this fashion, there have remained many ideologists and politicians anxious to preserve the essentials of the Stalinist system and introduce only administrative reforms – particularly in the USSR, but also in Poland and Hungary. However, administrative reforms are an inadequate solution, given the greater power over their own leisure time which ordinary people have acquired as a result of de-Stalinization. In Poland and Hungary the problem of luring the population into houses of culture is compounded by nostalgia among ex-cultural-enlightenment enthusiasts for the relatively recent spontaneous and self-organized club movements of the late 1950s to early 1960s in Poland and late 1960s to early 1970s in Hungary, backed by memories of the immediate post-war era. The Khrushchev period in the USSR is for some people a (fainter) equivalent. As Chapter Two has shown, the mid-1980s have witnessed an approximate repeat of these earlier bursts of de- Stalinization – accompanied by familiar attempts on the part of the authorities to over-organize and under-fund.

Chapter three

Changing content – changing goals?

Introduction

Chapter Two described how the need to reconcile control with an increase in popular input into cultural enlightenment created serious discrepancies and, sometimes, tensions, as many citizens and people employed in cultural enlightenment tried to jettison political socialization in favour of pure entertainment or non-political hobbies, the revival of national traditions or the adoption of Western fashions. Young people in particular seemed to be abandoning the ideology, and this caused particular concern to the authorities from the late 1960s onwards.

In such circumstances, the party became primarily concerned to assert sufficient control to ensure that houses of culture did not sabotage official socialization efforts by patronizing undesirable activities, rather than to positively develop political socialization. In fact, activities became increasingly depoliticized.The final stage of the process, which is occurring at the moment, is the powerlessness of the party to prevent houses of culture from being used for activities of an oppositional nature. At this stage, the house of culture has merely turned into a hall which can accommodate a spectrum of activities: it becomes difficult to pretend that it is an agency propagating the official ideology. This chapter discusses how the conflicting interests of party and public have been accommodated and reconciled, or not, and looks at the limits of acceptability. It is concluded that often the limits were, and often still are, very unclear and arbitrary. It examines the content of cultural enlightenment in the context of the development of different types of socializing activity, from the amateur arts which typified Stalinist cultural enlightenment to the computer courses and 'informal organizations' which are popular today. It concentrates chiefly on the impact of cultural enlightenment as addressed to individual citizens, rather than to social groups or classes; the social goals of cultural enlightenment are discussed in the final section.

69

It is difficult, even impossible, to know what is typical. Although some of the limited survey research does describe 'ordinary' practice, the more plentiful newspaper and journal articles tend to dwell on interesting and unusual types of work, not standard practice. Moreover, most of my interview and observational research was conducted in untypical areas: Budapest, Debrecen, Warsaw, Poznań, Moscow and Leningrad, which as major cities are particularly well endowed. Practice elsewhere is probably often much more conventional. One frequently reads and hears complaints about the unimaginative and pedestrian quality of cultural enlightenment, and its standardized character. For example, a Hungarian scholar claims that 'the yearly plans of a village house of culture in Abaúj [north-east Hungary] or Vas [on the Austrian border] hardly differ one from another, while the tendency towards uniformity is even more marked in the towns'. The same standardization was prevalent in the USSR in the 1970s and even in 1989.[1]

Amateur arts

Although groups of 'amateur technologists' did exist under Stalin, most cultural enlightenment was heavily oriented towards amateur arts. Songs, dramatic sketches, poems and other art forms were crudely saturated with political propaganda and demands for workers to raise their productivity. A typical description of amateur arts, referring to the participation of about two million performers in a national competition, reads: 'Amateur arts are a mighty instrument for the political socialization of the population. They vividly express the joy in life of the Soviet people; their strong patriotic feelings; their deep devotion and gratitude to the party of Lenin and Stalin....The force of this type of art lies in its mass scale.'[2]

The object was to force people to declare their support for the system, to watch their neighbours do the same, and to create a great emotional impression. Czesław Miłosz compares the significance of the Polish club under Stalinism to that of the chapel in the Middle Ages. 'People who attend a "club" submit to a collective rhythm, and so come to feel that it is absurd to think differently from the collective. The collective is composed of units that doubt; but as these individuals pronounce the ritual phrases and sing the ritual songs, they create a collective aura to which they in turn surrender. Despite its apparent appeal to reason, the "club's" activities comes under the heading of collective magic.'[3] Folk art – or what passed for it – was allotted a special place while jazz and other music of Western origin was largely outlawed, to the extent that there was a confiscation of saxophones in the USSR in 1949, and

Khrennikov, as secretary of the USSR Composers' Union, travelled round Eastern Europe on a musical inquisition.[4]

As Chapter Two described, after Stalin's death in 1953 Stalinist manipulation of amateur arts was subjected to scathing critical analysis in both Hungary and Poland. Novel types of amateur art emerged, particularly under the influence of greater access to Western developments in the arts and entertainment. Many Stalinist attitudes, however, lived on for years, and in some cases have survived to the present day. The 'more the better' approach is hard to extinguish, and through the 1960s and 1970s politicians continued to cite the high numbers of participants in amateur arts as an indicator of people's interest in building Communism and by implication, of the legitimacy of the regime. Figures were artificially inflated and the official statistics should be treated with caution.[5]

Another Stalinist attitude which survives, especially in the USSR, is the feeling that art should serve political campaigns. Why is it considered to be a useful instrument in campaigns, and is it in fact reliable and effective? An important advantage of artistic propaganda over lectures is considered to lie in the fact that it makes an emotional as well as an intellectual impact, on both spectators and performers. This is considered to be essential if propaganda is to succeed in changing citizens' inner, and often irrational, beliefs.[6] Hence the continuing importance of mass public festivals and the increasing tendency towards replacing lectures by debates or dramatized treatments of the same themes. Sometimes this type of socialization is presented as being like taking nasty medicine on a sugar lump. On the other hand, 'artistic' satire may be nastier than straightforward criticism. For example, satirical agitbrigade scenarios written about common problems, to be performed anywhere in the Soviet Union, are often accompanied by an instruction to insert the names of particular local offenders. Local film clubs also have a role to play by, for example, filming local drunken gatherings and showing their films in the house of culture.

There are particular situations in which emotional impact is much more valuable than intellectual argument. This explains the continuing use of amateur arts in the anti-alcohol campaign. For example, the anti-alcohol play *Champion*, written to be performed by amateur groups, arouses 'powerful collective disturbance'. Participants and spectators are intended to identify with the hero, an ex-boxer who, after an accident which disables him, turns to drink and bad company; or with the heroine, his loyal wife, who saves him with the help of doctors.[7]

Another field in which amateur arts have an important role is in Soviet anti-religious propaganda, in which the club is viewed as being in direct competition with the church, the synagogue or the mosque. Thus, for example, the opening paragraph of an article on cultural enlightenment in Tadzhkistan sets the scene and the problem: 'The lands of a prosperous collective farm border the edge of Dushanbe. On the farm stand a club and a mosque, almost next door to each other. But the mosque is always full to the brim, while the club has only a sprinkling of visitors.'[8] Clubs have a duty to win the faith of the local population. For instance, a 1982 official resolution 'On the work of cultural organs and institutions in strengthening atheist propaganda' ordered the cultural-enlightenment press to publish articles about good house of culture and atheist museum practice, announced a competition for one act plays on atheist themes, and declared that all amateur arts activities, including discos, were to be used in the struggle.[9] As this resolution suggests, Soviet clubworkers are perceived by the party to have a duty to raise visitors' consciousness by including atheist education as a component in all sorts of other activities. These may be lectures with titles like 'Mozart and religion' and 'How to use the works of Lev Tolstoy in atheist education'.[10] Alternatively, anti-religious propaganda may be combined with a fashion show or a concert of classical music to increase its palatability.[11]

Atheist propaganda seems to be regarded as one of the least appealing types of socialization. Even the people who are responsible for conducting it are notoriously uninterested and incompetent. The most creative type of anti-religious work is the organization of Communist rites and festivals. Since the 1950s, this has been an increasingly important part of cultural-enlightenment work in all three countries, although even here indifference among club workers has been reported.[12] To some extent, alternative rites have been moved to specialist institutions like wedding palaces, but many rites of passage and seasonal holidays are still organized by houses of culture.

Atheist propaganda was never mentioned to me in the course of interviews in any of the countries, nor was there any attempt to introduce atheistic elements into any events I have ever attended in a house of culture except for one Tchaikovsky concert in a remote village in rural Russia. One aspect of *glasnost* is increased religious tolerance and the opportunity for people to legitimately satisfy their curiosity about religion without necessarily having to attend an atheist lecture to do so. In April 1989, one evangelist priest was said to have been offered a constant flow of invitations to speak at houses of culture and even schools. On at least one occasion, religious pictures were exhibited and sold.[13]

I have no evidence of direct atheist propaganda as opposed to 'scientific education' actually being conducted in Hungary in recent years.[14] In Poland, the situation of atheist propaganda seems to be even worse, and in 1986, for example, even the very ideologically correct

Palace of Culture in Poznań hosted a concert of Negro spirituals sung by a church choir from Birmingham.

It seems to be a reasonable assumption that art makes more impact than a lecture. The propaganda potential of art was after all recognized long before the appearance of Soviet-style cultural enlightenment. Even if one ignores 'high culture' and the intent of individual artists, architects etc., more humble cultural enlightenment based on the same assumption is equally to be found in non-Communist countries, though often on a very small scale. Whether it is in the form of plays and puppet shows to educate British people about the viewpoints, feelings and rights of disabled people, or Ladakhis (in Northern India) about the benefits of solar energy, it is still a type of cultural enlightenment based on the same principle.

However, it is arrogant to assume that the effect of a piece of art will be wholly beneficial (from the point of view of its propagator). Artistic propaganda can only make an effect if it is well-written and properly pitched. If it is pitched too low, as so frequently occurs in the USSR, or as it was under Gierek, it becomes ridiculous. If it assumes too great a level of previous awareness of the issues or intellectual understanding it will be misunderstood. Moreover, it is unlikely to work if the audience is hostile to the theme addressed – for example, if it is contradictory to the prevailing political culture, as with much atheist propaganda or with pro-Russian propaganda in Poland or Hungary. Such efforts are often positively counterproductive. Moreover, even if the general values of the audience are correctly understood and sensitively approached, individual receivers vary so much in their responses that it is dangerous to assume that one can know in advance the precise effect of a piece of art.

Just because art is a powerful weapon but so difficult to manipulate, the Stalinist and, to a decreasing and uneven extent, successive leaderships have tried to closely monitor artistic events: that is, the repertoire of amateur arts has been controlled by censorship and restrictive regulations. The transitory nature of an arts performance as compared, for example, with a book, makes it much harder to enforce censorship regulations. For example, as was mentioned in Chapter Two, in January 1968 a Polish ideological official complained that much amateur arts work was totally devoid of ideological content.[15] An analysis of the programmes of three Polish houses of culture in 1968 suggests that this was indeed true.[16] In the USSR, control has been tighter: one example of official aspiration to control amateur arts was the review of amateur pop groups conducted during Chernenko's tenure as general secretary. The newspaper *Trud* commented in January 1985: 'The solution of the problem of young people's music must start off from the principle that not a single ensemble should remain outside the field of vision of specialists and the general public.'[17]

The actual process whereby the repertoire was controlled in the Soviet Union until the present confused era of *glasnost'*, when many regulations seem to have been allowed to lapse, was as follows. The leader of each arts group (the choir conductor, ballet master, etc.) was primarily responsible for the repertoire. The management committee of the house of culture also checked it, and ultimate responsibility in a state house of culture was borne by the director; in a trade union institution, by the management committee. Performances and disco programmes for which performers were to be paid or an entrance charge made also had to be registered beforehand with the culture department of the *raion* or town *soviet* and were informally checked with the relevant primary party organization and KGB section.[18] This applied even to circus and dance, but only a minority of events were subject to this regulation, since performances by amateur groups were usually free of charge.[19] The culture departments and the national copyright association VAAP were supposed to check out local performances to monitor the observance of the rules and republican ministries of culture had to report back to the USSR Ministry of Culture twice a year. However, there have been complaints in official resolutions that they were lax in their duties.

Censorship can never be absolutely effective and even in the Stalinist period some productions managed to slip through the net. For example it was complained in March 1953 that 'At the Zavodoukovsky forestry enterprise in Tiumen' oblast', the repertoire of the amateur arts collectives is checked by nobody. As a result a concert at the Lesnovsky club was accompanied by a vulgar compere and the drama brigade of the Zavodoukovsky club performed an anti-artistic play'.[20]

Concern about trivial and non-ideological amateur art, which seems to have been a feature of the 1950s and 1960s, was increasingly in the 1960s and 1970s replaced in all three countries by worries about ideologically unsound Western culture and, in Hungary and the USSR, by some anxiety about culture with a nationalist content. In Hungary, as has already been mentioned, a serious effort was made during the 1970s to both control youth clubs and foster acceptable cultural enlightenment more generally. In the USSR, a series of resolutions by party, state and trade union cultural authorities on amateur arts and their repertoire testified to top-level concern. In 1980 yet another resolution complained that too few repertoire pieces were being issued on the themes of the struggle for peace and friendship among socialist nations, and 'the discrediting of the bourgeois way of life was not always convincing.' There was also a shortage of works about the working class and about contemporary village life. The solution: more works on Lenin, the leading role of the party, current party decisions, the October

Revolution, the Soviet way of life, friendship among nations in the USSR, proletarian internationalism, the struggle for peace and the falsehood of bourgeois ideology.[21]

Many organizations produce works for the amateur repertoire, including professional artists' unions and specialised arts publishing houses. They may cover certain types of socialization more thoroughly than others: for example, the majority of the recommendations prepared by the All-Russian Methodological Centre for Cultural Enlightenment were said in 1981 to be 'in aid of production'. Titles included 'Clubs at the harvest', 'The club and the labour collective', 'Labour rhythms of the five year plan' and 'Clubs to the aid of socialist emulation'.[22] Some idea of the repertoire available may be gained from the Polish and Russian specialist journals (unfortunately the Hungarian journals are less helpful). A survey over one year produced the results shown in Table 1.

Table 1 Russian and Polish repertoire material, 1986–7

	Journal	
Type of socialization	Klub	Inspiracje
Moral (for adults)	9	1
Patriotic/military/peace	6	2
Labour	6	
Internationalist	4	
No apparent socializing aim	3	3
Ecological/cultural heritage	3	
Political	3	small item in 1
Anti-alcohol	2	
Exposure of bourgeois values	2	
Aesthetic	1	1
Educational	1	
Physical education	1	
Children's (occasionally of a moral nature)	5	5
Total	46	13

Sources: Klub, no. 13, 1986–no. 12, 1987; *Inspiracje (Biblioteczka Repertuarowa),* no. 7, 1986–no. 6, 1987.

Amateur arts ensembles are supposed to engage in 'aesthetic education' of their own members. However, research has shown that few of them do: they are too busy preparing for concerts to have time to do anything else.[23] Another activity which consumes the time of some amateur ensembles is travel, both within the country and abroad, especially to Comecon countries, but also to the West. This aspect of belonging to an amateur arts group can be a chore if it only involves visits to local collective farms. Since there is a statutory regulation for Soviet amateur groups to perform for the public at least once or twice a month, they inevitably do end up giving a lot of local concerts.[24] As this regulation suggests, amateur arts are permeated by a strong philosophy of service (in theory). Participants are socializing not just themselves but also other people. Arts trips can also open up unusual possibilities for travel. For example, in 1979 amateur collectives from the RSFSR visited Bulgaria, Czechoslovakia, Norway and Japan, and the possibilities to travel for Polish and Hungarian groups seem to be greater: a Hungarian amateur choir may participate in an eisteddfod, or a Polish non-professional dance group tour France, Spain and Portugal. Such trips are obviously an incentive to participate in amateur arts over and above (or in place of) ideological commitment. They also bring prestige to the institution with which the amateur group is associated.[25] In the Soviet Union, the trade union authorities had by 1981 become so concerned about the 'loss of working and study time' by amateur groups that they issued a resolution strictly confining participation in concerts and festivals to weekends and holidays and limiting the number of trips per year.

Participants in amateur arts and the public generally are supposed to benefit from visits from professional performing artists, painters and writers, who perform in ordinary houses of culture, often in settlements where there is no other access to professional arts. This type of cultural enlightenment should be able to draw on the traditions in all three countries of intelligentsia service to the people, but in practice it frequently seems to fail (particularly in view of the often far from comfortable conditions the artists face on their travels). It is more likely to succeed, however, where there is a sense of mutual benefit, and the visitors find useful contacts, have a good holiday or are well rewarded, as for example was shown by a survey of outreach work in the Kraków area in the 1970s.[26]

Art or entertainment?

Although discos are a phenomenon new since Stalin's time, Soviet cultural authorities have reacted towards their appearance in a purely Stalinist fashion and tried to keep them within the procrustean bed of cultural enlightenment. They first appeared in the late 1970s (somewhat after their appearance in Eastern Europe) and in the USSR provoked considerable worry and concern from those concerned about ideology, security (there were even demands that they be held in brightly lit rooms) and morals – all reminiscent of Stalinist reactions to jazz, or worries expressed in the 1960s about noisy dances frequented by 'youths dressed like Western cinema stars'.[27] However, perhaps because of the coincidental revival of cold war ideology in the early 1980s, there was a sustained attempt not only to render discos harmless but also to transform them into events of 'high ideological and artistic quality'. 'It is youth music which is most often used by bourgeois propaganda for ideological sabotage on a variety of scales. This is the reason why the disco had to become a field of active ideological struggle, a channel for propaganda and counterpropaganda.'[28]

Soviet discos were regulated in 1980, first of all by a joint ministry of culture and Komsomol resolution 'On measures for improving the activity of amateur associations, hobby clubs and discotheques' and then by a 'Model statute for the amateur discotheque'.[29] The amateur disco was defined as 'one form of organization of the population's leisure time, the development of amateur arts, the satisfaction of spiritual needs and interest in music on the basis of a comprehensive utilization of artistic and audio-visual technological aids'. The best discos 'create interesting, emotionally filled publicistic and informational programmes, which have a perceptible effect on the socialization and formation of the aesthetic tastes of young people'.[30]

The difference in theory between a disco and a dance is that a Soviet disco has some educational content. Presumably this is connected with the fact that discos are officially viewed as originally having been channels for Western propaganda, and the solution found has been to fill them with counter-propaganda. The alternative, to ban the fashionable 'disco' altogether and stick to dances, seems to have been discounted. However, the official concept of a Soviet disco differs from that possessed by most ordinary people (as the 1980 resolution complained). For the latter, a disco is merely a dance, preferably with Western music. For example, one Soviet house of culture director wrote to the specialist journal *Klub*: 'I myself am a Communist, but when a regular inspection committee demanded that our philophone club propagandize the materials of the party congress at discos, I was slightly bewildered...'[31] At one disco which I attended in Voronezh in 1982, the participants protested by dancing between the projector and the slide screen during the 'educational' sections of the evening.

The 1980 resolution criticized the lack of control exercised by cultural and Komsomol organs and, having lamented the small use made of classical and folk music in disco programmes, went on to warn that sometimes Western and *samizdat* materials were used in their preparation, with the commentary element 're-transmitting bourgeois culture, and quite frequently exerting a negative influence on the socialization ... of Soviet young people.'[32] A further resolution, published by the ministry of culture, Komsomol and VTsSPS in 1982, sounded even more alarmed: 'Many disco programmes which are prepared for public participation are not registered with the cultural organs. They rarely take patriotic themes or use Russian classical or contemporary Soviet music.' Responsible organizations were ordered to exert more control and to make available more methodological guidance to disco planners. However, by 1987 this was still not readily available. One house of culture director from the Altai krai was told by her 'local' methodological centre – a three hours' journey distant – that she could come to visit them and copy out by hand as many programmes as she would need (for a weekly disco). Even after a visit to the ministry in Moscow she was still bereft of printed materials.[33]

Despite lingering Stalinist aspirations, financial considerations – the 'need to fulfil the financial plan at all costs'[34] – have in all three countries always operated against too exclusive a concentration on heavy political propaganda or agitation. As a 1975 Hungarian report pointed out, 'economic compulsion often leaves them [houses of culture] no choice but to organize programmes which are often low in quality, devoid of socializing content, and purely for entertainment.'[35] Village houses of culture continue to survive on films and dances, while urban houses of culture also organize light entertainment and pop concerts, not always by 'official' groups, or popular films: 'the tasks of ideological and moral education require the showing of one sort of film, the box office dictates its own conditions'.[36]

In other words, whatever the desires of policy-makers, because of the inadequacy of state subsidies for cultural enlightenment, houses of culture have little choice but to succumb to public taste, at least once a month. (This corresponds with the findings of Starr in the case of jazz: Starr argues that the authorities have been compelled to accept the performance of first jazz and then rock in face of their enormous popularity.) In 1988 a new statute for houses of culture completely omitted to mention political socialization or ideology and opened to houses of culture the possibility of becoming self-financing. (See below.)[37]

In Hungary and Poland, entertainments offered by houses of culture today often do not attempt to include any socializing content at all, and certainly in Poland this has been true since the mid-1960s, if not earlier.[38] In both countries entertainment is recognized as a legitimate function of cultural-enlightenment institutions, although it can hardly be included within the concept of cultural enlightenment. In the USSR, on the other hand, there have been continued attempts to insert a socializing element or theme or merely provide an ideological label. For example, dances are often preceded by a thematic evening with slides and speeches about, for example, heroic youth brigades; a fashion show may be punctuated with satirical sketches and interrogation by the compere of members of the audience ('what is your definition of beauty?', 'how would you describe contemporary woman?' and 'men, should women wear trousers?'); a lecture on religious burial rites may be titled 'Graves as a minor architectural form and atheist-patriotic education'; or a concert by a famous pop star may be 'in honour of the Great Patriotic War'.[39]

An institutional reflection of the de-ideologization of popular culture and entertainment is the creation of Soviet 'leisure centres' and Hungarian 'free time centres'. Their very names suggest no concern with cultural enlightenment, although strangely enough this seems to be more true in the case of the Soviet centres than in the Hungarian ones. The two Hungarian institutions I visited were simply large and modern cultural centres aimed at young people in particular. The Soviet *tsentry dosuga* were, according to interview informants in 1987, still very much pie in the sky, but in theory nine hundred are to be built by the end of the century and run by *Rossatraktsion* of the RSFSR ministry of culture. In other words, they are not part of the cultural-enlightenment network.[40] The 'Temporary statute for leisure centres' published in 1987 defined their basic functions as being, in the following order, 'entertainment, stimulating creative activity, teaching leisure skills, health and physical culture, providing possibilities for people to meet, informational-methodological, and others.' As described in *Klub*,

> The leisure centre may contain halls for sport and spectator events, dances and exhibitions, fruit machines, fairground attractions, computers, sports training facilities, film, slide and video-film shows and discos; soirées, toy libraries, billiards and skittle alleys, swimming pools, sauna and solaria; radio-electronic, metal-working, carpentry, sewing and other types of workshop, studios for sound and video recording, photographic and cinema laboratories, hire points, buffets, bar, cafés, etc.[41]

Labour training and amateur technical work

'Labour training' or 'socialization for labour' is a traditional element of cultural enlightenment. Often it has been the most important element, or at least on a par with political socialization, from which it is sometimes difficult to distinguish. Its main objective is to raise productivity. The means to this end are the creation of better labour discipline and a better work ethic, increasing the prestige of manual labour and encouraging technological innovation. The increasing of labour productivity has been a constant need throughout the period. A further and increasingly vital objective of 'socialization for labour' is to interest and train people in new technology. Whereas in the past, cultural enlightenment devoted to labour training was often notorious for its crudity, today, the access available to computers in (some) houses of culture gives them a reputation for sophistication and a popularity which may even redeem their image.

The rationale behind the 'more cultural enlightenment = more productivity' equation is threefold. Propaganda makes workers motivated and enthusiastic; cultural activities deflect them from drinking and other unhealthy pursuits; relaxed workers work better.

Even today it is possible to find extraordinarily reductionist Soviet expressions of the first viewpoint, which is a good example of the 'old thinking', the type of clichéd false assumption which makes Soviet cultural enlightenment so inefficient. The Hungarian cultural authorities seem to have been the first to realize that this was a fallacy. In August 1956 the secretary of SZOT admitted that too much propaganda about production could have the effect of overkill: workers complained, saying that they came to the club to relax.[42] György Aczél ridiculed the old assumption in 1970 when he wrote that 'it is self-evident that a person's productivity will not be raised by even one per cent just because the previous evening he attended a Beethoven concert.'[43]

A more reasonable variation on the same theme is that a well-rested worker is a better worker, whether he has spent the evening before listening to Beethoven or watching a variety show. The only qualifying factor is that leisure activities must be 'rational': an evening over a bottle of vodka does not have the same effect. 'Proof' of the importance of providing good rest facilities has been found by various pieces of research. For example, some economists at enterprises in Perm' found that workers who were well rested after a day off performed up to 14 to 17 per cent better than those who were not.[44] Such evidence is frequently used to try to persuade factory administrations and ministries to honour their cultural commitments to their workers.

Labour socialization can take many different forms. To use a favourite Soviet expression, the 'whole arsenal' at the disposal of cultural enlightenment is employed, from songs and sketches about hard work or slacking to entire festivals. For example, the 'day of the communications worker' at the trade union of communication workers' Leningrad Palace of Culture in 1987 included speeches, amateur arts and flowers and applause for 'worker's dynasties' (where three or more family members were employed in the industry) and for colleagues who had worked at Chernobyl' after the accident of the previous year. Socialist brigades in Hungary also include economic and labour themes in their cultural work.

One form of work which is more directly related to the issue of productivity is amateur technical work. Amateur technical work is often associated with little boys making model aeroplanes or radio sets, and in the past it has not always been easy for adults to participate. However, amateur technical activity for adults in all three countries has in the mid-1980s become very much more a part of mainstream cultural enlightenment than it was before. Everywhere this development is connected with the arrival or expected arrival of the computer age and the need for computer training. So far, only very large or exceptionally enterprising houses of culture seem to have been able to provide computer training, and this is most widespread in Hungary.[45] In addition, in the USSR the Gorbachev era has witnessed a much more liberal attitude towards do-it-yourself work in houses of culture (partly in order to occupy male leisure time as an alternative to drinking). This development seems to have no parallel in Poland and Hungary, where, however, there are greater opportunities to engage in such work without help from the house of culture.

Hobby clubs, amateur associations and informal organizations

Amateur technical work is essentially an individual process, even if it is performed within a group, and frequently it is conducted for self-interested motives. There is no 'collective magic'. Increasingly too the collective magic has gone out of amateur activity as a whole, in arts as well as technology, and also in the borderline crafts activities which have become more and more commonly found in houses of culture.

Not only have leisure activities inside and outside the house of culture lost much of their collective character during this period; in a related development, those of an artistic character became more experimental. Part of this change was caused by changing fashions in all three countries. Mass choirs were out of fashion, bards like Okudzhava, Vysotsky and thousands of amateur imitators were in. Other forms of solo singing also grew in popularity. Lavish theatrical productions of the classics were replaced by small experimental theatre studios. No fashion is entirely explicable, but some secondary factors contributing to these changes were, as has already been mentioned, the rejection of Stalinist forms and an escape into family or individual leisure pursuits, an escape facilitated by the increase in individual flat and television ownership and higher levels of education.

A survey conducted USSR-wide in 1981–2 found that 'home-based amateur activity was everywhere far more common than amateur activity based in the clubs'.[46] Another survey, which questioned inhabitants of eight small Russian towns, discovered that 38 per cent of respondents participated in independent amateur cultural activities as opposed to 4 to 6 per cent in organized ones.[47]

By the late 1970s, Hungarian and Polish cultural-enlightenment specialists had come to accept that there was no reason why all amateur activities should take place in the house of culture.[48] In Poland, after

1981, the state was simply incapable of trying to exert any totalist aspirations to organize all leisure, even if the government had not embarked on a policy of 'democratization'. The Soviet survey of 1981–2 was an early indicator of a fact which has only become widely discussed under Gorbachev. There previously existed an almost ubiquitous prejudice among cultural officials and workers that there was something particularly desirable about organized, collective leisure; a belief which is no doubt still widespread, although today it is less fashionable to express it. This belief had an apparently rational basis in Soviet educational theory, with its emphasis on the role of learning within the collective, but it was also attributable to 'intellectual inertia'.

It is however a measure of cultural enlightenment's responsiveness to the 'needs and wishes of the local population' that houses of culture have been changing their programmes of activities since the 1960s to accommodate the new need for small-scale leisure activities and to control them. In the words of an author who discussed the 1981–2 survey, 'It is no accident that measures are being taken to draw this so-called unorganized amateur activity into participation in the All-Union Review of Amateur Arts of 1983–5'.[49] Since many of the new fashions were Western in fashion, there was an extra need for such control.

To some extent, the house of culture adopted a half-way approach, giving advice about hobbies without actually providing a home for them. 'In this way [according to a Soviet specialist], club life is a continuation of domestic forms of leisure pursuit, and so it becomes more possible to manage people's interests and regulate their social behaviour in the sphere of leisure.'[50] This seems to have become particularly common in Hungary, with advice sessions on, for example, building, interior decorating or gardening. At Debrecen, 'knowledge diffusion festivals' organized by the cultural centres arranged eighty-five advice sessions on matters as diverse as military defence, caged birds and fashions.[51] Hungarian houses of culture also offer advice on practical problems unrelated to hobbies, such as law, industrial law or careers.[52]

Middle-aged and elderly people in the Soviet Union are said to be more interested in 'utilitarian' activity than they are in the normal club fare. For example, many older survey respondents have expressed interest in the idea of talks on allotment gardening, a major spare time pursuit, although this is rarely encountered in Soviet clubs. (In Hungary it is a major activity: the HNF alone runs 600 gardeners' clubs with about 40,000 members.)[53] Surveys have shown that members of Soviet hobby clubs of an 'applied character' are mainly older people.[54]

Hobby clubs and courses in all three countries have become increasingly common types of organized leisure activity, supplementing for amateur arts to a far greater degree than has amateur technical activity. For example, in Poland the number of courses organized by the cultural-enlightenment network rose from 3,174 in 1960 to 23,993 in 1975, after which it fell to 19,721 in 1979.[55]

As early as 1972 the minister of culture of the RSFSR spoke of the need to encourage such types of activity:

> The ministry regards as a task of the first order for the immediate future the creation of amateur hobby associations in club institutions, especially *raion* and village houses of culture. These associations should be based on the genuine autonomous activity (*samodeiatelnost'*), in its wider sense, of their participants and should have a concretely expressed social objective.[56]

The social value of some of the new clubs was initially open to question, however. Collectors found that their acquisitive habits were not well-regarded in houses of culture – although by 1989 the national stamp collectors' society had acquired the right to elect a deputy to the USSR Congress of People's Deputies. It was only in 1986 that the commercial aspects of soviet hobby clubs' activity were regulated: for example, artefacts produced may now be sold in special shops. The June 1985 CC resolution about clubs called for the extension of popular services that bring in money and this is also required by the new five-year plan. By late December 1987 some amateur associations were alarming bureaucrats by their money-making abilities, even including winning contracts for research and development.[57] In Poland in 1986, several cultural workers whom I interviewed seemed persuaded that many participants of hobby clubs and courses were only interested in supplementing their incomes by, for example, selling macramé products on the private market. However, in general administrators and cultural workers welcome the opportunity to expand hobby clubs and courses because of the financial pressures on houses of culture, since such activities can be self-financing: fees can be charged for membership and enrolment in clubs and courses.

Hobby clubs and courses today often have little or no Marxist content. At the Palace of Culture in Poznań in 1985–6 there were the following clubs: contemporary thought, collectors, electronics, short wave radio, aeroplane modelling, boat- building, male choir, ballroom and other dancing, light music band, folk dance and song ensemble, bagpipers, photographic, film, art, tapestry, applied art, theatre lovers, literary, recital, theatrical, theatre of poetic song. In April 1989, the Old Town House of Culture in Warsaw was offering lectures on existentialism and a madrigals club. In April 1986, the Gutenberg House of Culture in Budapest had clubs for collectors of miniature books and stamps, a film club (whose programme consisted of two English films and one French one) and a club for the elderly; it also offered courses in sewing, gymnastics and karate, English and German. The cultural centre in a small town in Eastern Hungary in 1987 had clubs for weaving, embroidery, gardening and environmental protection. A 1987 Moscow questionnaire listed the following possible varieties: musical, drama, technological, crafts (knitting, sewing, macramé etc.), socio-political issues, collectors', international friendship, sport, physical exercise and health, military and patriotic, veterans of war and labour, atheism, gardening, hunting and fishing, family and marriage. At the same time actual houses of culture were more imaginative: one in Leningrad offered breakdancing, hairdressing and Japanese.[58]

Even in 1987, it was still considered desirable in the USSR that hobby clubs should include in their activities the various elements of socialization, such as Communist, labour, atheist or aesthetic education. This is apparent in, for example, the 1986–7 'cycle of events on a theme' for members of the philatelists' club at a Leningrad palace of culture. The cycle, called 'Stamp collections serving the people', included an exhibition 'October marches across the planet', a meeting on the theme of stamps and the Second World War blockade of Leningrad and an exhibition titled 'The Leninist course for peace'.[59] Often, however, such supplementary work is neglected.

The Polish and Hungarian authorities up to about 1980–2, and the Soviet authorities to the present day, have been keen to gather already existing informal hobby clubs under an official roof. The May 1986 Soviet regulations seem to have in part been a response to official worries about the extent of unregulated and harmful youth leisure pursuits: now, many more types of activity are permitted, but with the proviso that they register as being under the auspices of some official organization. (If the associations were allowed to register as independent public organizations, then they would achieve a more genuine independent status, and acquire the right to nominate deputies. However, as of late 1987 none of the registered non-formal organizations had acquired this superior status.)[60]

The possibilities for 'acceptable' hobby clubs have widened in the USSR, since the May 1986 regulations about hobby clubs and amateur associations allow them the possibility of finding a sponsor in *any* official institution. This considerably widens the opportunities for a hobby club to establish itself officially where the local house of culture has no space or time for it. However, there are still types of club which have difficulty finding a sponsor. Examples of these include collectors of proverbs, *matreshka* dolls or irons as well as political groups.[61]

Golubtsova, the deputy minister of culture responsible for cultural enlightenment, claimed in March 1986 that the number of amateur associations and hobby clubs in the USSR had roughly doubled in the last seven years.[62] An authoritative article in *Pravda* on 1 February 1988 said that there were 'more than 30,000 amateur groups and associations' and since then the number has certainly grown. However, despite the undoubted boom in amateur organizations, two qualifying remarks need to be made. The numbers available are almost certainly much exaggerated, first of all because houses of culture have been *ordered* by the ministry of culture to create amateur organizations, which in practice they have only been able to do by renaming old clubs or reporting the existence of fictitious ones. Second, although there undoubtedly is a tremendous amount of enthusiasm for creating such associations, often those which have been formed have not done much more than hold a constituent assembly.[63] No one knows the exact numbers of such clubs. In the USSR during the *glasnost'* period it is acknowledged that there are many thousand 'informal associations' which do not enter into official statistics.

Despite the fact that the exact numbers are impossible to establish, it seems clear that there has been a great increase in the number of informal groups operating outside the cultural-enlightenment establishment. In a handbook of informal organizations produced by the Moscow Popular Front in February 1989, only eleven of the 193 entries were formally attached to houses of culture, while a further fifteen met regularly in houses of culture.[64]

Why has this phenomenon occurred? Western analysts have a tendency to interpret the emergence of informal groups as a response to *perestroika*. However, this can only be partly true (more so of course of the most politicized groups), given that many of the informal cultural associations pre-date Gorbachev's accession. Their emergence is fully explicable only if it is seen also as a result of the crisis of confidence in official institutions existing in the early 1980s and, as a part of this, a reaction to the officially patronized hobby club movement. Since the house of culture was too over-regulated and too formal an institution to provide an acceptable setting for hobby clubs with a more sensitive agenda, such as rock music, many of the latter moved out of the official institutions into private flats and other unsupervised settings. Three Soviet specialists, writing in 1989, suggested that whereas in the early days of Soviet power a club was a small independent organization, while a cultural-enlightenment institution was designed to serve the broader public, from the 1930s to the mid-1980s the distinction had been lost. Club members became the objects of cultural enlightenment rather than its creators. Since 'clubs' were identified with official, discredited cultural enlightenment, new, genuine clubs (in the first sense) often prefer the labels 'informal organization' or 'initiative group'.[65]

However, some houses of culture/local authorities are in practice more liberal than others and may provide a roof for activities which other institutions would either avoid or destroy. Examples include the Akademiia House of Culture in Akademgorodok, Novosibirsk, which provided, and provides, a home for the patriotic association Pamiat' with whom it has jointly organized many events; Pamiat' members also participate in its folk groups. In Leningrad, a Centre for Creative Initiative, set up at the House of Culture im. Il'icha under the auspices of the city Komsomol committee in May 1986, encourages daring art forms (I was present, for example, at a reading of free verse and Polish religious poetry in spring 1987) and houses a number of leading informal associations, including Spasenie (architectural heritage), Memorial (de-Stalinization) and Del'ta (ecology).

Liberality in providing homes for unusual groups has frequently been reversed. For example, at a meeting of Novosibirsk house of culture directors in February 1989, an official from the party city propaganda department warned them to stop offering accommodation to all informal organizations apart from the Charity Society. (However, the Charity Society was also turned out of its office in a Palace of Culture after only one day, because it would not comply with the condition of excluding all believers from its membership.) In general, as one would expect, discussion clubs, Russian patriotic associations and ecological groups seem to find it easier to meet in houses of culture than do groups engaged in more directly political activity.[66]

In Poland the situation has been rather different, since semi-independent arts and patriotic cultural associations have been permitted to exist officially since 1956 (although subject to regulation and in some cases included within the party *nomenklatura*), and because, during the 1980s, the Church has provided a home for much unofficial culture – often of an oppositional nature. Nevertheless, houses of culture may sometimes play a role in hosting unofficial culture. For example, in Poznan in the mid-1980s one house of culture became popular for its organized meetings with cultural figures who had refused to join the new cultural unions. This sort of activity is definitely not acceptable to the authorities, whose attitude seems to be that while there is little which they can do about stopping independent culture, official state institutions must not be used for anti-regime activities. However, in 1988 they became much more ready to register clubs and other groups which in earlier years could never have hoped to become 'official'. For example, one recent beneficiary is a 'Union of Siberians' which is collecting materials about the experience of Poles exiled to Siberia: a scholarly enterprise which is clearly also political. Houses of culture today also host meetings at which oppositional views are freely aired, in protest, for instance, against a planned nuclear power station.[67] However, there remain all kinds of ways in which the authorities can hinder the new clubs from meeting. A notice posted in Warsaw

University in April 1989 complained, for example, that room space was not being taken away from the old, unpopular organizations to make accommodation available for the new ones.

In Hungary until the 1980s the official attitude was to be suspicious towards any type of independent cultural association, largely because of fears that they would provide a home for the same kind of activities as nationalist organizations in the inter-war period (or as Soviet patriotic associations today). Chapter Two discussed the attempt to revive people's colleges and the 1982 law on cultural associations. Because of the restrictions on legal autonomous activity, it seems likely that on occasion official cultural enlightenment was used as a cover for activities of an oppositional nature, but the only documented case to my knowledge before 1989 is that of the cultural centre in Lakitelek, near Kecskemét. The director of the centre, the poet Sándor Leszak, turned it into a place for writers' meetings which in 1979 produced demands for political and economic reform and in 1983 were the scene of controversial debates about the history of the Writers' Union. In late 1985 Leszak was dismissed for using the centre for 'counter-revolutionary' activities, in other words a speech made at a literary and artistic commemoration of the 1956 uprising. This also included the playing of a recording of Illyés reading his still banned 1951 poem 'A Sentence on Tyranny'. The meeting had been attended by people from all over Hungary, including some prominent poets, and although it aroused the condemnation of *Népszabadság*, the event was praised in the trade union newspaper and in *Köznevelés*, the organ of the ministry of culture.[68] Nothing could show more clearly the prevailing lack of precision concerning the boundaries of permissibility between 'tolerated' and 'forbidden' cultural activities. However, in the following year the Politburo attempted to impart some clarity. That Hungarian houses of culture have been more frequently used for oppositional meetings is suggested by the strictures of an unpublished Politburo resolution, dating from the latter part of 1986:

> The appropriate supervisory organs should prevent Houses of Culture and institutions from being used for holding hostile, politically harmful metings. The appropriate state organs should investigate the current regulations for giving permits to various meetings and programmes and should formulate proposals for ordering these with suitable political guarantees. The proposals should be discussed by the Agitation and Propaganda Committee and these should be the basis for effective measures in this respect.[69]

Of course, the Hungarian and Polish regimes have traditionally been so much more liberal than the Soviet one in their interpetation of what is acceptable in culture that it has long been unnecessary for activities like the reading of free verse to hide in houses of culture under false pretences. On the other hand, by 1988–9 the political situation had changed so radically that it was possible for genuinely oppositional independent groups, such as the reconstituted Smallholders' Party, to meet legally in houses of culture. The law on associations which was passed by parliament in January 1989 allowed any group of ten people to register an association as long as it did not possess weapons.[70]

It would probably be correct to suggest that the authorities' most frequent response has been – and probably still is – to repress novelties until it is quite certain that they have the official stamp of approval (as for example happened in the late 1970s in the case of Soviet discos). Even the *Pravda* article of 1 February 1988 admitted that this had been the pattern in the pre-*perestroika* era. So far, the regimes in all three countries have been able to maintain an uneasy balance between patronizing manifestations of nationalist and other types of semi-official or unofficial culture when it suits their purposes and suppressing it when it does not, but in the climate of *glasnost'* the latter alternative has become less feasible, and by 1989 was very difficult indeed, especially in Hungary and Poland. This must however be attributed not only to democratization and increasing public self-confidence, but also to divisions within the leadership over how to decide the limits of acceptability, and attempts by different wings of the leadership to exploit the informal organizations. (For example, liberals in the party leadership, anxious to ensure the radical character of the KPSS conference in June 1988, seem to have been behind the decision to make available the palace of youth and a house of culture to independent associations, which met to produce alternative conference theses, the so-called 'Public Mandate'.)[71]

The most important development from the political point of view is of course that of discussion clubs and campaigning organizations which articulate independent points of view on policy and, increasingly, politics.[72] These often undergo a metamorphosis from non-political cultural enlightenment, social or arts associations to political opposition groups, often in a situation of gathering political crisis (for example, the Petöfi Club in 1956). Of course, like voluntary organizations in any country, many associations which began life supposing their goals to be non-political later realized that the problems which they addressed demanded political solutions; in each period of rapid de-Stalinization there has been a constant dynamic between this internal realization and external political developments which make democratic political solutions increasingly feasible. This has led to tensions and splits within informal organizations as members disagree about the desirable degree of politicization.

The flourishing of such clubs in Moscow – by late 1987 there were said to be at least forty-eight[73] – was associated with their protection by El'tsin as First Secretary of the Moscow city committee of the KPSS. There were soon clear signs of discomfort at this liberalism, expressed by CC secretary Ligachev and others, and El'tsin's permissiveness may have been a factor in his eventual dismissal from the Moscow job (November 1987) and from the Politburo (February 1988). El'tsin's dismissal was the subject of a protest petition organized by the Club for Social Initiatives.[74]

The press campaign against Pamiat' in the summer of 1987 was the first clear indication of strong conservative reaction to 'abuse' of *glasnost*'; this was followed by the *Pravda* article '"Pamiat" and others' of 1 February 1988, which spelled out that any attempt on the part of the informal organizations to *unite* would be totally unacceptable; it criticized an August 1987 conference of independent clubs which had been organized by the Club for Social Initiatives at a Moscow house of culture.[75] However, the club movement gathered strength, with the formation of new associations and new joint conferences. While the majority of ecological groups and Russian patriotic associations seem to have been formed by June 1988,[76] from June onwards disappointed expectations for the 19th party conference and rising national minority unrest stimulated the growth of more overtly political groups, of cultural/nationalist organizations in the non-Russian republics and of energetic attempts to form popular fronts almost everywhere, including individual towns and areas in the Russian Republic.[77] By this point many of the radical clubs were blatantly political and had shed any resemblance to the art-lovers and collectors of proverbs with whom they had initially been bracketed; their story lies outside the scope of this book.

The Soviet cultural authorities' recognition of the importance of this phenomenon is reflected in their attempts to co-opt the leaders of the most important informal organizations by including them within the *nomenklatura*. Guidelines from above became more general in character and a new draft statute for clubs and houses of culture, which appeared in summer 1988, offered them greater independence and the possibility of approximating more closely to the informal organizations. They could be partly or wholly self-financing, have independent legal status, and could be leased out to co-operatives or groups of citizens. No mention is made of political socialization. The clubs' most important task is said to be to 'involve citizens in active public life'.[78]

The activation of the 'human factor' now seems to be the major ideological imperative. Control over the *content* of that activity is fast being removed.

Clubs and social policy

Often the issue of informal associations is seen as a 'youth problem' although of course not all those engaged in 'dissident activity' or discussion clubs are young. It may be that the regimes are over-ready to identify unacceptable behaviour with youth, suggesting that rebellion or dissidence is a passing phase in life and that, with a proper dose of official socialization, rebels can return to the fold.[79] However, given the widespread rejection of official youth organizations in all three countries (see Chapter Four), many of the new clubs have been set up by young people as alternatives. 'Youth culture' embraces a wide spectrum of activities, ranging from agitbrigades and pavement drawing competitions on the theme of 'peace' to activities which in some sense form a counter- culture, destructive of official socialization. These latter range from groups who wear swastikas and deface war memorials to dissident philosophers and poets.[80] There are many grey areas, and when a fashion is new, the authorities often take a while to decide whether it is a 'positive' or a 'negative' phenomenon. As Chapter Two described, young people have been turning away from official cultural enlightenment, and the official ideology, since the late 1960s; during the 1980s critical attitudes towards official culture found expression in the formation of new clubs and societies and of a common feeling 'of the necessity for struggle against shortcomings in society'.[81] (The author of an official Soviet information bulletin recommends a study of Dostoevsky's *The Devils* to illuminate the complex nature of youth problems today.)[82]

As in Western countries, there is an assumption in the USSR and Eastern Europe that the provision of officially-organized youth clubs can keep young people off the streets and out of trouble. However, Soviet officials seem to be hyper-suspicious of street culture, assuming that informal groups of teenagers may 'at any time' turn to immoral or criminal behaviour.[83] Cultural enlightenment is therefore called upon to prevent crime and drinking by providing a supervised, 'cultured' alternative. This is probably the major concern of cultural policy in the eyes of many bureaucrats. A vivid example is contained in the resolution of the VTsSPS of 28th February 1986, 'On serious shortcomings in the work of trade union club institutions in Omsk': 'In the course of 1985, the number of youths arrested for breaking the anti-alcohol laws has almost doubled. Out of 215 clubs, only seventeen organize alcohol-free cafés and buffets [and] ...a considerable proportion of young people spend their leisure time outside the houses of culture'.[84] The senior Lithuanian official responsible for cultural enlightenment wrote in August 1986: 'And what has been the effect of all these organized cultural events? Has drunkenness decreased in the countryside? How many teenagers have been put on or taken off the books in the inspectorates for the affairs of minors?'[85]

Young people, children and workers are special targets of cultural enlightenment. Other less politically important social groups, like women, or elderly or disabled people, have been relatively neglected (although less so in Poland and Hungary). This has meant that in practice groups like Polish peasant women or Soviet blind people whose needs are largely ignored by the regime have been able to organize their own cultural enlightenment in relative independence of official policy.

For example, where arts facilities are concerned, visually impaired people benefit from the attempt of the Soviet regime to include as much as possible of the adult population within the workforce. Blind people are provided with access to participation in non-professional arts activities in similar ways to ordinary workers, but under the aegis of the wealthy All-Union Society of the Blind (VOS) and its republican and local branches. VOS has the status of a voluntary organization, but runs its own factories and houses of culture. Blind people are in some respects at an advantage in comparison with other disadvantaged groups, in that they have an organization which can defend their interests. In Leningrad, many of the top VOS jobs in arts administration are held by blind people. The houses of culture engage in educational work among the public, sponsoring public performances by blind actors, dancers and musicians, with the purpose of making sighted people realize that blind people have a valid role to play in cultural life. This aspect of cultural enlightenment does not feature in any document or textbook on cultural enlightenment, but seems to have been adopted by VOS independently.[86]

Low priority groups in the USSR tend to be singled out for special treatment only when they can be used to solve particular problems: like contributing to family stability or the anti-alcohol campaign, as wives, mothers and grandparents; or inculcating patriotism, in the case of war veterans who are invited to visit schools and ceremonies of all kinds and provide 'patriotic education'. In recent years a more caring attitude has been emerging, which can be partly associated with the emergence of groups like *Miloserdie* ('Charity'). As in so much else, the Baltic states seem to be the most progressive in this respect. In Poland and Hungary, clubs for pensioners/the elderly[87] are much more widely organized and seem to be devoid of the manipulative approach characterizing such work in the USSR.

A good example of the manipulative approach to women's culture in the USSR is to be found in Central Asia where they are thought to form the most 'backward' part of the population and their 'emancipation' is a means of modernizing and Sovietizing local society. Women are therefore chosen, for example, to organize cultural life on collective farms.[88]

De-Stalinization and the house of culture

The Soviet approach to women's cultural enlightenment is fairly typical of official policy towards women in general. When the 'women's question' was still officially 'solved' (and even to a large extent during the Brezhnev era and up to today), cultural enlightenment was based on wishful thinking, using an idealized image of the ordinary woman. This ideal is of course familiar from other sources: woman as a perfect mother, as the strong moral and cultural influence within the family, the conscientious housewife, the sensitive partner, etc. For example, a guide to cultural enlightenment which was published in Penza in 1953 began by asserting that 'every woman has a family and children. Naturally, she is deeply interested in questions connected with the bringing up of children.' The guide therefore recommended the organization of lectures and talks on subjects such as 'How to develop the child's affection for work on the collective farm'. It was evidently assumed that childless and single women were not worth bothering about, or else that there were no childless or single women – a strange assumption, particularly in 1953, such a short time after the war. By 1984, however, a study of lecture propaganda conducted among women in the textile-manufacturing Ivanovo oblast' painted a more realistic picture. Young unmarried women are said to need to be educated for the family life which necessarily awaits them by lectures bearing titles such as 'The moral foundations of love in a socialist society', and some young women are said to be ignorant about child rearing or even opposed to having children, to have insufficient respect for the institution of the family and to be incapable of managing their finances and their spare time.[89]

In both 1953 and 1984 women were expected to aspire to be simultaneously perfect workers and mothers – the constant message of socialization addressed to women up to about 1988. (For example, the Penza booklet provides guidelines for a 'theme evening' titled 'Soviet women – active constructors of a Communist society'. The actual organization of the evening should be entrusted to a specially formed committee of leading women workers. The handbook lists the appropriate literature, facts and figures, materials for use in an exhibition and instructions on how to make a poster out of the photograph of a leading farm worker over the text of her story, for instance, 'How I managed to milk such a large amount' with accompanying statistics. The first item should be a lecture about the liberation of women under Soviet power, utilizing a quotation from Stalin: 'Only collective farm life could liquidate inequality and place woman on her feet.' Leading local women then talk about their work. The evening is concluded by an amateur arts performance and if desired a film: suitable titles include 'She defends her motherland', 'The distinguished potato grower' and 'Avoid dysentery'.)[90]

92

Cultural enlightenment in all three countries is much concerned with the need for stable families and therefore promotes collective family leisure pursuits at weekends. Increasingly too it has become concerned with breaking the isolation in which individual families live on urban housing estates and integrating local communities. This is a recent development in the USSR, where, for example, many town and borough festivals were organized for the first time in 1987.

In Poland, there has historically been particularly strong emphasis on integrative work, which is directly related to the experience of rebuilding the nation after the Second World War and to the industrialization which followed. For example, a study of cultural changes among the Silesian working class, published in 1982, was extremely positive about the role played by amateur theatre in the region, before the Second World War, after it and up to the present day:

> Amateur theatre played an especially important and complex role in the period after the war. These were not only cultural functions, but first and foremost national and social. The activity of Silesian theatres was in that difficult period an integrating factor for local people and those newly-arrived from other parts of Poland and from abroad. It was a way for germanified young people [who had attended German schools] to learn to speak good Polish. It was a source of historical and literary knowledge for all those who took part in performances or formed their audiences. Amateur theatres activized local society, involving young people first of all, and through them adults, chiefly parents.[91]

There are still areas of Poland which are undergoing industrialization, for example around Legnica. Here, culture is said to possess three basic roles: 'the integration of inhabitants, preventative action against manifestations of social pathology [defined as crime, family disintegration, alcoholism, drug-taking and prostitution] and equalizing access to culture.'[92] Whereas in Poland the concern seems to be largely with bringing together atomised individuals suffering from similar problems of alienation and uprooting from tradition, and creating a sense of community and national unity, in Hungary there is, in addition, greater awareness of the need to tackle the problems of targeted groups and individuals. For Polish cultural enlighteners, the social problem is perceived as being a political one. In Hungary, the acute nature of the social problems themselves seems to be the paramount cause for concern.

Hungarian cultural enlightenment has become involved with counselling work since the mid-1970s, under the joint stimulus of acute problems (high rates of suicide, divorce, alcoholism and neurosis) and openness to the West. Houses of culture run advice bureaux and also

93

clubs for groups like children in care, divorced people, alcoholics, overweight people and sufferers from heart disease. In general, one of the most characteristic features of what might be termed 'radical' Hungarian cultural enlightenment has been its assumption that the best way of introducing new people to cultural enlightenment is to give them total freedom to chose their own activities. This was the objective of the 'open house' experiment which began in the 1970s. Entrance halls, corridors and other spaces in houses of culture were provided with games, records, tape-recording facilities, looms, facilities for technical drawing, leatherwork and other occupations.[93] The idea was that members of the public who had previously been intimidated by cultural enlightenment would come in and use the facilities as they wished. Naturally enough, the experiments ran into many practical problems, but they also had some notable successes. The open house experiments aroused great interest among cultural enlighteners, and shared some characteristics of a movement, without however any fixed programme or, apparently, any attempt by the ministry of culture to impose one.[94] (The contrast with the USSR could not be greater.)

Conclusion

The history of attempts since 1953 to socialize Soviet, Polish and Hungarian citizens through officially organized, active leisure pursuits displays the fallacy of some key regime assumptions about the viability of the party's leading role. Party attempts to 'organize self-organized leisure' have rarely been successful in combining genuine popular acceptance with genuine party control. Even in the most Stalinist area of cultural enlightenment, amateur arts, popular participation does not imply that individuals accept official socialization policy. Often participants are more interested in art for its own sake or even in free holidays and other perks. As Chapter Four will show, cultural workers and local administrators often co-operate in pursuit of these goals. In addition, they frequently find themselves forced to patronize performances of light entertainment in order to meet their financial plans. (In the USSR such events often receive some kind of ideological figleaf of the type described earlier in the chapter.)

Official response to these difficulties has been to grudgingly and inconsistently open the doors of the house of culture to non-political hobbies, discussion clubs, advice centres and courses in practical skills for which there is popular demand. This tactic has the advantages of maintaining supervision over the population's leisure and of encouraging people to learn new skills which enhance their quality as workers. It has the disadvantage that the party's leading role is much reduced since it no longer dictates the content of activities and, moreover, is often forced to offer room to Western cultural influences and independent discussion which may be destructive of official socialization attempts. Sometimes the most popular events seem to be precisely those which run counter to official policy. Moreover, as in the case of amateur arts, the ability of the house of culture to maintain and control popular activities is uncertain. Many informal groups prefer to set up on their own.

The powerlessness of cultural enlightenment is compounded by two important factors. One is the almost universal shortage of money, the other the lack of clarity about borders of acceptability, especially in decentralized Hungary and (except in the 1970s) Poland. Art is always an unsuitable subject for regulation. When the party is weak and/or locked in debate, lack of clarity is at its greatest. By 1989, the limits of acceptability in all three countries were probably less clear than at any other time in the post-Stalinist era, and the possibility seemed very real of an almost total dismantling of the Stalinist system of political socialization through cultural enlightenment.

The use of cultural enlightenment as an instrument of social policy is becoming transformed as 'manipulators' give way to 'enthusiasts' and a more caring approach to individuals and communities is adopted. This is still a very partial and incomplete process. It is however a promising line of development, given the bankruptcy of Stalinist theories about the use of art for propaganda or the possibility of totally controlling people's leisure time, and the problems associated with much 'amateur technical work'. On the other hand, the tantalizing possibility remains that the house of culture may be able to recover its post-revolutionary legitimacy, based on literacy campaigning, by playing a leading role in the 'computer literacy campaign'.

Chapter four

Policy and practice 1: party and state

How and where is cultural-enlightenment policy made? How efficiently is it executed? Previous chapters naturally touched on these issues; this chapter will discuss them in greater depth. It will argue that policies emanating from the central party/state apparatus or Moscow have often been ineffectively executed, and even counterproductive. It examines how this has been gradually but only partially realized in all three countries and how a degree of local decision-making and greater responsiveness to public wishes has been permitted.

However, the scaling down of central directives has often failed to solve the problem. This is partly because the successful implementation of centrally-determined policy now depends upon the interests and priorities of local authorities and cultural workers, who may be unreliable or obstructive. A more widespread cause of failure is obstruction by the local population: even if central policy were applied energetically by the local authority (as it frequently is not), it might have little impact if few people attended the events which were organized. On the other hand, where decentralization is real and the local population becomes genuinely interested, cultural enlightenment may flourish, although rather as a branch of non-professional cultural activities than as political socialization.

Chapters Four and Five are organized from 'top' to 'bottom'. After considering the role of the Communist parties, this chapter discusses central and then local government, ending with a short description of the role of trade unions and other organizations responsible for cultural enlightenment. Chapter Five then turns to the directors and ordinary staff of the houses of culture and also examines the mechanisms for public input into cultural enlightenment.

The role of the party

How does the party exercise its leading and guiding role in the field of cultural enlightenment? The following sections will first examine party

96

membership within the cultural-enlightenment sector; then discuss guidance of cultural enlightenment by party members active in cultural enlightenment; and finally look at party guidance of cultural enlightenment by committees working outside cultural-enlightenment institutions.

Party membership in cultural enlightenment

As in all other areas of social and economic policy, the exercise of the party's leading role is largely the responsibility of individual party members and primary party organizations. Certain professions in Soviet-type systems are more highly saturated with party members than others, reflecting their priority status, as exercising greater power or requiring a greater degree of supervision and guidance. Many jobs within these professions are *nomenklatura* posts (that is, party appointments). Political socialization in general is one such area. For example, in the Soviet Union in 1983 about three-quarters of journalists were party members as were half of writers and one quarter of teachers.[1] How does the party membership of the cultural-enlightenment profession compare with these proportions? The answer to this question would give some clue as to how significant a branch of socialization cultural enlightenment is regarded as being. Ideally there would be included here an account of the extent of party membership at different levels of the cultural-enlightenment hierarchy, with a list of *nomenklatura* posts. However, only scattered and often imprecise information is obtainable in this sensitive area. It is particularly lacking for Hungary.

Party membership, and even more so, membership of the Communist youth organization, was rather high among cultural-enlightenment activists during the Stalinist period in Poland. It seems likely that the same was true of Hungary. In Poland, there was a purge of cultural workers who had been active before the Communist takeover and who were now considered politically unreliable, and their places were often filled by young activists. Evidence for a high degree of membership is suggested in Poland by the fact that cultural workers could be trained in a *party* school: the party school for cultural-enlightenment workers.[2] It will be remembered that in Russia too in the equivalent, post-revolutionary period of the 1920s and 1930s, young Komsomol activists had been in the forefront of cultural enlightenment. During the 'revolutionary' phase of socialization (to use Völgyes' terminology) the distinction which later emerged between political and cultural enlightenment was still very hazy. Enlightenment of both kinds was party work.

Although it is difficult to be certain, the situation during the 1940s to 1950s in Russia was probably similar to that which came to obtain in post-Stalinist Poland and Hungary. Once the system had been established and to an extent professionalized, it is probable that party membership became lower. Indirect evidence that this hypothesis is true is offered by the frequent complaints about staff to be found in the journal *Klub* from its inception in 1951 throughout the 1950s. Many cultural workers were said to be in their jobs 'by chance' (*sluchainye liudi*), which hardly suggests care in their selection on the part of party organs. There were complaints about their low level of political knowledge and trade unions were blamed for not being more careful about whom they appointed.[3] The entire period was marked by demands that the elected councils and management committees of houses of culture should play a much greater role in their affairs, supplanting inefficient paid staff: this too suggests that party membership among house of culture workers cannot have been high.

There may have been an increase in party membership during the 1970s, as more graduates joined the profession, although only a minority of cultural workers have ever had higher education. A complaint in 1972 about cultural workers' poor knowledge of Marxism-Leninism suggests little change from the earlier period.[4] In a work published in 1981, V. M. Striganov, deputy minister of culture of the RSFSR, lamented the fact that 'in many places the number of party members among these workers has displayed a noticeable decline'.[5] He did not however say during what period this had happened. The same work, an analysis of the survey 'The club worker today and tomorrow', produced the statistics shown in Table 2.

The percentage of KPSS members among club workers in this sample is 10.7 per cent, about the same as the national average among adults but considerably less than the average for the intelligentsia. Very few indeed hold 'elected' office (for example, secretaryships of party organizations). On the other hand, the level of saturation among higher education teachers and local government cultural officials is clearly high, with a particularly large number of the latter in responsible party positions.

The number of party members among ordinary cultural workers was said to be 'minimal' by a Ukrainian *obkom* secretary in October 1985. He went on to point out that if their authority was to be raised, more cultural workers should be admitted to the party.[6] Interview evidence and observation suggest that ordinary cultural workers are usually not in practice considered to be doing such responsible work that party membership would be a requirement, below the level of the senior administration. The fact that many of the cultural workers are women backs up this impression of lack of serious regard. Even today in small, especially rural institutions, where the director or only member of staff may be a girl of eighteen with secondary education or a retired person with primary education, he or she in unlikely to be considered a suitable candidate for party membership. Moreover, club workers frequently work such long hours, including many evenings, that party commitments would be an almost impossible extra burden, especially for women. Another factor is that many club workers would seem to regard culture and politics as two separate spheres, with their interests lying solely in the former. Such people are unlikely to become Communists or pursue a party career.[7]

Table 2 Party membership among Soviet club workers, cultural officials and Institute of Culture students and staff.

	Club worker	Expert[1]	1st year student	Final year student	Lecturer
Total no.	383	512	937	499	420
% Member of:					
KPSS	10.7	61.9	1.2	6.6	44.3
Komsomol	49.3	19.1	92.6	81.6	10.5
Non-party	36.0	18.6	5.3	11.0	44.9
Total	[95.0	96.3	99.6	99.2	99.7][2]
Party work					
elected post	–	22.5	0.2	0.4	–
permanent assignment	6.5	21.1	0.9	2.4	36.9
individual assignments	8.1	7.8	2.1	2.2	9.1
Komsomol work					
elected post	–	9.2	28.5	27.5	–
permanent assignment	21.2	7.0	38.3	16.2	6.9
individual assignments	21.2	7.8	18.9	22.8	6.7
Age: under 30[3]:	68.7	31.4	98.9	93.9	20.5

Notes 1. 'Experts' were raion level cultural officials. 2. Totals added by A. White: no explanation is offered in the book for the failure of these figures to add up to 100%. 3. Komsomol membership is open up to age 28.
Source: adapted from *Klubny rabotnik*, Tables 3 and 4, p. 102.

Unfortunately the available evidence is so limited that it is impossible to draw any firm conclusions on this subject. For Poland in the 1970s, there are quite contradictory indications. A collection of cultural workers' diaries for one month in 1977, *Z dnia na dzien*, reveals almost no information about party work undertaken by the writers, or whether they were party members. It would appear that only one out of the twelve was a Communist – this was the ex-director of a *województwo* house of culture. Two other diarists belong to the Peasant Party (ZSL).[8] On the other hand, a 1970 list of staff at Tczew Powiat House of Culture, temporarily functioning as a methodological centre, shows that two of the four cultural-enlightenment staff members, including the director, were members of the PZPR.[9] In the House of Culture in Leszno in 1971 there were six (unidentified) Communists, and six full-time cultural workers. These six workers may all have been Communists, therefore, although there were also other staff who could have been PZRP members.[10]

There are no house of culture positions mentioned on the only available list of *nomenklatura* appointments, that for Poland in 1972, although the heads of cultural associations – which are also cultural-enlightenment organizations and are supposed to work closely with houses of culture – are mentioned as being under the aegis of both the Central Committee and the regional party committees, and the directors of regional museums are appointed or approved by the regional party committee.[11]

During the 1930s in the USSR 'specialists from the leading clubs were included in the list of *nomenklatura* appointments of the leading personnel of the party *obkom*. Directors of some of the largest palaces of culture were included within the Central Committee *nomenklatura*'.[12] In the 1980s, according to interview information, only directors of houses of culture are normally expected to be party members.[13] One can probably add to these the senior administrators of large palaces of culture.

Primary party organizations (PPOs), where they exist independently in club institutions (that is, where there are three or more Communists) must usually be tiny, given the small size of most cultural-enlightenment institutions and presumably small number of Communists working in them. This was said to be the case in an article in *Sovetskaia kul'tura* in 1976.[14] Soviet PPOs in houses of culture were upgraded in status along with these on other educational and cultural institutions after the twenty-fourth party congress, being awarded the right of supervision over the administration. According to D. Jankowski, houses of culture in Poland in the early 1970s everywhere had primary party organizations.[15] Jankowski concluded that the Leszno PPO's discussions about house of culture activities 'undoubtedly influence the formation of the institution's programme of activities' and that 'informal interventions' by individual party members were also important and bore witness to the Communists' sense of responsibility for the house of culture's work.[16] Leszno was a particularly successful and popular house of culture at the time, and perhaps this was not unconnected with the large number of Communists on its staff. (See further below.)

Party members among activists in cultural enlightenment

Local party members are supposed to manifest activism by participating in house of culture administration and activities. Many Soviet activists are so involved, in a sense, in that many party members are involved in campaigning for local elections, and house of culture premises are frequently given over for this purpose, with entertainment provided for the 'electors' club'. There are also occasional newspaper reports of party members participating in more everyday house of culture activities. For example, *Sovetskaia kul'tura* in 1971 reported:

> The party committee and the club. One could cite many examples of their unbreakable connection. Let us take the Shchors collective farm. Here every festival and evening event is the close concern of the *partorg* Petr Andreevich Miroshnik. He writes scenarios, attends rehearsals and travels around with the agitbrigade as well. Young, energetic and cheerful, Miroshnik is highly respected on the *kolkhoz*.
> Another example: the *partorg* of the Voronovka state farm, Boris Iakovlevich Kol'chak, sings in the choir and runs a dance collective... It is unnecessary to add that the club enjoys his constant support and attention.[17]

However, many of such newspaper items probably fall into the category of socialist realist reporting: their purpose is to encourage activism rather than to convey an accurate impression of reality. One might speculate that party members are so often overburdened with other assignments that they have no time to commit themselves to low prestige work in houses of culture. On the other hand, house of culture work is of a type to attract genuine enthusiasts and volunteers, party as well as non-party. There must be party members who would find volunteer work in a house of culture a congenial 'assignment'.

Of two hundred leaders of prominent amateur arts groups in the USSR, 52 per cent were members of the party and the Komsomol.[18] A survey in five Polish *województwa* in 1983–4 of 369 volunteer workers in houses and centres of culture found that 24.75 per cent of activists were members of the PZPR, 9.2 per cent belonged to the Peasant Party, and 5.4 per cent to the Democratic Party.[19] So all parties were better represented than they were generally among the adult population with the SD the most over-represented and the ZSL the second most over-represented.[20]

Bearing in mind the very unsatisfactory nature of the evidence presented in this section, it is perhaps only possible to conclude that during the 1970s in Poland, all three parties may have been quite well represented among both cultural-enlightenment employees and activists, while in the USSR, according to the more useful survey material and interview evidence, the representation of Communists among ordinary cultural workers below the level of the senior administration was only average. This might bear out the suggestion already made that in the 1970s the Polish leadership was concerned to politicize cultural enlightenment (as well as to expand the PZPR). In the Soviet Union, it suggests that despite rhetoric to the contrary the party does not actually take cultural enlightenment particularly seriously by comparison with other socializing agencies. With this hypothesis in mind, the following sections turn to the question of party/state management of cultural enlightenment more generally.

Party management of cultural enlightenment: party committees and local party leaders

Whatever the level of party membership within the house of culture, the party's leading role is also exercised in the institution by the district/town party committee and its apparatus and through Communists serving in the appropriate local council and administration. In the party apparatus, cultural enlightenment, as a component of ideological work, falls within the remit of the propaganda or agitprop departments, and, it would seem, to some extent also of culture departments, where these exist.[21] The only possible exception to this rule is Poland, where a textbook published in 1982 named the cultural and the science and education departments of the Central Committee, and on the *wojewódkztwo* level the department of ideological and socialization work and the science and education department.[22] It would be a mistake, however, for other party officials and members to suppose that culture is only the province of specialists and none of their business. As a 1978 Hungarian textbook admonishes:

> We must struggle against the attitude that cultural work is unimportant – an attitude which still persists in many places, often on an unconscious level, but all the same inexcusably. Obstruction also comes from those party members who do not sufficiently recognize the social and ideological significance of culture, or who if they do, suppose that culture is only the concern of the higher party organs.[23]

Soviet club workers questioned in the survey 'The club worker today and tomorrow' reported very frequent contacts with the local party committee. These were assessed as 4.2 on a five-point scale, which was higher than with any other institution except the library and the school. Jankowski also refers to the close contacts between house of culture administrations and the local party organization in Poland in the 1970s.[24]

Party committees are supposed to not only supervise, but also display initiative in the conduct of local cultural enlightenment. One example of such initiative in cultural enlightenment which has been given press coverage is that of the Voroshilovgrad *gorkom's* 'Comprehensive programme for organizing the leisure of the working population'. After studying the leisure needs of the population and 'analysing the effectiveness of socialization work at place of residence' by studying local crime statistics, the *gorkom* launched its plan to improve facilities for propaganda, music and sport.[25]

The prominence given in the press to reports of party committees who do actively organize cultural enlightenment suggests editorial attempts to nag the many who do not. Complaints of neglect have been often voiced in all three countries throughout the period. For example, the parlous state of cultural enlightenment in Alma Ata *oblast'* (where seven clubs served 10,000 inhabitants) was attributed in 1985 'first and foremost to the fact that party committees in many *raions* of the *oblast'* have pretended for many years that there were no problems with rural cultural-enlightenment institutions'. When, episodically, they were forced to take some action, they would issue a resolution but fail to check that it was implemented.[26]

The problem of party negligence is often attributed to the party's over-involvement in economic matters at the expense of ideological work. Not surprisingly, it is difficult to find evidence from party sources about how much attention party committees pay in reality to cultural enlightenment. One party source contrasts the active measures taken by party committees in the Cheliabinsk *oblast'* to stop industrial and agricultural specialists quitting their posts with their total lack of concern when a club or library employee does the same.[27] Presumably party committees assume that the house of culture has no role to play in improving the local economy, which is *their* chief concern. In other words, they do not believe the assertions of ideologists that cultural enlightenment significantly increases productivity and disregard the evidence of sociologists that recreational and rest facilities do the same. It may be too that party members assume that no one goes to the house of culture, hence they do not represent a potential security risk and there is no point in monitoring them closely. The urban, intelligentsia and male bias of the KPSS may partially explain neglect of a service which is largely run by women for rural dwellers.

The goodwill of the local party leader would seem to be of fundamental significance for successful cultural enlightenment. A recent unpublished Soviet survey concluded that the interest of the regional leader was the only *essential* factor in determining the success of local cultural-enlightenment institutions.[28] One such well-intentioned party leader was El'tsin, who during his tenure as *obkom* secretary in Sverdlovsk patronized the building of a *narodny dom* (an interesting and possibly unique example of a *Soviet* politician harking back to a pre-revolutionary model of cultural enlightenment).[29]

In Hungary, 'numerous examples convince us that the moral support of one or two political, state or economic leaders can help to solve what had seemed to be hopeless causes'.[30] Jankowski also considers this to be a vital factor in Poland and gives as an example of the goodwill of local leaders leading to successful house of culture work the case of the Leszno House of Culture.[31]

The state administration

It would be artificial to draw too clear a distinction between the party and state administrations. One very clear illustration of their inseparability is provided by the history of the 1958 MSZMP cultural directives, which still today form the basis for official (party/state) cultural policy. Originally these directives were intended to be issued as a *state* document, prepared by the ministry of culture from spring 1957 onwards in consultation with academics, party committees, journalists and others. Then in March 1958 'it was decided' that the directives should be a *party* statement about culture and after a debate in the Politburo the directives were finally presented to the Central Committee by György Aczél, in his double capacity as deputy minister of culture and head of the MSZMP working party on culture.[32]

On the other hand, one occasionally reads of a quite curious lack of co-ordination between party and state administrations. For example, the head of a *raion* cultural department, herself a member of the audit commission of the town party organization, complained in a letter to *Klub* in 1987 that despite the fact that 'the town soviet cultural department is closely linked with the propaganda and agitation department of the party *gorkom*... we often receive directives from them [separately] which are mutually exclusive'.[33]

More often, complaints about lack of co-ordination concentrate on the fact that one or both institutions are not pulling their weight: that is, these are complaints about the absence of direction, rather than about contradictory directives.

This section on state administration will consider each country in turn, dealing first with central, then with local government.

USSR

The ministries

The ministry of culture exists on both all-union and republican levels, with most important directives emanating from the USSR ministry (often in conjunction with the national trade unions council (VTsSPS) and Komsomol). Since its establishment in 1953 the ministry of culture has been responsible for cultural enlightenment. How is cultural-enlightenment policy made and implemented within the ministry? *Sovetskaia kul'tura* in two articles in June 1986 revealed some inform-ation about how the ministry and its party organizations worked, with a detailed description of their energetic activities in the aftermath of the June 1985 resolution about club institutions. However, despite these efforts, there was little attempt to check on the implementation of ministerial policy, to make sure that there had been practical follow-up from all the seminars and other activities. As a result, at the end of 1985 'the USSR ministry of culture was subjected to severe criticism for its unsatisfactory implementation of the resolution about clubs'. The newspaper articles in June 1986 concluded that this failure to check on implementation was a serious weakness permeating the entire work of the ministry. The head of the cultural-enlightenment department, Tiutikov, complained that:

> at some place along the chain from ministry to club there are weak links where our influence sometimes breaks. The regular KPSS *inspektors* also feel this skidding sensation in the practical implementation of the [ministry of culture] collegium's resolutions, our instructions and letters about methodological matters and the directives about the analysing and putting into practice of new methods.[34]

In July, two senior ministry officials accepted the criticisms made by *Sovetskaia kul'tura* (which concerned other areas besides cultural enlightenment). Shortly afterwards, Demichev was dismissed as minister and replaced by Zakharov; other officials were also replaced. Between 1 August and 1 December 1986 the central apparatus of the ministry underwent a 'socio-political testimonial'.[35]

It would be interesting to discover which links Tiutikov suspected to be the weak ones. The *Sovetskaia kul'tura* articles of course suggest that the very first link in the chain is not too reliable. Although the stereotyped quality of both criticism and praise in Soviet journalism makes the accuracy of reporting often difficult to judge, it is often possible to find out something about the nature of weaknesses at each level, and this should help towards assessing where policy implementation breaks down. The rest of this section on the state administration, and Chapter Five, which is about policy-making in the house of culture itself, address the question of the location and nature of weak and strong links. However, by 1989 the state cultural administration was being criticized publicly for attempting to direct culture at all, and some district cultural departments were liquidated.[36]

At the same time as the USSR ministry of culture was criticized, central control over the *republican* ministries was tightened: 'There is a strengthening of ties between the ministry and the union republics. The practice of sending out workers from the central apparatus on trips to the localities is being perfected.'[37]

In particular, something had been going very badly wrong in the culture ministries of Central Asia, although obviously a blind eye had been turned to corruption there by more agencies than the USSR ministry of culture alone. In the ministries of culture of Tadzhikistan and Turkmenistan, the ministers, their deputies and the members of the repertoire committees all wrote talentless plays and forced the amateur and professional theatres of both republics to perform – or pretend to perform – them; altogether, such plays could amount to as much as 75 per cent of the total repertoire. One minister (aping Brezhnev?) even awarded himself a state prize. All this was not only a case of vanity, but also highly lucrative business. The situation of cultural enlightenment generally in Turkmenistan was described as shocking in September 1986. In November and December Kazakhstan, Kirgizia and Tadzhikistan all came under fire for their lack of concern for cultural enlightenment.[38]

Soviet local government

Chapter One of this study mentioned the so-called 'principle of last priority' (*ostatochny printsip*), according to which culture is always awarded last place in plans for investment. This subject is too familiar to be worth going into in detail. This is an area in which local soviets are particularly powerless *vis-à-vis* the central ministries, since they themselves often lack a sense of priority where culture is concerned. They more often prioritize housing, nursery schools and other 'immediate' social needs. New towns are a particular source of complaint. For example, in Togliatti in 1985, one of the city's three very large boroughs (the Avtozavodsky *raion*) was entirely without clubs, houses of culture, cinemas or theatres: all the socio-cultural funds had been spent on housing, schools and other services.[39] Agriculture makes its own demands, and farm managers and local soviet chairmen are often described as being too concerned about the harvest to worry about its effects on culture, even when ministers of culture try to remedy the situation. For instance it was claimed in 1963 that for as long as anyone in the Mari ASSR ministry of culture could remember, clubs had shut down in spring and winter to serve as storehouses for grain and vegetables; when a journalist entered the office of a deputy minister of culture he found him rather pitifully asking the chairman of a *raion* soviet: 'Why haven't you cleared the peas out of the clubs? You know how many months in a row we have failed to fulfil our cinema plan!'[40]

A regulation about cultural complexes published in 1985 unambiguously gave the local soviets control over all local cultural activity.[41] The July 1987 law giving soviets greater power over their budgets was an attempt to reverse their traditional lack of power *vis-à-vis* the central agencies. This would certainly seem to be necessary in the sphere of local cultural spending, judging by the evidence of a remarkably uniform barrage of complaints from local soviet cultural department heads which were published in *Klub* in 1987. Cultural enlightenment is among the responsibilities of the local cultural department head and often seems to absorb much of his or her time (especially, of course, in rural areas where there are often no theatres, art galleries or other 'professional' cultural institutions).[42] Most collective farm chairmen (according to the diary and letters in *Klub*) have little respect for the department head and he or she has to spend most of the time running about from office to office, 'kneel at the feet of the economic managers' and unsuccessfully try to sort out problems connected with finance, equipment and repairs. One letter writer blamed this on the managerial incompetence of the department head – 'people are appointed to the job of department head because they can sing, play musical instruments or dance'. One department head, from Belorussia, pointed out what seems however to be the 'root cause' of her own difficulties and those of her colleagues: 'the status of the *raion* cultural department'.[43] (This, it will be remembered, is despite the fact that almost a quarter of the local officials in the survey recorded in Table 2 held 'elected' party offices.) The *Klub* editors felt compelled to remind their contributors (unrealistically?): 'Dear comrade department heads, after all, it's you who are the bosses, you are the council executive committee employees, and councils now have sufficient rights to enable them to implement *perestroika*. If some rights are still lacking, then it's possible to "take" them, as an experiment.'[44]

Of course, *raiony* vary in size and importance: the status of a *raion* head in a borough of Moscow is almost certainly higher than that of someone working in a country district. Similarly, the importance of town-level cultural departments must be very varied. The only town department head to write to *Klub*, from Novaia Kakhovka in the Kherson *oblast'*, said that she identified with all the diarist's problems. She also added the extra 'social burden' of the department head: his or her outside commitments, many of which are in effect ex officio and which grow as one ascends the local government hierarchy. Her own included, among others, the following positions: member of the Novaia Kakhovka party organization audit committee; member of the bureau of the party organization for cultural institutions; leader of the Novaia Kakhovka school for the ideological *aktiv* on questions of the propaganda of culture and art; deputy to the Novaia Kakhovka town soviet; member of the *gorispolkom* (town soviet executive committee) standing commissions for the anti-alcohol struggle and for work with foreign students; member of the *gorispolkom* commission for work with juveniles; member of the commission for rites; member of the *gorkom* of the trade union of cultural workers; president of the Novaia Kakhovka Soviet–French Society; member of the presidium of the Novaia Kakhovka primary organization of Znanie and of the Society for Protecting Cultural and Historical Monuments.[45]

In 1979 the average paid staff of a *raion* cultural department consisted of one to three people. The *raion* is perceived to be the weakest link in the chain of methodological centres.[46] This is hardly surprising in view of all the difficulties the *raion* departments seem to face. In some areas this problem has been tackled on an experimental basis by the establishment of direct contacts between Moscow and the *raiony* (compare the bypassing of county governments by the NI in Budapest, which prefers to establish direct contacts with villages). On the other hand, contacts between the central methodological centres and the *oblast'* centres are said to be good, implying that there is a lack of co-ordination between the *oblast'* centres and the *raion* cultural departments and houses of culture.[47]

Conclusion: USSR

Perhaps the most striking fact to emerge from this material on local Soviet cultural administration is the lowly status of the *raion* head of department. By 1989, he or she was even dispensable, as cultural departments shut down.[48] However conscientious the official may be, he or she obviously faces immense difficulties in implementing ministry policy: this is a 'weak link'. Connected with his or her status is the still more interesting suggestion that very often these people have been trained as dancers or musicians rather than as ideologists. They may think of themselves as being involved in 'culture' rather than 'political socialization'. The fact that cultural enlightenment remained in the ministry of culture when other agencies of political socialization, such as cinema and television, left it is again suggestive of this identification. On the other hand, within the present USSR ministry, the cultural-enlightenment department is the most highly saturated with Communists, suggesting that it is the most politicized of those which are left. Once again, the situation (and the realization of policy goals) is confused by the ambiguous nature of cultural enlightenment referred to in Chapter One. As will be seen below, the identification of cultural enlightenment with 'culture' rather than 'ideology' becomes stronger as one moves down the hierarchy from minister to ordinary citizen.

Poland and Hungary

Chapter Two described how Polish cultural enlightenment was extensively decentralized from 1958, the powerlessness felt by the central authorities in the 1960s, Gierek's attempt to recentralize by weakening the *województwo* leaderships and firmly orienting cultural enlightenment towards campaign-centred mobilization (imposing detailed central directives), and finally the weakened position of the ministry of culture and art in the 1980s, when it almost seems to have abdicated from any attempt to treat cultural enlightenment as ideological work.

The concern, or lack of the same, of *local* government with cultural enlightenment up to 1972 is one issue discussed by Jankowski in his study of cultural enlightenment in the Leszno area (1977). Jankowski examined 'official documents' dating from 1965 or before.[49] For the period up to 1972 he found only two(!) which were concerned with the cultural aspirations of the local community (dated 1965 and 1971); and one of these was issued by the People's Unity Front. Other documents were concerned merely with improving the 'material base' of local institutions for which the council was responsible, although these documents could give some indication of priorities:

> On the basis of this information it is possible to assert that... the local authorities assessed as being most important the need to satisfy people's desire for entertainment, the need for social integration through the formation of a feeling of connection with the traditions of the subregion and the requirements of readers.
>
> At the same time, these documents bear witness to the local leadership's lack of realization of the great range of cultural requirements existing within the local community. Moreover, the local leadership did not attempt to play any role in the local network of cultural institutions as a whole, but limited itself to organizational questions which were the direct responsibility of the people's council. Neither did it make any attempt to encourage any survey research into the cultural needs and interests of local inhabitants.

It was only half way through 1972, after the lead given by the sixth PZPR congress, that the local government and party organs began to take a more active interest in local cultural affairs: an interest which

Jankowski suggests they maintained up until the time he was writing (1976–7) – although he only cites evidence up to 1974.[50]

After the collapse of much of the trade union cultural- enlightenment system in 1980–1, some local councils took it over and ran it themselves. In Legnica, this was said to have led to a much diminished service.[51] In the period after 1981 local councils have however frequently been reported to be too busy trying to cope with economic problems to have time to spare to concentrate on cultural enlightenment.

One of the most interesting aspects of decentralization in Poland is the connection between local and national patriotism. It is hard to avoid the conclusion that because of the politically sensitive nature of manifestations of *national* patriotism, opportunities to display local patriotism, for example, through regional cultural societies, became more important as a substitute. The Gierek leadership's attempt to impose pro-Soviet propaganda on cultural enlightenment was bitterly resented. In Hungary, where the memory of national cultural traditions like the people's colleges and sociographic camps remained only a memory for many years, the attraction of such forms proved to have great survival capacity, despite the suspicion of the Hungarian leadership. As in Poland, the introduction of such typically Hungarian forms within a local community may be a way of making a nationalist statement while insisting, as some of the NI radicals for example do, that small deeds are for the sake of small communities or as a step towards the wider democratization and reform of Hungarian society.[52]

As in Poland, Hungarian cultural administration was extensively de-centralized after 1958. Also as in Poland, the results disturbed officials in Budapest. For example, in 1966 a Central Committee official complained that there was need to overcome separatist and 'anarchic' tendencies in pursuit of common goals: there should be no slackening of centralization in ideological work.[53] As Chapter Two described, during the 1960s numerous attempts were made to reassert central control and this was partially achieved with the imposition of the new institutional structure in 1968.[54] In 1977, however, Imre Pozsgay admitted that the ministry of culture had practically lost control over its subordinate institutions: it was rather the county authorities who dictated policy.[55]

Hungarian councils vary greatly one from another in their political complexion and this is reflected in their differing cultural policies. Moreover, a survey of house of culture directors in 1986 revealed a great variety of different types of relationship with the local council. On the one extreme, there was at least one case of severe neglect by the council. 'We have absolutely no system of information [from the council]. Not one of our administrative superiors was ever inside our house of culture.' More often, however, the council was viewed as playing an overly protective, distrustful and even obstructive role, taking a long time to make decisions and making almost impossible the introduction of real innovation. One blunt expression of this opinion stated: 'The council's administrative mechanism is incapable of supporting innovative methods'. Moreover, the councils had a habit of showering the directors with 'ad hoc' orders and regulations. The end result was to stifle initiative. One director explained bitterly: 'If the local council doesn't like what I'm doing, then I'll do anything to win their approval. Sometimes it's easiest if I do nothing at all and let things drift on of their own accord...'[56]

The obstructive power of county councils in Hungary is perhaps even greater than is the comparable power of regional and republican councils in Poland and the USSR, although there is no way of proving this impression in any quantitative fashion. What is clear is the great variety in practice between local authorities which – as Chapter Two suggested – makes it so dangerous to generalize about 'Hungarian cultural enlightenment'.

Trade unions and other organizations

To a large extent, the trade union cultural-enlightenment network merely replicates that of the state, and many important resolutions about cultural enlightenment are issued jointly by state and trade union authorities. There are historical differences in the organization of state and trade union institutions, as a result of which union houses of culture in the USSR are sometimes claimed to be more 'democratic'. However, such differences are not really very significant, and as Chapter Two showed, at various times the state has taken over trade union institutions (Poland in the 1950s and after 1981) or vice versa (in the USSR under Khrushchev). Had the USSR ministry of culture been abolished as some observers expected in the early 1960s, the state network might have been taken over entirely. In 1987 the existence of two separate networks in the USSR was once again under serious consideration in the Central Committee.[57] Why, given the parallelism between the work of state and union institutions, has the dual network been maintained so long? One obvious answer is the inertia and conservatism which make it so hard to get rid of any irrational administrative division. Another is the revolutionary tradition of union cultural enlightenment. However, the main reason must surely be a financial one: the state simply could not afford to run the union network in addition to its own.

Almost every social and mass organization bears some responsibility for cultural enlightenment, although in most cases cultural enlightenment is only one of a multiplicity of functions of the organization responsible. So, for example, a secretary of the KISZ Central Committee in 1970 rebutted criticisms that KISZ had been too little involved in directing youth culture by pointing out that 'KISZ is not a cultural, but a political organization'.[58] KISZ maintains the same standpoint today; however, this is a very disputable position. The activities of 'political' youth organizations in all three countries have a large cultural element; they run their own clubs, patronize their own artistic ensembles, for example, pop groups, and frequently co-operate with other organizations such as state cultural organs and trade union councils in issuing resolutions and regulations. They are supposed to co-operate with local cultural-enlightenment institutions in organizing cultural events, although such co-operation is not universal: departmentalism and parallelism play their part here as well. One outstanding example of successful co-operative work was the activity of the Polish rural youth union in the 1960s; this success was based on enthusiasm and spontaneous initiative of a type often displayed only by *unofficial* youth groups, such as those operating in all three countries today. One characteristic feature of unofficial Soviet youth groups today is their insistence that they left the Komsomol because of its over-bureaucratic approach: yet another indication that the emergence of the club movement under Gorbachev is largely a product of the previously inadequate organization of cultural enlightenment. Since the early 1980s KISZ membership has also been declining, as many of its former members join independent groups. The official Polish Students' Union (ZSP), never the most popular of organizations in the 1980s, seemed doomed to near extinction by 1988–9. A survey conducted by the ZSP in late 1988 or January 1989 revealed that only 20 per cent of members would remain within the ZSP if other independent organizations were permitted to function.[59]

In a sense, the youth organizations have more responsibility than any other mass social organization for cultural enlightenment, since young people form the majority of consumers and since the 'ideological struggle' with the West is most pronounced in the area of youth culture. However, other organizations also play a prominent role. One of these is the HNF in Hungary, which has its own network of clubs and also organizes festivals and other types of cultural enlightenment with regular houses of culture.[60] The work of the HNF often contains a strong patriotic or nationalist element: for example, it was the HNF which was partly behind the initiative to re-establish people's colleges. In Poland, the regional cultural societies are probably the most important cultural enlightenment organizations outside the houses of culture. Judging by the *nomenklatura* list, they would seem to be considered politically more important even than the main palaces of culture. Like the HNF, they have a patriotic quality, although this is a blend of local and national patriotism. In the Soviet Union, there is nothing similar to either. Cultural enlightenment is much more narrowly dominated by the state, trade union and Komsomol networks: additional organizations confine themselves to one aspect of cultural enlightenment. Examples of such organizations are DOSAAF and VOOPiK (with responsibility for military training and the preservation of historical monuments, respectively). Lecture propaganda in all three countries is the responsibility of specialist Knowledge societies: Znanie, TWP and TIT. These have a special role to play in co-opting intellectuals to participate in cultural enlightenment and in atheist propaganda, although the latter would seem to be nowadays a minor part of the work of TIT and in Poland is shared with the Society for Disseminating Lay Culture (TKKS).

In addition, responsibility for cultural enlightenment also lies with a motley of organizations concerned with various components of ideological work: patriotic, ecological, artistic etc.

A 1984 survey of members of the Hungarian Association of Cultural-Enlightenment Workers (MNE) showed that more than half of the sample considered the irrationally divided and overlapping jurisdictions and powers of the various bodies concerned with cultural enlightenment to be a serious obstacle.[61] This has been a common complaint throughout the whole period under consideration, in every country. Yet, are rationality and efficiency the most important criteria? The main problem of cultural enlightenment in Soviet type systems is over- bureaucratization and standardization. In such a situation, staleness may be avoided, at the risk of confusion, by the participation of several organizations at once. The HNF, for example, tries to play just such an invigorating role in the cultural enlightenment of other institutions. Moreover, purely financial considerations operate. Many of the most successful cultural-enlightenment events are large festivals which could not be afforded by one organization working alone.

Chapter five

Policy and practice 2: house of culture staff and the public

It is probably the house of culture staff who form the weakest link in the chain of command from the ministries and who are at the same time most responsive to the tug of the local community. They are in an invidious position, since it is they who have to cope with the reality of the contradiction within the ideology, which on 'higher' levels is still within the realm of rhetoric. On the one hand, they are expected by their superiors, and even to some extent by the population, to do no more than provide a service. On the other hand, they are expected, more fashionably, to provide the setting in which the population can organize its own leisure, with their guidance and help.

This chapter discusses in turn the house of culture plan; the objectives of director and staff and their responsiveness to public demands; and cultural-enlightenment workers' social status. It then examines public input into cultural-enlightenment policy through public management committees, other voluntary work in the house of culture and opinion surveys. Finally, some general conclusions are suggested, drawing on evidence presented both here and in Chapter Four.

Compiling the plan

In all three countries throughout this period cultural workers have been supposed to respond to directives from central and local government about the broad outlines and content of their programmes, and to suggestions or orders from local authorities and social organizations about specific events. But at the same time throughout the period everywhere the actual programme has never been entirely laid down from above: institutions have a say in compiling their own plans, and are responsible for writing them themselves, although naturally they are approved by higher authorities. What differs between countries and over time is the proportion of freedom and compulsion involved in compiling the plan, and, connected with this, the degree of responsiveness to local wishes.

In the Soviet Union (but not, it would appear, in Poland and Hungary), central directives to be used in the composition of plans concern not only the content of cultural enlightenment, for example, the type of socialization work involved, or themes of particular campaigns, but also forms of organization such as types of club operating within the institution. Thus, after the issue of the May 1986 regulations about amateur associations, houses of culture received orders to set up a certain number of hobby clubs and amateur (*liubitel'skie*, literally 'from love') associations: the absurdity of *ordering* people to create clubs 'from love' was satirized by the journal *Klub* in July 1987.[1] In the short term it could only be done by creating fictitious clubs or changing the names of existing clubs and lecture courses. One house of culture director suggested: 'But even the people who "from on high" sent down orders for these figures understood that probably we would only "write them in". Or perhaps they did not understand?' Conversely, it is often extremely difficult to set up new types of club which are not covered by directives: for instance, in 1987 this created an extreme shortage (relative to demand) of Soviet skateboard clubs.[2]

However, *perestroika* also creates new problems: house of culture directors do not like to be told by the ministry 'decide for yourselves' even if it is only to fix the price of membership for an amateur association. As one director pointed out in the *Klub*, they knew from bitter experience how risky it was to take decisions for themselves: they had yet to be persuaded that decentralization was for real.[3]

Planning in Hungary is sometimes a haphazard affair. A study of Budapest houses of culture in 1975 found that:

A good half of the *workplans* do not reflect any serious thinking about cultural policy or pedagogical objectives, and most of the plans confine themselves to generalities. There are institutions where there is no plan of work....Most of the plans more or less adhere to formal requirements, but more than half do not include a budget, two-thirds have no plans for the work of clubs within the house of culture and altogether 50 per cent mention the improvement of material and personnel resources. Only half the plans included a concrete time schedule for planned events.[4]

With regard to the provision of cultural facilities for workers in particular, one respondent replied that Budapest houses of culture 'work in the spirit of central policy guidelines, but no one has time to really work out what this policy should be, how it should accord with real needs and aspirations.' The authors agreed that 'a great deal is demanded of the cultural-enlightenment workers, and expectations of them are often unreal. They have to spend much of their time on administration and organization.' In their official working hours they can spend extremely little time on the real tasks of cultural enlightenment.[5]

The director

The director has considerable input into the plan, and bears the main responsibility for its implementation, so his or her aptitudes and attitudes are a key factor in what occurs. At one extreme, he or she may be very committed, full of ideas and energy; on the other, lazy and totally uninterested in culture, someone who has made a failure of some other career, perhaps because of an alcohol problem, and regards the directorship of a house of culture as a comfortable niche.[6] Or he or she may fall somewhere in between and be conscientious, but unimaginative: such a person may not realize that in order for cultural enlightenment to be effective, the official framework of red-letter days and traditional types of event and activity promulgating the operative ideology is insufficient – however secure and comforting a guide it may be to the cultural worker.

The 'committed' director is often someone with a great deal of imagination and an elastic interpretation of 'culture', interested in organizing women's self-defence classes and yacht races (Poznań) or deep sea diving and archaeological digs (Leningrad). The people I met, like the diarists who contributed to the Polish collection *Zdnania dzień* were almost all enthusiasts of this type.[7] They were also 'enthusiasts' for the broad egalitarian social and cultural objectives of cultural enlightenment, and rather seldom repeated the slogans of the *operative* ideology. I heard of many directors of the opposite, apathetic sort – particularly the predecessors of the people I interviewed. This image of the lazy director seems to be something of a stereotype among cultural workers, although it is only occasionally confirmed in the press. For instance *Sovetskaia kul'tura* claimed in October 1964 that village clubs were often run by people whom the authorities should not have appointed 'even at gunpoint' and cited the case of a Tadzhik who neglected his club for days on end to sell melons at the market.[8] There is no way to assess the extent of such negligence.

I have little evidence about people in between the two extremes: perhaps indeed only the enthusiasts or the totally blasé survive long in cultural-enlightenment work. The turnover rate of staff in general in cultural enlightenment in all three countries has been consistently high, with the profession thus dependent on continual fresh cohorts of enthusiasts. A Soviet club director wrote in 1985: 'Most often it is enthusiasts who come to work in cultural-enlightenment institutions, but after a couple of years' work only a scrap of enthusiasm remains.'[9]

I asked directors of houses of culture in all three countries about the origin of particular clubs and items in their programme. Sometimes they mentioned instances in which members of the public had approached them with suggestions, but very often, usually after thinking for a while, they decided that the club or event in question had been their own personal idea or that of their colleagues or friends. In the largest houses of culture, there is sometimes a special planning department. House of culture directors may confine their activities to those which they feel confident about organizing, which, in a small club with not very well qualified staff may mean a very limited choice of activities. An article in *Sovetskaia kul'tura* in November 1985 attributed the frequent lack of sophistication and the over-emphasis on children's activities to staff shortcomings:

> The 'childish' level of much of what goes on in the clubs is, alas, only to be expected. Cultural workers' performance depends on their knowledge, experience and age. And after all, often they are only eighteen or nineteen, with no experience, and with the knowledge which they have acquired in the cultural-enlighten-ment *uchilishche* (tertiary college) far too limited for them to transform the club into a real hearth of culture. Far from every young woman *uchilishche* graduate succeeds in winning the respect of adults, which is why she devotes her attention to small children....And before the time the young women have grown up and acquired some experience, they have already left the club because of the poor pay or living conditions or because of family commitments, and new, inexperienced young women take their places...[10]

The head of the Lithuanian ministry of culture cultural-enlightenment department described the same 'problem' in August 1986:

> Many young graduates have begun to come to work in collective and state farms, and not only agricultural specialists....In large collective farms we have artists, architects and even the occasional landscape gardener. How can a nineteen-year old cultural-enlightenment *uchilischche* graduate hope to establish contact with such people? And many such little girls are not only incapable of conversing with such people as equals, but are even afraid to approach them![11]

One suspects that 'little girls' working in club institutions find it difficult to organize not only intellectually sophisticated cultural events but anything at all, given this type of attitude combined with the propensity of Soviet administrators to arrange things through informal channels and networking which may be inaccessible to women, especially if they are new to the job. A Soviet survey of house of culture directors revealed they 'prefer to discuss business with other institutions and organizations... not through the public management committee [the official channel, see below] but by the "more reliable" channel of personal contacts: friends, relatives or family.'[12]

Staff responsiveness to public demand and general objectives

As previous chapters described, during the post-Stalinist period house of culture programmes have been supposed to become more responsive to popular demands, expressed through institutions such as the public management committee. As Sándor Boros, Hungarian deputy culture minister, put it in 1978, 'We used to really impose culture on people: we told them what they were interested in and needed. This has to stop. We request the house of culture workers to shape their activities and offerings in response to the needs and aspirations of the house of culture visitors.'[13] Cultural workers have not always responded to the new demands that they be more responsive to local wishes. A speaker at the National Cultural-Enlightenment Conference in Hungary in 1984 pleaded for house of culture workers to stir themselves from their desks and instead of thinking up their plans in their offices, go out and talk to the public.[14] A *Sovetskaia kul'tura* editorial on 21 August 1986 complained, surely with some exaggeration, that at the moment it was still the case that 'absolutely everywhere the club workers dictate their own conditions to the visitors, permit or forbid, behave towards people disrespectfully and in a bureaucratic fashion'; while in 1987 a letter to the Polish journal *Inspiracje* complained of 'the administration of culture from offices with soundproof doors'.[15]

In the present climate of official approval for a more democratic approach, directors often seem to feel some discomfort if they do not utilize opinion surveys before arranging their programmes. However, directors often vindicated themselves by pointing out that they and their colleagues have an accurate conception of what the local population would like, since their job involves constant contact with local people and with local organizations, as well as more academic knowledge gained from the methodological literature. This is a fairly convincing argument, although on occasion the house of culture may quite naturally make mistakes and display lack of thought and sensitivity. For example, the Poznań Palace of Culture arranged a series of dances during Lent which hardly anyone attended: this was described to me as having been purely a mistake.[16]

An extension of the argument that the house of culture staff know the population's needs already is that they know them better than the public does itself. They have the ability to articulate and realistically formulate aspirations which many members of the public may only vaguely sense.

To continue Boros's remarks, quoted above: 'Our obligation is to satisfy existing aspirations, but we must also pay attention to those cultural needs which haven't yet been consciously realized.'

The problem with this argument is that it tends to become circular: articulating unfelt needs is a short step from the normative approach which Boros began by criticizing. In practice, because of their own aptitudes and inclinations, cultural workers may introduce activities which had not occurred to the local public, not because they necessarily want to 'further their cultural growth' but simply because they want to do something innovative. New ideas may be Western in origin; often they are the latest fashion (although not necessarily yet among the general public). A Polish house of culture director expressed his aims for his institution: 'Fashions sweep across Poland like bombs. I want them to explode in this house of culture.' This is a far cry from all the warnings in official documents about a decline in public taste and insidious Western influence. On the other hand, it is surely what many, especially young, people in all three countries would like their houses of culture to provide. Other directors looked backwards for inspiration. For instance, the director of the Palace of Culture in Poznań (Poland's largest house of culture) said that she wanted to follow and revive local traditions. This aspiration was shared by cultural workers in all three countries. Again, it is in harmony with real public wishes.

In the early 1970s, apart from the director and former director of the Leszno House of Culture in Poland, the staff members had difficulty in formulating the more basic goals of their work. Most of them wished to form habits of cultural participation and popularize good 'cultural' entertainment. They failed to mention many of the goals listed in the new house of culture statute, such as the formation of socialist morality or a scientific world view. In this, they differed little from the local officials (including the PZPR propaganda secretary and head of the cultural department (!)) who were also interviewed. 'In both cases, there predominates a narrowly pragmatic approach to these goals and no reference is made to Marxist axiology. This bears witness to insufficient knowledge in this sphere, and the lack of deep philosophical, sociological or pedagogical interests.'[17] A survey by a Moscow research institute disclosed a similar lack of ability to relate to the basic goals expressed in regulations and official resolutions.

In practice, house of culture arts collectives displayed a limited sphere of tasks as compared with those perceptions of the social functions of amateur activity which have become fixed in public consciousness and are formulated in normative documents and philosophical works. The main, and often the single goal is in practice the achievement of artistic results.[18]

A survey of which the results were published in 1980 revealed that 'practitioners of club work are far from always able to perceive what goals inform the events they organize'.[19] Another survey discovered that 97.4 per cent of a sample of 380 leaders of adult amateur arts groups were uninterested in educational processes and were only concerned with the standard of final performance.[20]

The status of cultural-enlightenment workers

Frequently the poor state of cultural enlightenment is blamed on the incompetence of house of culture employees. However fair this assessment (and those employees I met did not strike me as incompetent), the low regard in which they seem often to be held is a factor discouraging many from persisting with their chosen career. A 1987 survey of cultural workers found that almost a third of them wanted to change career, not as was usually assumed because of poor material conditions, but for 'psychological reasons': complaints expressed included 'no one takes us seriously' and 'there are too many cultural know-alls about'.[21] The low prestige of the profession is a major reason for this high turnover rate and also helps explain why the house of culture staff have difficulties liaising both with the local authorities and with the local public.

A survey of 130 trade union cultural workers in Leningrad in 1976–7 showed that they were most dissatisfied with their work conditions and pay and with their social standing, related to public estimation of the value of their work. The authors conclude that 'the social position of the trade union club worker is marginal. Formally he is included among the workers in culture and education, but in practice he is a member of a labour collective occupied with production work corresponding to his branch.' His different sphere of work from the rest of the collective 'makes his position not entirely secure, and compels him to again and again try to prove his usefulness and defend his work against those who consider it of secondary importance.' As a result, he often suffers from a sense of grievance which affects the way he conducts his work.[22] The 'Club worker' survey reported similar attitudes to social standing, as shown in Table 3.

In other words, 57.2 per cent of cultural workers and 66.1 per cent of first year students rated the social prestige of their work somewhere between 'very low' and 'not very high', while 83.8 per cent of lecturers and 85.4 per cent of final year students did the same. This is a very negative assessment. In June 1985 the secretary of the VTsSPS requested members of the party, soviets and social organizations to treat cultural-enlightenment workers as members of the creative intelligentsia: in other works, strongly suggesting that at present they are not.[23]

Table 3 'How, in your opinion, is the profession of cultural worker regarded in society?' (%) The status of cultural-enlightenment workers in the USSR.

	Cultural worker	1st year student	Final year student	Lecturer
Very highly	3.9	7.2	1.4	1.9
Highly	21.2	16.3	6.8	7.1
Not very highly	46.0	48.0	45.5	50.0
Lowly	8.1	12.9	25.5	19.5
Very lowly	3.1	5.2	14.4	14.3

Source: Klubny rabotnik, p. 119, Table 28.

The social status of Hungarian and Polish cultural workers would seem to be equally unsatisfactory, if one may judge by the constant complaints which they make in the pages of the press. The NI claimed in 1985, on the basis of research, that even 'senior house of culture workers occupy the last ranks of the intelligentsia'. In Poland, the 1984 law about culture diffusion specifically attempted to raise the prestige of cultural-enlightenment workers. In 1987 deputy minister of culture Cłapka claimed that this had been achieved 'as is emphasized everywhere'. This was confirmed by a specialist journalist fairly critical in other respects about the effect of the law, who said in January 1987 that the status of the profession had been 'significantly raised'.[24]

Why is it that cultural-enlightenment workers are held in low regard? Does this reflect society's regard for cultural enlightenment? In my opinion it does: this is one of the main reasons for their low status. As this study shows, there is plenty of evidence to confirm that cultural enlightenment is frequently neglected and despised by both authorities and the public. There are also, however, other reasons why cultural workers and by extension cultural enlightenment suffer in public and official esteem. The most important of these are their gender and their level of education.

It is obvious from some of the instances already cited that a contemptuous attitude towards cultural-enlightenment workers, and, by extension, cultural enlightenment, may be based on unfair assumptions. This was the case of the Soviet situations described above, when the mere fact that the club worker was a young girl was assumed to mean that she could not perform her job. A similar attitude is displayed in a Polish study of village clubs: 'Clubs often become the workplace of "failures" (especially girls) with a vocational education, who for various reasons do not take up work for which they were trained.'[25] In general, interview information and observation both suggest that part of cultural enlightenment's low prestige is attributable to the fact that there exists a widespread perception in Poland and the USSR (although not apparently in Hungary) that it is a 'woman's profession'. This connection was, however, vigorously denied by some of my interview subjects. To my knowledge, no research has been conducted into the subject, although it is said to be in Poland the 'unspoken assumption' of both research and popular writing that the feminization of the profession is a problem.[26]

Where does the 'problem' really lie? As with 'women's professions' in general, causation is of a circular nature. Because women work in cultural enlightenment, it is not prestigious, therefore it is ill-paid, therefore women work in it; but of course the lack of prestige and money also have other causes. However, it is possible to find out at least a little about the actual proportion of women working in the profession. If it is large, then, I would argue, assertions that this is a cause of cultural enlightenment's low prestige probably have a certain validity. From a variety of evidence[27] it seems to be fairly clear that in the USSR and Poland cultural enlightenment is indeed a profession with a high number of women, but not in the same category of saturation as, for example, catering or clerical work. Shishkan classes 'cultural' workers in her third category of occupations divided according to female saturation, that is, those where women form 50–70 per cent. This seems to be reasonable, although given the fact that many managerial positions in cultural enlightenment are held by men, among ordinary cultural-enlightenment workers the percentage of women may in some areas be even higher than 70 per cent.[28]

In many cases the failings of cultural-enlightenment workers are attributed to their poor level of education. Once again, it is not a fair assumption that just because a cultural worker is uneducated he or she is not going to be able to implement official policy. There are many accounts, for example, of successful village clubs run by poorly educated but well-respected and enthusiastic local people. However, greater control over cultural enlightenment is naturally associated by the regime with the formation of a better-informed and socialized corps of workers. In 1970, three per cent of club workers in the USSR had higher education.[29] During the 1970s, educational levels among club workers improved, as degree courses and refresher courses, seminars and other types of training became more widely available. However, in 1978, 3.7 per cent of club workers (possibly in the RSFSR only) were said to have higher education, while only 2.1 per cent of the club workers questioned in the 'Club worker' survey held degrees.[30]

Poland and Hungary witnessed an increase in the number of graduates entering cultural enlightenment work as specialist degrees were established during the 1970s. Many, however, had humanities degrees of various kinds, rather than a specialized qualification. As in the USSR, graduates show a strong inclination to work in urban areas. A survey of cultural-enlightenment workers and librarians graduating from the Debrecen Institute of Education in the mid-1970s showed that two thirds were working in the towns and only 6.4 per cent in small communities.[31]

The number of graduates produced bears little relation to the number actually working in cultural enlightenment. The benefit of developments in training has frequently been lost because of the high turnover of cultural workers and the reluctance of cultural-enlightenment graduates to accept jobs in backward rural areas. In the RSFSR, this problem seems to be even more acute than it is in the case of schoolteachers or librarians, with a turnover rate of around 30 per cent. In the USSR there are frequent press reports about graduates who either leave shortly after arrival at their new village job or else never turn up at all. Dozens of lecturers at the Tashkent Institute of Culture are said to make yearly forays into the surrounding countryside in search of missing ex-students.[32]

The cultural-enlightenment worker: conclusions

The picture which emerges of the average club worker is of someone who is interested in doing creative work in the arts and believes that there is also public interest in doing the same. The realistic club worker knows that the job is not a prestigious one, especially in Poland and the USSR. This lack of prestige is partly related to the fact that many Polish and Soviet cultural- enlightenment workers are women, and also to the fact that some workers – especially in country areas – are not very well educated. However, a more important cause is connected with the dual nature of cultural enlightenment as both culture and ideology, and the fallacies this breeds. The public often sees cultural enlightenment as ideological work and the cultural worker as an ideological hack. As has been shown, this is far from always the case. Most cultural-enlightenment workers are more interested in 'culture' than in propagating the operative ideology. Their superiors have a clearer idea of this than does the general public, but this does not help, since from the point of view of the cultural authorities at the top cultural enlightenment is essentially ideological work – cultural workers are a 'weak link', the 'key problem of cultural enlightenment', because they are not doing their job. As was shown in previous sections, local government officials may have a more ambiguous point of view.

Public participation

Self-management is one of the most important methods of achieving didactic and socializing objectives and is closely connected with the active self-education of its participants.[33]

123

This final part of Chapter Five discusses the weakest link in the chain from minister to citizen: the last link of all. On first sight it would not, however, appear that this weakness was caused by any absence of *attempt* on the part of the regime to involve citizens in the making and execution of cultural enlightenment policy. How real are such attempts and how well do they succeed? How else does the public influence the making of cultural-enlightenment policy? This section examines in turn the concept of participation; public management in the house of culture; the role of activists; and the use of opinion surveys. The chapter ends with some conclusions about policy making and its execution in cultural enlightenment.

One of the most efficient means of socialization is generally assumed, in Soviet-type systems, to be for the object of socialization to be engaged him- or herself in socializing others. It is hoped that participation in officially-sanctioned activity will engender a sense of identification with official values and with the regime and develop social responsibility and initiative. These aspirations may be contradictory, as for example Barghoorn and Remington point out.[34] In practice, however, in cultural enlightenment this possibility of contra- diction, though real, when as so often happens regime and public expect- ations differ, is limited in significance by the formalized nature of much 'self-management'. In houses of culture, this formalization is often a special disadvantage. In a local council, for example, the fact that powerful local party leaders participate ex officio is to the council's advantage. To an institution like a house of culture, the fact that local officials participate in the management ex officio (in all three countries) often brings no such benefit. The officials regard the duty as one of the least of many (see Chapter Four, on the official from Novaia Kakhovka!), while the over-representation of ex officio members on small management committees means that there is very limited possibility for energetic public activists to play a role. This seems especially unfortunate in view of the fact that cultural enlightenment is in many respects a particularly suitable (and relatively harmless) area for public involvement.

There has never been a law on participation in culture in the USSR of the type of the Hungarian 1976 law on cultural enlightenment or the Polish one of 1984 on the dissemination of culture. Both these laws reflect a realization by the regime of the significance of assuring popular activity in the cultural sphere, and of taking positive measures to improve access to culture. This was a retreat from the traditional assumption that the introduction of a socialist regime had *ipso facto* democratized culture. The fallacy of this assumption had been especially acutely realized in Poland, and, as was described in Chapter Two, the neglect of culture had become a significant political problem by the early 1980s. In Hungary, Pozsgay, with his particular concern for energizing new social forces, seems to have been very much the driving force behind the 1976 law. After his transferral from the Culture Ministry to the Patriotic People's Front (HNF) in 1982,[35] the momentum to improve cultural participation was partly lost. The 1976 official commentary published with the law on cultural enlightenment stated that:

> Building on the results of old-style cultural enlightenment (*népmüvelés*), but abolishing its obsolete elements, the law desires to promote the constant and active participation in culture of the entire population. This is in the interests of every citizen, and at the same time is in the public interest: it is something affecting the whole of society, an essential element for the further development of Hungarian society.[36]

Article 2.1 of the 1984 Polish law explained that:

> The goal of cultural diffusion is the enrichment of the human personality, the formation of citizens' ideological, moral and patriotic principles, of socialist relations and foundations in public life, the strengthening of ties between individuals and the development of cultured behaviour in work, leisure and everyday life.[37]

'Participation' in cultural enlightenment may take two forms: simple attendance at the house of culture or helping to make policy and run the institution. In practice the dividing line between these forms of participation is not always clear, since the active members of collectives within the house of culture have opportunity for informal influence over how the house of culture is run. Moreover, simply by attending an event or club in sufficient or insufficient numbers the public may be able to influence what is provided, especially as in the course of time houses of culture in all three countries have been required to find a greater proportion of their income from their own profits. However, it seems more convenient to consider evidence about attendance in Chapter Six, which is about the effectiveness of cultural enlightenment. The rest of the present chapter will examine more active means of involvement.

The assumption that participation is an effective means of socialization is central to the political system in all three countries. In practice, however, the regime has almost always taken care to control forms of public participation, fearing the emergence of values and policies inimical to official socialization policy. As we have seen, the history of houses of culture shows that these fears have not been groundless. However, public influence over cultural enlightenment seems to have been most often exercised through consumer power, and only in rare periods of intense social involvement in cultural enlightenment through the official organs of 'democratic' public management. In practice, like so many other forums of public participation, these have frequently been neither powerful nor democratic. The chief institution in which such participation formally takes place is the so-called 'public (management) committee' or 'council' of the house of culture. The committee in all countries is intended to act as a 'bridge' between the house of culture administration and the public, who are thereby given the opportunity to provide input into the house of culture programme and monitor the institution's work.[38] In practice, the committee is often a one-way 'bridge', a transmission belt, between the local party/state apparatus and the professional house of culture staff. (In Poland, there is genuine public management only in village clubs run by volunteers.)[39]

Cultural enlightenment is in particular need of public participation in management, given that one of the major objections ordinary citizens – especially young people – have against it in its present form is that they do not like to have leisure activities imposed on them. Cultural-enlightenment specialists too, especially in Hungary, are adamant that the old concept of a 'cultural service' is outdated and that the population must organize its own leisure time in the house of culture. The role of cultural workers is simply to facilitate this. However, the traditional frameworks for public participation may not necessarily be the most suitable; for example, it is often unwise of houses of culture to try to force youth culture into traditional forms of self-management: youth groups are organized according to their own rules.[40] In both the USSR and Hungary there is an observable trend towards greater official trust towards new types of autonomous, smaller-scale cultural enlightenment institutions. In Poland, semi-autonomous institutions already existed: what is really new there in the last decade is the role of the church and the underground in housing flourishing alternative cultural groups.

Public management committees in their old form have not been a success because of their insufficient powers and frequently undemocratic character. However, this does not necessarily mean that they will be formally abolished. They still remain the most appropriate form of controlled public 'participation' in the eyes of the many remaining conservatives in cultural-enlightenment administration. There is obviously a need for more useful channels for the public to express its 'cultural needs'. Some of these will now be considered.

Activists in the house of culture

There are numerous other ways in which volunteer activists can help in cultural enlightenment, some of which are more voluntary than others.

One of the major forms of voluntary work is that conducted by members of the intelligentsia, who are co-opted into the system/able to share their knowledge, or earn some spare cash, by giving lectures for the societies for disseminating popular knowledge: Znanie, TWP and TIT. These are mass organizations organizing work on a very large scale indeed which despite their many shortcomings must qualify as one of the largest arenas for volunteer cultural-enlightenment work.[41]

Volunteers may also teach in arts groups or hobby clubs, or do a range of odd jobs around the house of culture. They perform many of the same functions as volunteers in British arts centres, and wherever arts are short-staffed, this is surely likely to be the case. Volunteers are often enthusiasts for their particular hobby rather than consciously model citizens: it is quite misleading for Soviet sociologists to throw them indiscriminately into the category of 'vanguard citizens'.

The informal mass of activists, like the formal management committee, is intended to sound out the needs and wishes of house of culture visitors or of potential visitors and relay them to the house of culture.[42] This function may also be performed by trade union organizers or people on the management committees of blocks of flats.[43] Interviews with house of culture workers showed that many felt that informal channels of this type were the most useful. However, a more 'scientific' approach is now in fashion.

Opinion surveys may be conducted for one of at least three reasons. Either there is a practical need to find out the requirements of the local public, or there is some more abstract scholarly purpose, or there is a political reason why it is desired to measure the 'spiritual growth' of the population. In practice, there is a certain amount of overlap between the three types, especially the second two. This final section will consider surveys conducted by cultural-enlightenment institutions in their own vicinity for 'practical' purposes, since it is through these that the public has most direct input.[44]

A survey conducted by the Higher Trade Union School of Culture in Leningrad found that of a sample of 464 directors of club institutions, 50.85 per cent regularly and 43.7 per cent occasionally took part in studying the 'requirements, interests and desires of the public' (unfortunately no more detail is supplied).[45]

More frequently, a less satisfactory picture is painted. It is difficult to estimate how widespread survey work actually is. In the USSR, the republican methodological centres often do not themselves receive reports about research which is actually being undertaken at the local level.[46] On the other hand, Hungarian county methodological departments based in cultural centres, especially those in Budapest and Debrecen, regularly undertake sophisticated research. They employ full-time research staff and include research within their yearly plans.[47]

Although local surveys are largely a phenomenon of the 1980s, as early as 1965 some houses of culture are said to have been experimenting with them and to have used the results in drawing up their plans for future work. For example, in 1965 one of the biggest Leningrad palaces of culture asked its visitors at the New Year what they had liked during the past year, what they had thought of innovative forms of work, and whether they had suggestions for improvements. The Dnepropetrovsk Students' Palace of Culture and another unnamed institution asked the same types of question, requesting opinions on specific sorts of event. Some houses of culture were said to send out several mini-questionnaires a year, others held regular meetings with visitors to discuss practical matters like the timing of events. Yet other institutions held evenings under the rubric 'By the request of our visitors'. Well in advance, they pasted posters around enterprises and housing estates announcing the theme of the evening and inviting suggestions as to what celebrities, films or concert pieces should be included.[48]

Of the types of survey conducted today, the simplest is to make available a book for comments, which may be displayed in a prominent place after a performance with a request attached for feedback.[49] Alternatively, visitors may be requested to express their feedback by completing a formal questionnaire.[50] The disadvantage of these methods is that they give no indication about the wishes of non-attenders and so cannot extend the house of culture's local net. An extension of the same method is to gather together the local public, or a section of it, to ask them on the spot for their ideas. This is said to have been very successful in some Soviet institutions. On the other hand, an attempt to do the same in Leszno in Poland was a total flop: no one turned up for the meeting. When some of the people invited were asked afterwards why they did not come, they said that it was the business of the house of culture to provide a programme, not theirs.[51] Alternatively, the local population may be requested to formulate their wishes in writing. In Voroshilovgrad in the early 1980s this method was very fruitful. For example, it led to the creation in the city of an office of the 'Leisure' organization, and to the establishment of 'musical soirées': concerts introduced by professional musicologists and consisting of pieces chosen by the local public.[52]

Many Soviet amateur surveys make extensive use of open-ended questions.[53] Short questionnaires of this type can be useful: for instance, one director of a house of culture on a Poznań housing estate employed such a questionnaire to find out what foreign languages local people would like to learn. A survey produced in 1987 by the Moscow City Methodological Centre to assess local needs went to the other extreme of using huge lists of possible answers and offering 2,500 residents the

128

possibility of spending hours deciding their opinion on every conceivable leisure activity.[54]

Soviet local surveys sometimes use a methodology employed for mass surveys developed by the Arts Studies Research Centre. This combines 'what is' with 'what should be'. The cultural wishes and habits of the 'vanguard' group in the area, the activists of various kinds, are studied on the assumption that this group will necessarily increase in size and influence, and long-term cultural plans are drawn up accordingly. A Tadzhik survey, for instance, included in this group 16 per cent of the urban and 9 per cent of the village residents in its sample.[55]

Club workers are often said to be unfamiliar with the techniques of survey research. One Institute of Culture lecturer, writing in 1978, lamented that no Soviet institutions of higher education taught survey skills,[56] although this is now on the syllabus in some institutions, such as the Leningrad Institute of Culture, where lectures are delivered by none other than the eminent sociologist Iadov, and at Debrecen University in Hungary. Another contributor to the same 1978 collection urged the need for houses of culture to enlist the services of professional sociologists working in institutes and factories.[57]

The difficulties house of culture staff face in producing their own questionnaires include much simpler, practical problems, particularly lack of copying facilities. One Uzbek house of culture arts director spent three weeks typing out copies and carbon copies of a questionnaire for assessing people's wishes.[58]

A Soviet author claimed in 1978 that 'many' enterprises had embarked on cultural surveys among their workers as part of a wider effort at their 'passportization'. At the Zhdanov tractor factory in Vladimir, for example, more than five hundred engineers and technicians and also most of the Komsomol members had their own 'creativity plans' for 'raising their level of culture'. Every year the holders of these plans had to give an account of how successfully they had been fulfilled.[59]

Policy and practice: some conclusions

The most important development in policy formation and execution since Stalin's death has been the increased extent of popular input and freedom of choice for the house of culture staff. Popular participation is not often very successfully exercised through formal channels (the public management committee), but more usually through informal influence on house of culture staff, and increasingly through opinion surveys. Being more interested in culture than in ideology, cultural workers often identify with the aspirations of the local public rather than with officials – although they may have a more elitist perception of culture and dismissive attitude towards light entertainment than does the ordinary house of culture visitor.

These trends have complicated causes. One important reason for them is of course the increased opportunity for public participation which has occurred more generally since Stalin's death. But some developments within cultural enlightenment have also played their part. One is the continuing 'cultural' bent of the club workers, despite their increased level of education. The most important, however, has been the propensity of ordinary citizens to vote with their feet and by quitting the house of culture in great numbers forcing the authorities to take their views seriously.

However, although the inability of many cultural-enlightenment institutions to attract an audience is the weakest link in the chain from the central party/state apparatus, local government officials are often remiss in their duties or else too interested in culture and too little in ideology, too low in status or too poorly educated, to be effective agents of official socialization.

At all levels, the party, which should be most concerned about the effectiveness of political socialization, is negligent in its handling of cultural enlightenment. However, where there is a local party leader with a special interest in cultural enlightenment, the improvement can be dramatic.

Chapter six

The effectiveness of cultural
enlightenment

Introduction

> The evidence of numerous sociological surveys shows that the
> house of culture is the last place in which the average citizen
> wishes to spend his free time and where he expects to be able to
> fulfil his aspirations.

> Barbara Parobczak, 'Z domami kultury czy bez?', *Kultura i ty*, no.
> 2, 1981, pp. 5–6

If Parobczak's assertion is true, then cultural enlightenment must be
deemed a total failure. However, Polish houses of culture in the years
immediately before 1981 were probably at their nadir of popularity: this
was a time when such extreme statements were probably more true than
at any other (with the possible exception of the mid-1950s). The overall
evidence as to the success of cultural enlightenment is more complex
and contradictory than Parobczak suggests. This chapter will look at the
evidence and draw some provisional conclusions. In doing so, it
contributes at least a little more to the pool of existing knowledge about
the effectiveness of ideological work.

The simplistic beliefs about cause and effect which characterized the
Stalinist period persisted in cultural enlightenment for many years after
Stalin's death. As a consequence, some rather straightforward methods
were suggested for measuring the success of cultural enlightenment. For
example: 'The effectiveness of cultural enlightenment in the
countryside can be measured in tonnes of grain and cotton and centners
of meat and milk'.[1] This chapter, however, will not discuss either tonnes
of cotton or centners [100 kg] of milk. In order to assess the
effectiveness of cultural enlightenment, it will first discuss how to
define its objectives, and then measure how successfully these are
achieved. Neither is a simple task.

The first objective of cultural enlightenment is to involve all
members of the population. Thus, in order to determine success in this

one objective, it is useful to measure the number of people exposed to cultural enlightenment, and if possible the degree of their exposure. Many surveys do precisely this. They will be discussed below. This approach is obviously a sensible beginning. If no one is involved, there is nothing to measure. Problems, however, set in after the aim to involve everyone in *house of culture* activities disappeared in Poland and Hungary around 1979–80. It is much easier to measure participation in houses of culture than it is in the more informal organizations which are now considered to be acceptable. For the earlier period, however, and for the USSR to the present day, surveys about house of culture attendance are useful. If nobody among the local population attends the house of culture, or if it is padlocked all year round, or if the planned and advertized activities actually fail to take place, then there is no cultural enlightenment to measure. Even if 30 per cent of the local public visits the house of culture from time to time, it is still highly problematical to talk of success, when the stated aim is to involve everyone.

Other surveys assess the extent of cultural participation as a whole, not just cultural enlightenment. These broader surveys also give some indication as to the effectiveness of cultural enlightenment. If no participation at all is recorded in *culture*, this must be considered a failure on the part of *cultural enlightenment*, which bears responsibility for introducing citizens to culture and involving them in cultural activities.

On the other hand, as many observers have pointed out, a quantitative approach carries many dangers. First of all, statistics are often unreliable, and second, more may not necessarily mean better. If a huge audience gathers in a house of culture to attend a meeting of the nationalist society Pamiat', this is not a success for Soviet cultural enlightenment. Moreover, the 'more equals better' approach leads to the very simplified attitude towards the potential of cultural enlightenment which was typical of the Stalinist era. The more concerts about Rákosi, the more people loved him. Obviously this was not an entirely naive point of view, especially at that time, when it was still possible to create an atmosphere of 'collective magic'. It has however led to much unintelligent cultural enlightenment since.

Cultural enlightenment under Stalin, Rákosi or Bierut was unquestionably successful in two very important senses: the 'masses' were introduced to selected aspects of the cultural heritage, and a large proportion of the population – particularly the politically important categories of workers and young people – were coerced into declaring their support for the regime through participation in amateur arts. However, as has been shown in previous chapters, this second aspect of success was short-lived. On a deeper level, it was very counterproductive, since it destroyed the credibility of cultural enlightenment for many years to come.

Since the 1950s, cultural enlightenment has become more sophisticated and responsive to popular needs, which means that it is faced with many different objectives to meet and consequently it has become increasingly difficult to achieve success. To some extent, all the preceding chapters have been concerned with definitions of objectives, and it has been shown that these are manifold, changeable and contradictory. A member of the public, a cultural worker, and a politician may make quite different assessments of the same event or institution in accordance with their very different aspirations for it. Each person who has his own expectations of cultural enlightenment will probably define success in terms of the fulfilment of those particular expectations. Thus participants, cultural workers and ambitious factory managements often aim for achieving a professional standard of performance, while politicians and theoreticians consider that the goal is rather participation and 'all-round development': the fact of participation, and its exploitation for socialization work, rather than the artistic standard gained, are the most important factors. Because objectives are so varied and even confused, it is difficult if not impossible to find adequate ways of measuring effectiveness.

The main focus of this study is on cultural enlightenment in a political context, and the objectives with which it is most concerned are those which are possessed by the political leadership. Since they tend to view cultural enlightenment as an instrument for solving problems, such as 'liquidating vestiges of the past', then measuring the incidence of such problems or vestiges should provide evidence for the success or otherwise of cultural enlightenment. The lower the crime figures or the number of religious believers, the better the house of culture. Such a technique is sometimes employed. However, there are of course enormous problems with this methodology, which render it useless.

First, there is only limited evidence to show that cultural enlightenment is successful at solving such problems, although there is obviously a wide degree of variety here. Youth clubs may be more successful than discos about the twenty-seventh party congress or atheist propaganda lectures, while the latter, or lectures designed to inspire love of the Soviet Union in Poland and Hungary, may be positively dysfunctional.

Second, it is almost impossible to separate out individual factors which cause change: is the decline in religious belief caused by factors common to all modern industrial societies, or can it be attributed to successful socialization? Most Western analysts favour the first point of view, while most Soviet ideologists would assert the second. A further complexity is introduced by the fact that the citizen is being socialized by many agencies at once. Is cultural enlightenment more or less important than television, for example? Television reaches far more of the population, yet cultural enlightenment may be a far more powerful agency of socialization for those who actively participate in it. These complexities detract from the usefulness of the only work to offer a detailed methodology for assessing the effectiveness of different types of socialization: *The Evaluation of Ideological and Political Socialisation Work in the Localities* by Z. I. Dzhibladze, a book published in Tbilisi in 1986 in 1,500 copies for use in town and *raion* party committees.[2] Dzhibladze suggests behavioural indicators for measuring success, with some for each component of socialization. They include, for example:

- political socialization: the proceeds made by the showing of films on socio-political topics;
- atheist education: the number of weddings and christenings performed;
- internationalist and patriotic education: the incidence of evasion of military service; the number of weddings between members of different national groups;
- labour education: the number of industrial disputes; the overall quantity of scrap material and medicinal herbs and fruits collected by schoolchildren; the number of graduates not working in the jobs to which they were assigned;
- ecological education: the number of forest fires.

(In late 1984-early 1985, a similar methodology was used in a survey of about 28,000 inhabitants of Georgia. In general the results were encouraging: by these indicators at least, socialization was effective. Cultural enlightenment, however, scored very low indeed.)[3]

There is a dearth of research enquiring into the immediate impact of particular types of cultural enlightenment, even though this is surely what the regimes would most like to know. One exception in Poland was a survey conducted in 1981 which asked respondents whether the local house of culture had influenced the formation and development of their cultural interests. Slightly over a third of the 57 per cent who attended the house of culture said that they had acquired new interests in the arts which the house of culture had done most to popularize, with light music heading the list. A house of culture in Łódz (1978–84) and three of the best in the Lublin *województwo* (1980–1) were said – on the basis of two separate pieces of unspecified empirical research – to have had no influence at all on the formation of cultural interests of the local population.[4]

Paradoxically, cultural enlightenment is often most successful in the eyes of the population when it is least so in the eyes of the regime. Thus, if cultural enlightenment is depoliticized, public attitude surveys may register a high level of satisfaction with cultural enlightenment and to some extent by extension with the state which provides it. Clubs devoted to 'Oriental culture', for example, have little in common with Marxism-Leninism. On the other hand, satisfaction with one club or institution does not necessarily mean that the population translates satisfaction with a particular house of culture into satisfaction with the regime. As was suggested in Chapter One, quite the opposite is often true.

The survey evidence about satisfaction with particular cultural-enlightenment activities is frustrating because, naturally, it very rarely directly addresses questions such as what people think of the concept of cultural enlightenment or how far their attitudes towards it are coloured by memories or myths about the Stalinist period or hostility towards the Soviet Union. Usually questions about dissatisfaction are not of the open-ended variety, nor can it be expected that any survey which did produce such evidence would be accessible to a Western scholar.

The quantitative approach

At the twenty-seventh party congress in 1986, Gorbachev, drawing on an analogy from the Soviet economy, complained that 'A serious impediment in the ideological sphere is the prevailing "gross output" approach'. In cultural enlightenment as much as in other sectors of the ideological sphere there has been a constant preoccupation with the production of impressive statistics, sometimes to the detriment of more useful activities. Indeed, cultural-enlightenment workers in all three countries complain that they waste too much time compiling statistics instead of getting on with the job.

Unfortunately, however, statistics produced on the basis of reports by houses of culture and cultural administrators are only of limited reliability and perhaps should be entirely disregarded. There is strong pressure on everyone concerned to produce ever more impressive results, partly because cultural workers' pay to some extent depends on how well their house of culture is used, and the Soviet press even carries tales of how honest house of culture directors report lower figures than in the past only to have their reports rejected by the local cultural department with the instruction to produce a report which shows 'progress'.[5] However, one's confidence is somewhat restored with regard to the most recent period by the fact that in all three countries the national statistics have actually shown a decline, although perhaps this conceals a very drastic crisis.

Statistics are 'cooked' not only by cultural workers and administrators concerned for their jobs and salaries, but also in order to score a political point, since statistics about house of culture attendance and, particularly, involvement in amateur arts are a stock indicator of political success. Conversely, the June 1985 Central Committee resolution which recognized a serious decline in attendance at houses of culture was registering one facet of a political crisis.

Even supposing that the statistics on which they are based are accurate, the conclusions drawn from impressive figures under Stalin are open to doubt, since the 'voluntary' nature of such participation was rather artificial in the prevailing atmosphere of terror. Some attendance was certainly involuntary, as in the case of schoolchildren and soldiers. These groups remain captive audiences up to the present day: children and students in organized groups form, for example, a large proportion of the attenders of Soviet anti-religious films.[6] At least one house of culture director has been criticized in the press for 'forcibly inviting' children to attend his house of culture in order to make up for the 'visitor in short supply' (*defitsitny posetitel'*).[7] Attendance for adults not doing their military service may be more or less obligatory at ceremonial occasions – anniversary festivals, rites of passage, and so on – which are held in the house of culture. Where children are the main performers, audiences may consist largely of their parents: a not entirely 'voluntary' attendance.[8]

However, as we have seen after Stalin's death attendance at houses of culture did become in general voluntary, and houses of culture were faced with considerable competition from television, professional theatre and other cultural institutions – so it is valid up to a point to use participation as an index of success. Of course, such competition is considerably greater in urban areas, particularly large towns. A rural dweller who prefers not to watch television and wishes to attend a concert or play often has no choice but what is being performed at his or her local club.

Surveys about the extent of attendance at houses of culture may approach the problem from one of two angles. They may find out from the house of culture how many visitors it receives, or they may find out from a sample of the population whether and how often they visit the house of culture and what they do there (obviously this makes a difference, given that some activities are little concerned with socialization). In theory the first approach should be more reliable and less impressionistic, but as was noted above, the tendency for house of culture staff to inflate figures detracts from the usefulness of such statistics, while the second variant – that of questioning a sample of citizens – has produced useful results, within obvious limitations. The following section will discuss briefly the situation in each country, drawing on both official statistics gathered from houses of culture and surveys of visitors. The evidence is far from satisfactory, but it allows one to draw a few tentative conclusions.

From the late 1970s, scholars in the *USSR* were aware from their research into individual cultural habits that attendance had been falling off. This led them to perceive a crisis in cultural enlightenment and need for *perestroika* which, however, only became evident in the official statistics in the early 1980s, and was only articulated outside the specialist literature after Gorbachev became general secretary. In 1977, a survey in the Gor'ky *oblast'* showed that less than half the population visited clubs.[9] In 1984, more than two-thirds of the urban population were said to never visit clubs.[10] In September 1985, only just over half the population were club attenders,[11] while in early 1987 'The national average is for them to be only one third full...'.[12] Surveys which enquired into the regularity and type of attendance found for example that in 1977, 8 per cent of inhabitants of Smolensk *oblast'* participated in amateur arts; a 1985 survey showed that 49 per cent of respondents attended houses of culture, but only 7 per cent regularly; also in the mid-1980s, in some parts of Tadzhikistan 0.9 per cent of the population participated in amateur arts. From the official nationwide statistics,[13] 4–5 per cent would seem to be the maximum (and improbable) figure of Soviet citizens participating in amateur arts. With the exception of those for Smolensk, these must be considered extremely low figures, in view of the effort the Soviet regime has put into persuading the population to participate in amateur arts. In March 1989, *Sovetskaia kul'tura* reported that specialists had predicted that attendance per head of population at cultural institutions of all kinds would fall by half by the year 2000.[14]

Turning now to *Poland*, official national statistics published in *Rocznik Statystyczny* show that the number of participants in artistic and educational clubs peaked in 1970, with 1,130,400 members represented out of a population of 32.7 million, which would be one out of every twenty-nine Poles, if the figures were accurate and if no one person belonged to more than one group. Since both 'ifs' are unlikely to be true, the figures are probably lower. Research conducted in country areas of the Kielce *województwo* in the early 1970s showed the marginal role played by cultural-enlightenment institutions in local cultural life. In the absence of research into participation in the later 1970s, no firm conclusions are possible. By 1979 only about 2 per cent of the population at most were members of collectives in houses of culture; even fewer attended courses (530,300).[15] No official data are available for after 1979, which can only suggest that since then the picture has been worse. Moreover, house of culture activities have become even more of a children's activity than they ever were before. Whereas in the mid-1970s primary school children formed 40 per cent of the total participants in cultural institutions, a decade later their proportion had grown substantially, in some institutions to as much as 80 per cent.[16]

Surely this makes the number of adult regular visitors something very much less than 1 per cent.

Research conducted in the 1980s shows clearly the decline in popularity of cultural enlightenment. For instance, the three best commune cultural centres in the Lublin area in 1980–1 were found to be suffering from a steady decline in membership of their clubs which had set in after 1977.[17] In Górzow in 1981 and 1984 there seemed to be almost a boycott by the adult population.

> Whereas in the past, people of all ages had been greatly and genuinely interested in the activities ...of the cultural centre, one now witnesses universal indifference on the part of people of working age. Not only do they not participate actively in any way – neither do they come to any shows or concerts. (Most of the members of the house of culture collectives are under twenty-five.)[18]

Statistics for participation nationwide in *Hungary* vary.[19] However, the extent of involvement in cultural enlightenment as indicated by individual studies suggests that here too the more modest statistics are likely to be the more accurate. Probably attendance is slightly better than in Poland and slightly worse than in the USSR. The press carries many worried comments of cultural-enlightenment specialists about declining participation in culture since the 1970s, caused by the economic situation.

In Budapest in November 1975, there were altogether 27,850 participants in various types of house of culture activity, apart from spectators at performances and visitors to dances.[20] These figures are in keeping with the Polish ones, given that the whole number of participants, allowing for overlap, were hardly likely to form as much as 1 per cent of the Budapest population, and the proportion engaging in amateur arts much lower. However, since Hungary has a much older population than Poland, percentages of the total population reflect more adults.

The following section will consider the evidence about the types of people who actually do attend houses of culture.

Attendance, by social group

As we have already seen, figures about house of culture attendance have only very limited value in their disaggregated form and can be quite misleading. Overall figures may include a very high percentage of children, in which case the house of culture cannot be said to be satisfactorily fulfilling its primary function of adult socialization. It is important to ask who remains 'outside' cultural enlightenment. Which social groups particularly need help and encouragement to participate?

The first category consists of those who find it hard to participate in any sort of cultural activity, even cultural enlightenment. These include peasants, long distance commuters (an especially serious problem in Hungary), the parents of small children and disabled people. In their outreach capacity, houses of culture have a special duty to make efforts to involve such citizens. The other, often overlapping, category consists of people with little education who, it is believed, need to be 'introduced to culture'.

The Polish sociologist of culture, Kloskowska, has suggested that the population can be divided into three major categories according to their degree of exposure to culture. In her opinion (published in 1981), the only almost ubiquitous form of cultural activity in Poland is exposure to the mass media. About 60 per cent of adults probably have sporadic contacts with other types of cultural activity, while only some hundreds of thousands are regular participants in 'high culture'. If this hypothesis is correct, the situation can hardly be viewed as showing success for cultural enlightenment.[21] In a 1983 booklet, the Hungarian sociologist János Tóth suggested that the evidence was that only skilled workers with established roots, students and intellectuals were interested in the widening of access to high quality culture.[22]

In the Stalinist period, workers were probably the social group most frequently exposed to cultural enlightenment, although a Hungarian trade union leader complained in 1956 that even so, state cultural institutions had made too little impact on moulding working class culture. (He recommended that they should be more responsive to the workers' own wishes). As for the intellectuals, they hardly used the houses of culture.[23]

During the Khrushchev period (and particularly in the 1960s) the professional journal *Klub* was full of articles about the need to involve intellectuals, particularly the village intelligentsia, in cultural enlightenment. There were also occasional comments about the need to attract more workers, for instance in the newly created 'universities of culture', which were said to be badly attended by 'workers engaged directly in material production'.[24]

However, during this period, the more frequent assumption seems to have been that Soviet workers at least participated sufficiently in cultural enlightenment, relative to other groups. The major new concern was with people who did not work for a state enterprise, such as housewives, pensioners and people working on distant farms and pastures. Particular urgency was created by the opening up of the Virgin Lands.[25] In Poland and Hungary during the late 1950s and early 1960s, much attention was focused on the peasantry. In the Polish case, this was largely due to spontaneous initiatives by rural communities and the

Rural Youth Union. In Hungary, it was connected with the campaign to persuade peasants to join the co-operatives.

The remainder of this section will discuss the extent of participation by different social groups since the mid-1960s. It will focus in turn on age and gender; educational level and social class; and geographical location.

Age and gender

Research in all three countries shows that children and young childless people form the bulk of house of culture visitors. When an explanation is offered for this phenomenon, it is the obvious one that people in the over-25 age group tend to have family and work commitments which severely limit their free time. However, even if they do have time to participate in house of culture events, they often find themselves excluded. ('I'm too young to be an old woman!' was the headline over one letter from a thirty- three year old would-be dancer.)[26] Despite the scattered and fragmentary nature of the evidence, it seems clear that cultural enlightenment has failed to involve a large proportion of the working adult population, especially and increasingly in Poland. This is the section of the population for which cultural enlightenment has most responsibility: children and students have other opportunities for participation in culture/socialization, while pensioners are not very significant politically. One group which has not been studied properly is that of working adults with grown up children, a group which contains a large proportion of the people with power and influence in society. Sometimes it is included with the 'middle-aged', at others with 'the elderly'.

Although it is difficult to draw conclusions from the existing evidence, there is no reason to suppose that there is any sharp difference in overall levels of participation between men and women, apart from the facts which do emerge from the evidence: women with young children find it particularly hard to participate, and elderly visitors include a large number of women. However, it is hardly necessary to seek survey evidence only to prove such obvious points. The occasional references to the desirability of providing crèches at houses of culture are evidence of efforts to widen access for younger women. There is considerable segregation within the house of culture. Certain activities are almost exclusively the domain of men (for example, radio repairs) or women (embroidery). Occasionally, houses of culture attempt to involve men in traditionally female tasks, by for example arranging cooking competitions between spouses, but this is hardly a major branch of cultural enlightenment.

Social class and education

The Leningrad cultural-enlightenment specialist, Triodin, concludes that the results of most surveys into the composition of amateur arts and other house of culture collectives show a majority of schoolchildren and students, white collar workers and members of the intelligentsia. 'Cultural workers face the problem of actively involving workers and peasants in the house of culture.'[27] Information about the social composition of Soviet house of culture visitors is difficult to find. One survey of which the results were published in *Klub*, which involved a questionnaire completed by ninety-five manual and 123 white collar workers in a Moscow factory, discovered that more than twice the number of manual than white collar workers were ignorant of the house of culture programme and 14 per cent of the manual workers did not attend the house of culture 'because of lack of need for cultured leisure'. Moreover, the less educated respondents showed a marked preference for entertainment (and only 6 per cent wanted to attend 'spoken journals' – the only specifically ideological activity which seems to have been on offer).[28] A survey of Soviet small towns showed that on the whole, it was the more educated sections of the population who visited the houses of culture, although they were more likely than other groups to be episodic visitors.[29] This is therefore a confusing result: it might indicate that better educated people were better socialized or that they simply used the house of culture as another theatre or cinema without becoming too closely involved in any attempt to socialize them.

The Polish sociologist Tyszka found that the intelligentsia was characterized by almost total involvement in cultural activities, and also contained the highest proportion of members in the 'most culturally active' category. Intellectuals formed the majority of members of cultural societies in both 1971 and 1986.[30] In Kraków in 1968, 10 per cent of those visiting shows were workers, 26 per cent were 'otherwise employed' – presumably intellectuals rather than peasants – and 31 per cent were students.[31] In Kashubia in 1970–1, members of the intelligentsia, especially schoolteachers, were the most frequent visitors to houses of culture. (See the last two columns of Table 4.)

Tyszka found that one social category in Poland was, in general, completely uninvolved in any type of cultural activity. These were manual workers who did not even possess a primary education. Tyszka also found in a study of the small town of Konin that even manual workers who had a primary education usually confined their cultural activities to contact with the mass media and that they often existed in a 'cultural vacuum', spending their spare time either doing nothing or else drinking vodka. This was surely a classic example of failure on the part of the local clubs in their outreach capacity. The cultural-enlightenment specialist Kargul describes the existence of this group of disadvantaged people on the fringe of society as evidence of the 'dysfunctioning of the socialist state'.[32] He points out the danger of ignoring poverty as a cause of non-participation in culture and draws attention to the experience of one club for elderly people which was always full, largely because it offered generous quantities of free tea.[33] An Academy of Sciences survey of miners and metalworkers in lower Silesia in 1973 showed that less than 1 per cent of a sample of 6,627 participated in an amateur arts ensemble or in adult education unconnected with their work.[34]

Table 4 Attendance of 992 Kashubians at houses of culture, clubs and *swietlice*, 1970–1, by socio-professional status and place of residence (to nearest %)

| Social group | Residence (N) | None | Frequency of contacts | | | |
			Once yearly/ less	Twice yearly	Several times a month	Several times a week
Farmers (148)		80	4	8	7	1
Workers						
	(154) country	66	4	4	10	16
	(185) town	87	6	4	2	1
White collar						
	(128) country	66	6	8	11	9
	(189) town	83	4	5	5	3
Intelligentsia*						
	(21) country	31	23	46	–	–
	(50) town	29	–	34	31	6
Teachers						
	(62) country	44	8	16	24	8
	(55) town	13	10	29	34	14

Source Sopuch: 156.
Note: *Only including graduates (in 1971, secondary schoolteachers did not have to be graduates)

A 1971 Hungarian survey revealed percentages of groups with different educational qualifications as shown in Table 5. The sample was much better educated than the population as a whole. The authors conclude that the houses of culture have failed in their mission to involve the least educated in culture.[35]

Thirty-three per cent of the users were workers, as compared with 36 per cent of the population as a whole. Thirty per cent were white collar/intelligentsia, as compared with 13 per cent. Students and schoolchildren were over-represented by a factor of four, while retired people were significantly under-represented.[36] However, this could be because of the wide network of separate clubs for elderly people in Hungary. Factory houses of culture managed to attract a large number of 'their' workers although not when workers lived an inconvenient distance from the institution.[37]

Table 5 Hungarian house of culture users, by education

	% pop., 1970 census	*% interviewed visitors*
Less than 8 yrs	48.3	5.0
8 yrs, vocational ed.	31.8	56.0
High school	15.6	31.0
College, university	4.3	8.0

Source **Kerekes** *et al.*: 3.

In Budapest in November 1975, amateur arts groups were said to include a 'relatively high number of qualified workers and students at vocational colleges' but very few manual workers.[38] Fifteen per cent of members were graduates, as compared with 6.5 per cent of all Hungarians over 25 in 1980.[39] In 1983, 33 per cent of total participants were workers of various kinds, although in state institutions these constituted only 19 per cent – again suggesting that factory workers do attend 'their' houses of culture.[40]

Surveys rarely consider separately the participation of subgroups within the intelligentsia. One exception is the work of L. Módra, who concluded from his study of rural intellectuals in Baranya and Hajdú counties that:

> As regards cultural centres, we found that these are frequented by intellectuals with less schooling. This assumption is proved by the fact, that the healthworkers, who showed the greatest activity in every [other] area [of cultural pursuits], rarely or never go to the cultural centres.[41]

Conclusions regarding social groups

Three main conclusions can be drawn from the available evidence. One is that in Poland and Hungary the least educated groups remain outside the orbit of the house of culture. This may be true in the USSR, but the evidence is too limited to make any conclusions. Second, another, often unstated, fact seems to be that despite the concern of sociologists for disadvantaged groups, it is in fact the participation of the working class – the most politically important – which is often used as a measure of success. Here the evidence is conflicting. Workers obviously under-participate, in relation to their proportion of the population, but seem to participate more if there exists a trade union house of culture which actively sets out to involve itself in the life of the enterprise and/or is solicited to do so by factory managers. It would be helpful to be able to distinguish between different types of worker, as sociologists in all three countries do under other circumstances. Bearing in mind Módra's findings about rural intellectuals, it seems that it might also be helpful to know more about the participation of different strata among this group too. Do the more educated not go to houses of culture as frequently as the less well-educated members?

The third, tentative, conclusion is that although members of the intelligentsia as a whole are over-represented among house of culture visitors, especially if students are included in this category, they may often be only occasional attenders. The intelligentsia would therefore be somewhat removed from the most intensive socialization: possibly by choice, but probably also simply because of better possibilities for pursuing cultural interests independently. Since intellectuals are most exposed to official socialization in other circumstances (for example, through party membership) their participation in cultural enlightenment cannot be considered to be of major importance, except in so far as they have a duty to provide it for other social classes by giving lectures or voluntarily running arts clubs.

Ease of access and publicity

Television and radio have equalized access to culture on a scale which houses of culture could not hope to emulate. For some purposes, there is no longer any rationale for providing an even network of cultural-enlightenment institutions and indeed in both Poland and Hungary the numbers have been allowed to decline. The reverse is true of the Soviet Union. However, in all three countries there is still a commitment to redressing regional inequalities. Of course, even where there is a cultural institution, it may function more or less adequately, be open during the summer or not, open only during working hours or only in the evening or all day ... the variation is endless.

Polish writers seem to be particularly aware of the difficulties faced by rural dwellers in reaching houses of culture over bad roads and long distances.[42] A survey conducted in the Russian Republic in 1974 showed that more than a third of the population of the Non-Black Earth region lived more than half an hour's walk from the nearest club. 'During the time of impassable roads and blizzards, i.e. 4–6 months of the year, the cinema and club are inaccessible.' At the time, only a quarter of such villages were serviced by clubs on wheels.[43] A direct correlation between frequency of visits and travelling time to the house of culture was discovered in the 1971 Hungarian survey.[44]

These and similar surveys discussed so far in this section give useful information about the extent of participation among different groups of the population, and suggest some reasons why people do or do not participate, connected with age, gender, level of education, social class and geographical location. However, participation is also influenced by more incidental matters such as whether the house of culture is open at convenient times (which is often not the case), and how and to whom the activity is advertised.

The method of advertising is quite a significant factor in determining who comes to the house of culture. Effective advertising may take various forms, from the director of the *kolkhoz* club who goes down to the village shop the one day a week that bread is delivered and invites the local inhabitants individually,[45] to the colourful and well-printed monthly programmes that sit on the cloakroom counters of large Budapest houses of culture. Budapest and Moscow have listings magazines which mention houses of culture, although *Leisure in Moscow* is difficult to obtain unless one has a subscription.

Evidence of concern about advertising is much more frequent in the Hungarian specialist literature, as one would expect from the generally greater awareness of the need for good publicity and attractive advertising in Hungary. In all three countries, personal invitation is considered to be the most effective method of drawing an audience to the house of culture, although this of course introduces an element of selectivity on the part of the house of culture staff. Sometimes they may simply invite their friends or contact acquaintances in local schools, youth organizations, and so on. If they are trying to reach a wider audience, they use the local radio network or ask the post office to distribute leaflets to people living in the neighbourhood.[46]

Motivation, attitudes and satisfaction

The type of survey described in the previous sections gives us no insight into matters which would really provide some idea of the success or otherwise of socialization: why people participate, their attitudes towards socialization and whether or how they think cultural enlightenment could be improved (although figures for attendance at particular types of event give some indication of trends and fashions). Why do people visit the house of culture or not? Soviet survey questions often assume that the public consists of model citizens, and respondents tend to choose the more officially acceptable from sets of acceptable answers. The most frequent response among residents of Pskov and Leningrad *oblasti* was 'For help in the rational organization of my leisure time' ('meeting other people' came third.) By contrast, the preferred response among 2,872 club visitors in the *Club worker* survey to the question of what they considered most important in the work of the club was 'the creation of conditions for relaxation and entertainment'. Second came 'the conducting of ideological work and socialization among the population'. Among club workers and local cultural officials, this ordering was reversed.[47]

A much wider range of possibilities was put to a group of 8,170 Hungarians from different parts of Hungary, who answered the question 'Why do you visit the house of culture?' with what would appear to be disarming honesty. (See Table 6.)

Table 6 'Why do you visit the house of culture?' The responses of 8,170 Hungarian house of culture users.

1.	33% My friends and acquaintances go there too
2.	29% The house of culture is near where I live
3.	25% It provides suitable entertainment
4.	24% It helps me improve my general level of culture
5.	21% To practise my hobby
6.	19% You can have a good time there relatively cheaply
7.	13% You can find programmes which cater to various individual interests
8a.	12% The programmes are well-advertised
8b.	12% They provide up-to-date information about political, economic and cultural affairs and the possibility to debate freely and exchange opinions about such matters
8c.	12% To meet other people of my age and discuss our common problems
9.	10% To extend my professional knowledge
10.	8% To satisfy my urge to be creative and active
11.	6% There are no other cultural institutions in the neighbourhood
12.	5% All members of the family can meet their friends here
13.	2% My living conditions are such that it is impossible for me to meet my friends, amuse or educate myself [at home]

Source Kerekes: 37

The literature tends to assume that if people do *not* attend this is caused by some outside obstacle – connected with the deficiencies of the particular club, home circumstances or age. Unfortunately there are few surveys which directly address the issue of popular satisfaction, although a large Soviet survey conducted in the mid-1980s found that among urban dwellers 29 per cent were satisfied with their local clubs, 16 per cent were dissatisfied and 55 per cent found it hard to say (presumably because they did not frequent the clubs!)[48] However, high levels of satisfaction are not necessarily a measure of success. Dissatisfaction may be a better indicator that official cultural policy has been successful in awakening cultural aspirations, as a study of the Kraków area in the 1970s suggested.[49]

Attendance (or non-attendance) at houses of culture seems to be largely a matter of habit and local popularity. My own informal survey of acquaintances not involved in cultural enlightenment professionally usually elicited a response which can only be described as snobbish. On the other hand, there are institutions at which attendance *is* fashionable. Miścicki concluded from his survey in south-east Poland in the late 1960s that attendance at particular institutions was largely dependent on whether this was considered 'the done thing' in the neighbourhood.[50] Interview evidence and observation combine to suggest that it is, however, very much a matter of chance whether or not someone becomes involved in house of culture activities. It does not necessarily reflect general attitudes towards the regime and its socialization policy. Moreover, there is a very wide range of reasons why people do become involved, as the 1971 Hungarian survey, for example, suggests (see Table 6) – and many of these are unconnected with socialization.

There is evidence that there is likely to be resistance among adults towards activities which are too overtly socializing. A KISZ conference delegate in 1988, for example, challenged 'the regime in power... to acknowledge that it cannot achieve anything among us [young people] through trivial propaganda, because we do not have the mentality of subjects under Stalinism.'[51] Polish scholars often seem to take this type of attitude for granted (with reference to the 1970s), while the more honest Soviet ones make a point of spelling it out. Experienced Soviet club workers are reported to take the attitude that 'what eccentric adult will come to the club if he's told that he will be socialized all over again?' even though that is what the club workers may be intending to do to him.[52] 'Some' administrators and scholars questioned in a nationwide survey in 1982–3 'categorically rejected the socializing function of clubs on the basis that "no-one goes to the club specially to be socialized"'.[53]

Another scholar refers to the same phenomenon: 'In the club, the business of socialization is complicated by the fact that the majority of club visitors have a neutral attitude – and some have even a negative one – to their club and to socialization work conducted on its premises.'[54] In recent years – following the criticism expressed in the June 1985 resolution – there have been some sharp comments to the same effect in the press. For instance, the trade union newspaper *Trud* reported on 12 July 1985 that the incompetence of club workers led to 'the forming of an ironical attitude on the part of the public towards cultural institutions and their potential for influencing productivity and towards socializing measures [in general]'. *Pravda Vostoka* commented acidly on 3 January 1986 that 'there is no way in which club activity can be described as attractive to young people'. *Sovetskaia kul'tura* on 12 October 1985 pointed out that young people were simply bored in the club: they had no wish to be 'enlightened'. Three specialists writing for the Russian ministry of culture journal *Kul' turn-prosvetitel' naia rabota* in March 1989 stated that

> official cultural-enlightenment institutions have discredited themselves in the eyes of the population, especially of young people....People used not to visit clubs because they had an allergy towards official forms of cultural-leisure events and their content.... Surveys show that around 85 per cent of the population believes that such institutions are unnecessary in principle, since they do not satisfy social needs for cultured leisure.'[55]

Obstacles to success: finances and personnel

Cultural officials, club workers and the public often have different views about what hinders success in cultural enlightenment. The respondents in the survey of Soviet small towns answered the question 'What is the most important measure to take to improve club work in your town?' Most were in favour of expanding services; more than 25 per cent mentioned the 'material base' and only 14 per cent 'cadres'.[56] In other words, answers from the public differed from the recipe offered by many officials and specialists, who consider cadres to be the key problem of cultural enlightenment: thus adding additional confirmation to the conclusions suggested in Chapters Four and Five of this book. Members of Hungarian Association of Cultural- Enlightenment Workers felt that the priorities for their association were to give professional guidance to cultural workers and to ensure that their opinions were solicited when cultural policy was made.[57]

The most frequent obstacles identified in surveys and other sources are the lack of resources of various types – space, money, staff, building materials, and perhaps most importantly, heating fuel: many are the complaints of how hard it is to attract Russians to an unheated house of culture in the middle of winter.

In all three countries the opinion is frequently expressed that a general panacea for solving cultural enlightenment's problems is to make them more self-financing. Those who advocate such a solution link the low prestige of cultural enlightenment to its cheapness and image as a state-provided service rather than a prestigious consumer good – 'people value more what they pay for'. Increasing the self-financing elements also, it is said, will lead to democratization, since the programme will be more responsive to the market, and of course it will also solve the financial problems of the house of culture. This is the philosophy behind the 1988 Soviet draft statute on clubs, which allows houses to be partly or wholly self-financing, leading to 'the replacement of command-administrative methods by economic methods'.[58] As in Hungary, staff pay is to depend on the extent to which the institution is financially independent. However, the expansion of paid services has not yet brought the hoped-for results. One problem is that the cultural-enlightenment system often cannot actually provide entertainments for which the public wants to pay. The director of the Park of Culture and Rest in Khar'kov was reduced to buying a crocodile and a python to pull in the crowds because the park's more conventional offerings were rejected by the local public. 'The scale of paid services in parks is to be increased by three times during the current five-year plan, and by ten times by the year 2000. But how, if there are no decent amusements, but only old and rusting scrap metal?'[59] Another problem is that poor people and children are more frequently excluded from cultural enlightenment as houses of culture become more dependent than ever on meeting a financial plan.[60]

In addition to their continual problems with money and staff, houses of culture are becoming ever more disadvantaged because of new public expectations that leisure activities must be dependent upon or be accompanied by sophisticated technology. Traditionally the public does not expect average or small houses of culture to provide much, although one exception to this rule was the case of television in its early days. The houses of culture have potential trump cards in videos, computers and other technology which is privately owned by only a small, if increasing, minority of the population. However, it is only in Hungary that this card seems to have been played to any great extent.

There is always going to be a problem associated with the fulfilment of rising expectations. Cultural and technological provision may improve, but expectations may rise still faster, so that people refuse to participate even in an improved system. Cultural expectations seem to be higher in Moscow and Leningrad, hence dissatisfaction is also greater than in smaller cities, despite far superior cultural amenities: 'understanding the sources of support for the regime requires serious empirical study of the relationship between objective conditions and subjective evaluations of the quality of material life'.[61]

Conclusion

As has been shown, it is much easier to determine the objective conditions promoting success or failure than it is to find useful evidence about subjective evaluations of the socialization provided by cultural enlightenment. The whole subject is complicated by the illogicality of many popular evaluations. In Poland and Hungary, and even sometimes in the USSR, the cultural-enlightenment system is part of the 'first society', something official/unreal/disliked, and despite the fact that for

149

some people, who happen to be involved in a particular institution, these activities may be part of the 'second society' and therefore authentic, *even they* often do not approve of the system as a whole. On the other hand, for many Soviet people who do identify with the system and its ideology, both doctrine and operative ideology, cultural enlightenment as a whole may still be something which is unpalatable because it is seen as being 'childish' and 'primitive': a service badly provided by the state, rather than an activity to which the intelligentsia can and should be committed. Paradoxically, the strongest commitment, on the level of the doctrine, is in Poland. Here, there would seem to be a real commitment to equality of access to culture, and also the awareness that it is a field for independent intelligentsia activity, as it was before the Communist takeover.

The illogicality of many people's attitudes is well illustrated in the article from which the quotation at the beginning of this chapter was taken. Although Barbara Parobczak claims that the house of culture is the last place where the average citizen would wish to spend his free time, she concludes her article:

> Although it is true that there are many [houses of culture] which we never even notice and have no meaning for us, there are on the other hand a few – especially in small settlements, like Tarnogród, Kurów and Zdzilowice – which we would certainly find it hard to do without.[62]

Is the whole concept of state cultural enlightenment perhaps inherently contradictory?

Chapter seven

Conclusions: the death of
Communist cultural enlightenment?

> The point is to encourage initiative, to develop free time so that
> it's really free, with the greatest possible freedom of choice.
>
> Specialist at the All-Russian Methodological Centre for Popular
> Creativity and Cultural Enlightenment, Moscow, 1987.

This final chapter discusses comparative aspects of cultural
enlightenment, drawing conclusions from Chapters One to Five. These
concern the nature of de-Stalinization, both as a universal experience
and as one individual to each country, and the connection between de-
Stalinization and popular and regime attitudes to cultural enlightenment.
The chapter then sums up the conclusions of Chapter Six about the
effectiveness of cultural enlightenment. Finally, it questions an
assumption so far implicit in this book, that de-Stalinization has been a
continuing (if uneven) process, and demonstrates that within cultural
enlightenment this is indeed true.

De-Stalinization

In this book, de-Stalinization has been viewed as a continuing and
incomplete phenomenon. The comparative study of cultural
enlightenment in three Soviet-type systems during the period from
Stalin's death to 1989 sheds light on the process of de- Stalinization in
general and within each country in particular. Three facets of de-
Stalinization stand out in sharp relief. First, the authorities' control over
leisure time was weakened as a consequence of the decreasing level of
terror and increase in attention to consumer needs (in so far as the
regime defined these to be 'rational'); technological developments like
the spread of television; and increasing contacts with the West (which
continued under Gierek and Brezhnev despite other 're-Stalinizing'
feature of their regimes). The authorities' loss of control was manifested
in a 'privatization' of leisure pursuits, which became increasingly
responsive to Western fashions and concerned with national

(pre-revolutionary) cultural traditions. Second, the initial phase of de-Stalinization under Khrushchev did not succeed in absolving the party from blame for the horrors of Stalinism or in legitimating the post-Stalinist system. The example of public contempt for cultural enlightenment up to the present day shows how deeply implanted such feelings were during the Stalinist era. Third, within cultural enlightenment itself – an umbrella covering numerous areas of ideological work – there has been significant depoliticization. This has been accompanied by democratization of a kind, as the public has acquired more say as to what may count as cultural enlightenment, largely by voting with its feet against Stalinist-style cultural enlightenment and forcing cultural authorities to become more responsive to society's real needs and wishes.

Each of these three facets will be examined briefly in turn, together with some associated phenomena.

First, one of the main conclusions of this work is that the privatization of leisure, in other words a *social development* which was only the indirect consequence of decisions concerning de-Stalinization, has made more impact on the evolution of cultural enlightenment since 1953 than have top-level decisions. Khrushchev's advocacy of public initiative in cultural enlightenment was premature under Soviet conditions at the time. However, the Gierek regime's attempt to impose a Stalinist-type mobilizational pattern of officially organized leisure activities was too late to succeed: it only accelerated the population's retreat into independent leisure pursuits. Administrative reorganization of cultural enlightenment in all three countries during the 1960s and 1970s failed to win back the public into the houses of culture. By contrast, pursuits such as home television-viewing, attending discos and tending allotments became increasingly popular everywhere.

The rise in educational levels among the population, together with the still insufficient number of university places, resulted in another important social influence on cultural enlightenment: public demands for a more sophisticated type of art than that of the agitbrigade, and for more practical forms of adult education such as courses in foreign languages other than Russian. 'Free universities' within the cultural-enlightenment network compensated for the deficiencies of the regular school curriculum and the shortage of university places. Hand in hand with increased educational levels went increased urbanization, including the partial urbanization of rural leisure patterns.

Second, although in practice the de-Stalinization of leisure has been substantial, all three regimes have been unable to uproot public mistrust so deeply implanted in the Stalinist period. Stalinist policies in cultural enlightenment were dysfunctional. (Paradoxically, mistrust is greatest in Poland, where the Stalinist experience was the shortest: but here it was reinforced by disillusionment with Gomułka's failed reforms and with the cynical manipulation of Gierek.)

All three countries (and especially Hungary and Poland) have allowed criticism of Stalinist cultural-enlightenment practice, as of other selected aspects of Stalinism, but they have not succeeded in winning public faith that post-Stalinist cultural enlightenment is substantially different from its predecessor. The Stalinist stigma attached to cultural enlightenment was not removed even by successful official or semi-official initiatives such as lectures preaching the 'Soviet way of life' in the USSR in the 1970s, or by the club movements in Poland and Hungary in the early 1960s and late 1960s to early 1970s respectively.

Of course, the association of cultural enlightenment with Stalinism is not its only handicap, as far as concerns attitudes. The low priority attached to culture by the party and state bureaucracies is reflected in public attitudes. As was shown in Chapter Five, such attitudes are partly connected with the perceived 'feminization' of cultural enlightenment in the USSR and Poland and low educational levels among club workers. The low status of cultural enlightenment is also said to be connected with the fact that much cultural enlightenment is either cheap or free, and therefore assumed to be worthless.

Third, increased opportunities for the privatization of leisure and negative public attitudes towards cultural enlightenment both contributed to a serious decline in adult participation in cultural enlightenment and particularly in amateur arts, traditionally associated with political socialization. Cultural enlightenment became an increasingly ineffective part of the system of ideological work. (This occurred despite the fact that it was still necessary: television viewing, as *passive* exposure to propaganda, could only partially substitute.) As activities like hairdressing, Japanese language, break dancing, astrology classes and sex counselling invaded the houses of culture, political socialization was pushed into the background, despite the fact that many activities were still packaged as part of the official socialization effort, particularly in the USSR.

How did this depoliticization occur? As Chapters Four and Five suggested, the pressures for depoliticization came largely from the public, but also from house of culture employees with interests similar to those of their clients, and even from some local cultural officials and specialists who were hardly distinguishable from cultural-enlightenment workers (and whose career patterns sometimes overlapped). Central directives designed to increase public self-management in the house of culture also played a role in the process, although informal public inputs into the house of culture plan have been more significant than officially-sponsored public management committees. Local cultural administrators and house of culture employees, together with some academic enthusiasts, have often attempted to return to pre-Stalinist socialist and intelligentsia aspirations to open access to culture (rather than indoctrination), for example, by organizing local festivals for the whole community, and by using cultural enlightenment to address the particular needs of disadvantaged groups like blind or elderly people.

New initiatives have often been small in scale and based on the principles of self-organization and spontaneity. The Polish club-cafés of the early 1960s, Hungarian open house experiments (1970s–1980s) and cultural associations (1980s) and some Soviet youth clubs in the 1980s are good examples of such initiatives. They represent both a recognition of popular resentment at the over-organizing, 'dictatorships over needs' approach to Stalinist cultural enlightenment and a return to traditional, small-scale forms of cultural activity dating back to a period when cultural enlightenment was not a service provided by the state. Often the removal of Communist propaganda from cultural enlightenment has entailed a return to local or national cultural traditions liquidated under Stalinism, such as regional societies or peoples' colleges. Individual houses of culture have also successfully adapted to new public leisure interests, and – where resources permit – have provided access to technology still unavailable to most citizens such as videos and computers. (These are most widespread in Hungary and least so in the USSR.)

In other cases, persistent attempts by cultural officials to organize all public leisure activities have driven 'informal associations' or clubs of people with similar leisure interests to more congenial homes outside the official cultural- enlightenment system. The blossoming of informal groups concerned with culture, politics, the environment and other areas over the past few years must be viewed in the context of the depoliticization of official leisure activities and of new opportunities for independently organized leisure. The informal organizations are not phenomena connected only with *perestroika* and/or the dissident movement, but have deeper and more extensive roots. Crude attempts to maintain the party's leading role in public leisure activities were counter-productive.

The problem is even wider, since it is not only the informal organizations which have left the houses of culture. The adult public, by neglecting to attend houses of culture at all or else patronizing only discos, pop concerts and other non-ideological activities, has influenced the content of house of culture programmes. Houses of culture financial plans, and often club workers' salaries as well, depend on satisfactory attendance. This is probably the major factor influencing the depoliticization of cultural enlightenment, rather than the volition of those organizing it at any level.

154

Public attitudes to cultural enlightenment

These conclusions have inevitably already mentioned public attitudes more than once, but in a general and over-simplified manner. As Chapter Six suggested, attitudes are in fact highly complex and frequently contradictory. On the one hand, there is a tendency to reject cultural enlightenment as 'Stalinist', 'unsophisticated' or 'childish' – three often interchangeable terms which reflect not only memories of the Stalinist period, but also resentment at the primitive propaganda so often provided in the post-Stalinist era – as well as the real decline in adult involvement in cultural enlightenment. On the other hand, there is an expectation that the state should provide access to culture, and recognition of the need to guarantee equality of access to culture for both individuals and communities. In other words, the humanist, not Stalinist, values of the socialist ideology *are* accepted and these feed on the pre-Communist political culture, as was suggested in Chapters One to Two. Where individual institutions can satisfy these needs, and persuade the local community of their 'authenticity', cultural enlightenment is popular and successful. However, such local popularity does not legitimate the whole cultural-enlightenment system.

Regime attitudes to cultural enlightenment

Chapter One classified cultural and ideological officials as either 'enthusiasts' or 'manipulators', depending on which aspects of the ideology were most important to them, the egalitarian doctrine or the instrumentalist operative ideology. It is dangerous to overgeneralize, especially since practice varies greatly even within one country (for example, between Hungarian counties), and since some officials at local level seem to be unconcerned with the ideology. However, it seems fair to conclude that the instrumental approach, attempting to dictate needs, has been increasingly ineffective. On the other hand, officials who are ready to respond to the public wish for entertainment or enthusiasts seeking to satisfy real social needs have become increasingly common-place. However, there remained and still remain many Stalinists, especially in the USSR. These 'manipulators' have often responded to their decreasing influence over the public by *pretending* that they control the activities which actually take place, which in many cases represent real public needs or at best some kind of compromise. Pretence is achieved by labelling any activity which takes place in a cultural-enlightenment institution as 'cultural' and squeezing it into some category of socialization. Thus a kitchen shelf made in a house of culture raises the level of political culture and contributes to labour education. This is part of the ritualization of ideology upon which many observers have commented. It is particularly marked in the USSR.

The emphasis in all three countries has come to rest on accepting any harmless leisure activity as positive, while attempting to liquidate harmful influences such as Western disco music or mysticism in Hungary (see Chapter Two). However, even this degree of control is difficult to achieve, given the limits to which post-Stalinist regimes can actually control leisure time and the absence of either the will or the money to provide an adequate state cultural service of a popular nature (for example, one which supplied every house of culture with computer games).

By the end of the 1970s, cultural-enlightenment specialists and officials in both Hungary and Poland were concluding that totalist aspirations to involve the entire population in cultural enlightenment were pointless.[1] Houses of culture should be arts or community centres open to those who wished to make use of them, and the creation of small clubs operating freely within the houses of culture was encouraged. In the USSR, the emphasis during the Gorbachev period is increasingly similar, as the quotation which heads this chapter suggests.[2]

The effectiveness of cultural enlightenment

The pre-Stalinist history of cultural enlightenment in all three countries, and the post-Stalinist experience of groups conducting independent or oppositional cultural enlightenment, suggest that cultural enlightenment can be successful only on a relatively small-scale and self-organized basis. State cultural enlightenment which attempts to impose a uniform service everywhere is bound to fail to do anything more than create a fiction of public involvement. By its very nature, cultural enlightenment demands a commitment to real private or local goals and inspiration and creativity which the state cannot provide ready-made.

State cultural enlightenment has been unsuccessful in attaining its goals. Although access to culture has been widened, only a small section of the population, chiefly its younger and better-educated members, participates in official cultural enlightenment, and, even where individual houses of culture successfully involve the local population, the public perception of state cultural enlightenment as a whole is negative. In Poland and Hungary, it is associated with an illegitimate regime, and in all countries it is viewed as 'primitive' and associated with childhood or Stalinism. Although in practice the de-Stalinization of cultural enlightenment has been substantial, all three regimes have been unable to overcome public mistrust so deeply implanted during the Stalinist period. The evidence as to cultural enlightenment's effectiveness in changing behaviour in other ways is too poor for conclusions to be drawn. Probably there are somewhat fewer alcoholics or forest fires as a result of house of culture propaganda, but success must always depend on a haphazard combination of circumstances.

De-Stalinization and re-Stalinization

To many East-Central Europeans, de-Stalinization ended in 1968, when attempts to reform the system from within were recognized to be fruitless. Writers, philosophers and political scientists began during the 1970s to emphasize the links between Bolshevism and Stalinism, to see a 'totalitarian core' which remained immutable within the partially de-Stalinized system, and to explore ways in which a civil society could be recreated as a force for extra-systemic change.[3] At the same time, some Western scholars, notably Jerry Hough, were emphasizing the lines of continuity between Khrushchev and Brezhnev in areas such as political participation. Was de-Stalinization an ongoing process or is it more appropriate to emphasize the ending of serious attempts at reform after 1968, until the current era of *perestroika*?

In the history of Soviet and East-Central European criticism of the existing system, 1968 is undoubtedly a watershed, marking a psychological turning point and change in strategy for reform from revisionism to dissent. In the scholarly debates, on the other hand, the conflict is largely over emphasis. De-Stalinization was an uneven process and proceeded at different speeds, sometimes going into reverse, in different areas of political, social, cultural and economic life in different Soviet-type systems. This book has argued that in cultural enlightenment, the significant force for change was social developments originally set in motion by the initial round of de-Stalinization in the mid-1950s. The party lost a part of its leading role in organizing private leisure time and was forced increasingly to retreat from attempting to saturate public leisure activities with political, or any type of, socialization.

However, as has been suggested, the road from 1956 to *perestroika* was far from smooth. In Hungary, the gains of 1956, even including Politburo permission for the resurrection of people's colleges, were succeeded by several years of semi-Stalinism during which cultural enlightenment served the collectivization campaign, in traditional Stalinist fashion, and by years of suspicion about the re-emergence of national(ist) forms of cultural enlightenment – suspicions which have not yet been overcome. In Poland, on the other hand, substantial gains in cultural freedoms made in 1956 were only gradually eroded, and cultural enlightenment enjoyed considerable freedom from ideology (largely because the state could not afford to subsidize it adequately) until the Gierek period, which marked a sharp increase in political socialization and even sovietization. In the USSR, the Brezhnev era was marked by an absence of real attempts to reform the cultural-enlightenment system; the only reforms were administrative reorganizations. The patriotic flavour of much cultural enlightenment with its stress on a proper work ethic, the stability of the family and its propaganda of success was reminiscent of the Stalinist period.

However, not all the gains of the immediate post-Stalin era were discontinued and elements of continuity predominate in the organization of cultural enlightenment. During the latter 1960s and 1970s the regimes continued to emphasize the role of smaller-scale institutions such as clubs and amateur associations, audience participation in ideological work (debates rather than lectures) and other more 'democratic' types of activity, and the importance of public management committees. In other words, this was controlled public participation within the framework of the party's leading role, as in other areas of public life. In Hungary, the 1976 law on cultural enlightenment marked an especially urgent attempt to activate this kind of controlled participation.

As we have seen, change in the content of cultural enlightenment was however forced by changing patterns of leisure outside the party's control. The really vital difference from the Stalinist period was that the regime did not now have the power to subject society to a cultural enlightenment of its choosing.

Where are the parameters of reform? In Poland in 1956–8 and again in 1981–2 cultural-enlightenment institutions were spontaneously liquidated, as collective farms had been in 1956. In the post-Stalinist years there have been advocates of such a policy in all three countries. 'Will the revolutionary wind of *perestroika* sweep away cultural-enlightenment institutions?'[4] Such destruction might constitute a reform of the Soviet-type system, though it would be a denial of the possibility of reform of state cultural enlightenment.

What are the limits of de-Stalinization, if cultural enlightenment is to be preserved as such? Cultural enlightenment as it exists in a Soviet-type system consists of three main elements. These are belief in the need to equalize access to culture, belief that access to culture changes human behaviour, and belief that the party should control both processes, deciding what constitutes suitable 'culture'. In Fehér, Heller and Márkus's terminology, this is cultural 'de-enlightenment', since genuine enlightenment lies in the individual's freedom to make up his or her own mind.[5]

In non-Communist countries (and even in NEP Russia) there exists and existed a type of cultural enlightenment consisting of the first two elements only. A club is an independent institution. In such a system different and often competing philosophies influence the nature of the culture. In other words, there is cultural pluralism. In such systems the state normally exercises a lesser or greater degree of negative or positive censorship: it is almost inconceivable that there should be no state engagement, especially where the state subsidizes the arts.

As has been shown, the process of de-Stalinization has involved a move back from the first type of cultural enlightenment towards the second, with substantial erosion of the party's leading role. Increasingly the important issues are those confronting any system where the state only partially subsidizes and partially controls the arts.[6] The leading role frequently exists more in fiction that in fact. The logical next move, which the toleration of 'informal organizations' shows is already in process, is to abandon the fiction of the leading role. In other words, this is to sanction pluralism in cultural enlightenment, making free time 'really free'. Since the leading role is already largely fictional in cultural enlightenment, unlike in other parts of the system, cultural enlightenment could make this critical adjustment with relative ease. It now seems that it must do so. How it makes the adjustment will be an interesting test case, given that the nature of 'socialist pluralism' is the key issue of *perestroika*.

Notes

Abbreviations

DKwPL:	Domy Kultury w Polsce Ludowej, (1985).
IBAE:	Information bulletin on adult education, (Budapest).
Klub:	both the journal *Klub*, which existed until the end of 1963, and *Klub i khudozhestvennaia samodeiatel'nost'*, which replaced it in January 1964.
RFE and *RL*:	Radio Free Europe and Radio Liberty Research Bulletins. SR: Situation Report, BR: Background Report.
SK:	*Sovetskaia kul'tura.*

Introduction

1. *1 Ogólnopolska Partijna Konferencja Ideologiczna-Teoretyczna*, 1982, p. 518.
2. See, for example, the definition in *Bol'shaia Sovetskaia Entsiklopedia*, 1973, p. 599, entry 'Kul'turno-prosvetitel'naia rabota'.
3. For example, Gorzka (1985, 1988), Fitzpatrick, (1970, 1978), Kenez (1986), O'Connor (1980) and Pethybridge (1982). There are two comparative monographs by Soviet and Polish scholars, neither very analytical: Genkin, *Kul'turno-prosvetitel'naia rabota v stranakh sotsialisticheskogo sodruzhestva* 1984 and Połurzycki, *Rozwój Oświaty Dorosłych w Państwach Socjalisticznych* 1981.
4. Kargul Z *Teoretycznych Problemów Pracy Kulturalno-Oświatowej* 1986, pp. 57–9; *Népmüvelés*, no. 9, 1956, p. 5. The sphere mentioned was atheist education.
5. *O Upowszechnienie Kultury i Oświaty. Materialy Krajowej Narady Działaczy Kulturalno-Oświatowych w dn. 18–19 Grudnia 1958 r.*, 1959, p. 17.

Chapter One: De-Stalinization, ideology and leisure policy

1. See 'Mass expectations and regime performance' by Walter Connor in Bialer (ed.) *Domestic Context of Soviet Foreign Policy*, 1981; Brian D. Silver, 'Political Beliefs of the Soviet Citizen: Sources of Support for Regime Norms' in Millar (ed.) *Politics, Work and Daily Life in the USSR: A Survey of Former Soviet Citizens*, 1987, p. 132; Alfred Meyer, 'Assessing the ideological commitment of a regime' in Nogee (ed.) *Soviet Politics: Russia after Brezhnev*, 1985. On the social compact, see, for example, Alex Pravda, 'East-West interdependence and the social compact in Eastern Europe' in Bornstein, Gitelman and Zimmerman (eds) *East-West Relations and the Future of Eastern Europe*, 1981.
2. For a fuller discussion, see Chapter Six.
3. Stephen White, 'The effectiveness of political propaganda in the USSR', *Soviet Studies*, vol. 32, no. 3, 1980.
4. See for example George Schöpflin, 'The political structure of Eastern Europe as a factor in intra-bloc relations' in Dawisha and Hanson (eds), *Soviet-East European Dilemmas*, 1981, p. 65.
5. Hollander, *Soviet Political Indoctrination*, 1972, pp. 20, 7. The comparison with original sin is Margaret Mead's.
6. See Hyman, *Political Socialization*, 1959, p. 46.
7. Vladimir Shlapentokh 'Bi-level concept of Soviet Mentality and the Quality of Soviet Sociological Data' unpublished paper, 1983/4.
8. Taras, *Ideology and the Socialist State*, 1985, p. 235.
9. For the 'Soviet way of life', see Zaslavsky, *The Neo- Stalinist State: Class, Ethnicity and Consensus in Soviet Society*, 1982; for useful discussions of these distinctions, see White and Pravda (eds), *Ideology and Soviet Politics*, 1988.
10. Heller (ed.) *Lukács Revalued*, 1983, especially pp. 100, 105, 184–7.
11. *SK*, 27 August 1985, p. 1.
12. Völgyes, in Völgyes (ed.) *Political Socialization in Eastern Europe*, 1975, p. 14, estimated the 'degree of indirect party control over political socialization in Eastern Europe' in the early 1970s using indicators such as 'party censorship activities, party control over communication media, amount and types of non-ideological cultural events, the performance of non-Communist plays, operas and musicals'. He concluded that there was a high degree of control in the GDR, Romania and Czechoslovakia, a medium degree in Poland and a low degree in Hungary.
13. *L'Unità*, 9 April, 1985.
14. József Kargul, 'Autorytet domu kultury' in *DKwPL*, p. 139.
15. Béla Kása in *Népmüvelés*, no. 10, 1985, p. 13.
16. Kargul, op. cit., p. 140.
17. Elemér Hankiss, '"Második társadalom?"' in *Valóság*, vol. 27, 1984, no. 11.
18. See, for example, the works by Stephen White listed in the bibliography, and Ellen Mickiewicz, 'Political communication and the Soviet media system' in Nogee (ed.), op. cit.
19. Zaslavsky, op. cit., especially chapter 2.
20. Mary McAuley, 'Political culture and communist politics: one step forward,

two steps back' in Brown (ed.) *Political Culture and Communist Studies*, 1984.

21. See, for example, the chapters by White and Schöpflin in Brown and Gray (eds) *Political Culture and Political Change in Communist States*, 1979 and Michael Waller, 'What is to count as ideology in Soviet politics?' in White and Pravda (eds), 1988, op. cit., pp. 29–32.

22. Williams, *Culture*, 1981, p. 13.

23. See, for example, Czajka, *Z Problemów Teorii i Metodologii Uczestnictwa w Kulturze*, 1985, chapter one, and Vitányi, *Obshchestvo, kul'tura, sotsiologiia*, 1984, p. 103; for the second opinion, see Niżnik, *Społeczne Przesłanki Projektowania Działalnosci Kulturalnej*, 1983, p. 18.

24. Arnol'dov, *Sotsialisticheskaia kul'tura*, 1984, p. 16. I use the term 'non-material culture' to translate *dukhovnaia, szellemi* and *duchowa/ symboliczna*. The latter is the term favoured in contemporary Polish writing.

25. For example, Szczepanski's definition is 'the totality of products of human activity, material and immaterial, the values and ways of behaviour, accepted in social groups and transferable to other groups and to succeeding generations'. *Polish Society*, 1970, p. 147. For similar definitions see Vitányi, op. cit., p. 99; Arnol'dov, op. cit., p. 12.

26. Dupré, *Marx's Social Critique of Culture*, 1983, p. 5, p. 278 and Conclusion.

27. Vitányi, op. cit., pp. 104–6.

28. Stalin's pronouncements about linguistics are published in *The Essential Stalin*, 1973, pp. 407–44.

29. See, for example, Fitzpatrick (ed.), *Cultural Revolution in Russia, 1928–1931*, 1978.

30. See Robert Tucker, 'Stalin and the uses of psychology' in *The Soviet Political Mind*, 1971.

31. Brezhnev, *O Kommunisticheskom vospitanii*, 1975, vol. 1, p. 14.

32. A comparative survey of notes and bibliographies shows that Soviet works mention Western writings considerably less often than do Polish and Hungarian. They also rarely refer to Polish and Hungarian writers. On the other hand, they quite often co-author works with Bulgarian scholars. Polish and Hungarian works more frequently refer to each other, but often include little or no reference to Soviet authors.

33. Mentioned in Káposztás *et al*, *A kulturális szféra tervezése*, 1974, p. 439.

34. Gorbachev, *Perestroika* 1987, p.82. On 'raising the level of culture' under Khrushchev, see Gilison, *Soviet Image of Utopia*, 1975, pp. 72–4.

35. Kaczocha, *Rozważania nad Modelem Kultury Socjalistycznej w Polsce*, 1981, p. 105.

36. *Moscow News*, 19 March 1989, no. 12, p. 7.

37. See Archie Brown, 'Soviet political culture through Soviet eyes' and 'Conclusions' in Archie Brown (ed.), op. cit. In my opinion the difference between the Western and Soviet concepts is greater than Brown suggests. Soviet politicians' use of the term is not merely 'evaluative' (see p. 192) but is being used within a quite other context (as indeed Brown suggests in his discussion of Soviet attitudes towards 'culture').

38. Burlatsky, *Lenin, gosudarstvo, politika*, 1970, p. 327.

39. Strumilin, 'Mysli o griadushchem'. *Oktiabr'*, no. 3, 1960, p. 142; Moskoff *Labour and Leisure in the Soviet Union*, 1984, p. 19.
40. Quoted by William Turpin in *Problems of Communism*, no. 6, 1960, p. 34.
41. 28 January 1960, p. 1.
42. Page ix. Moskoff devotes a chapter specially to leisure (chap. five) and also discusses rural clubs on pp. 183–4 in the context of rural leisure facilities.
43. For a discussion of the Hungarian concept, see Káposztás, op. cit., p. 32. The unfortunate fate of cultural and social amenities in Soviet town planning is discussed by William Taubman in *Governing Soviet Cities: Bureaucratic Politics and Urban Development in the USSR*, 1973, esp. p. 71. This problem is of course common also to Poland. The declining priority accorded to cultural investments in Poland in the 1960s and 1970s was a politically significant public grievance: see chapter two.
44. Moskoff, op. cit., p. 81.
45. E. Goldhagen, 'The glorious future – realities and chimeras' in *Problems of Communism*, no. 6. 1960, p. 18.
46. Mickiewicz, *Soviet Political Schools*, 1967, p. 173. 'Political enlightenment' is the name for party education.
47. *Chelovek, svobodnoe vremia i profsoiuzy*, 1980. pp. 162, 1984, p.166.
48. *Current Digest of the Soviet Press*, 1983, no. 24, p, 10.
49 *Voprosy ekonomiki i upravleniia kul'turnym obsluzhivaniem naseleniia*, 1979, pp. 50–1.
50. Ibid., pp. 88–9.
51. Ibid., p. 27, p. 29.
52. Weinberg, *Development of Sociology in the Soviet Union*, 1974, p. 94; Grushin, *Svobodnoe vremia – aktual'nye problemy*, 1967; *Svobodnoe vremia. Velichina. Struktura, Perspektivy*, 1966; 'Tvorcheskii potentsial svobodonogo vremeni', *Kommunist*, no. 2, 1980, p. 75.
53. Papp Gyorgyné, 'Az ötnapos munkahét és a megnövekedett szabadidö', *Budapesti Népmüvelö*, no. 1–2, 1984, p.48.
54. Ziegler *Environmental Policy in the USSR*, 1987, p. 36.
55. Alfred B. Evans 'The decline of Developed Socialism? Some recent trends in Soviet ideology', *Soviet Studies*, vol. 38, no. 1, 1986, pp. 13–14.
56. *Klub*, no. 1, 1986, p. 14.
57. *KPSS v rezoliutsiiakh* (3rd edn), vol. 8, p. 290.
58. For recent trends in ideology regarding foreign policy, see Stephen Shenfield's chapter in White and Pravda (eds), 1988, *Ideology and Soviet Politics*, op. cit.
59. See, for example, Smol'skaia, *Massovaia kul'tura*, 1986.
60. *Pravda*, 16 June 1985, p. 1.
61. *Közmüvelödés* was the term used in the 'Law on Cultural Enlightenment/ Culture and Education' of 1976 (published in Népmuvelés, no. 12, 1976, pp. 3–7.
62. Hutchison and Forrester, *Arts Centres in the United Kingdom*, 1987, p. 24.
63. Interview with D. Jankowski, Poznań, March 1986.
64. 'Tipovoe polozhenie o klubnykh uchrezhdeniiakh sistemy Ministerstva kul'tury SSSR', passed by the USSR ministry of culture, 2 February 1983, published in *Sbornik rukovodiashchikh*, 1983, p. 330.

De-Stalinization and the house of culture

65. *Kul'turno-prosvetitel'naia rabota*, no. 7, 1988, pp. 7–8.
66. *SK*, 7 August 1986, p. 3.
67. By 1989, even Soviet writers were using a variant of Fehér, Heller and Márkus's useful concept of 'dictatorship over needs'. (*Dictatorship over Needs*, 1983.) See, for example, *Kul'turno-prosvetitel'naia rabota*, no. 3, 1989, p. 17.
68. D. M. Genkin and P. A. Podbolotov in *Kul'turno- prosvetitel'naia rabota v sisteme ideologicheskoi deiatel' nosti KPSS*, 1984, p. 24.
69. The Soviet scholar is V. E. Triodin. See *Ty prishel v klub*, 1980, p. 130, 'Gyámkodó' (patronising) is the epithet used by Ferenc Balipap in 'Be(le)menjünk-e a nyitott házba?', *Mozgó Világ*, no. 7, 1985, p. 22.
70 Népmuvelés, no. 4, 1987, pp. 3–8.

Chapter Two: A brief history of cultural enlightenment

1. Recent research by Jeffrey Brooks shows however that towards the end of the old regime this gap was significantly narrowing. Brooks, *When Russia Learned to Read*, 1985.
2. Such as 'popular readings', girls' schools and public libraries.
3. Pinalov *et al*, *Istoriia kul'turno-prosvetitel'noi raboty*, 1983, p. 36.
4. Ibid., pp. 50–1.
5. Ibid., p. 35.
6. Ibid., p. 50.
7. Today this is the Railwaymen's House of Culture, 63 Tambovskaia ulitsa.
8. Interview information at the House of Culture and Pinalov, p. 49.
9. Ibid., p. 52.
10. *Kul'turno-prosvetitel'naia rabota*, 1969, p. 33.
11. Pinalov, op. cit., p. 59.
12. See, for example, Lee, 'Voluntary teachers', 1987, for a suggestion that the tradition did indeed persist.
13. On youth groups, see Diane Koenker, 'Urban Families, Working-Class Youth Groups, and the 1917 Revolution in Moscow' in Ransel (ed.) *Family in Imperial Russia*, 1978.
14. Gorzka, 'Proletarian culture in practice', 1985, pp. 6–7. On workers' clubs in general, see her book *Arbeiterkultur in der Sowjetunion am Beispiel der Industriearbeiter-Klubs 1917–1929*, 1988.
15. Kenez *Birth of the Propaganda State*, 1986, p. 57.
16. *Kul'turno-prosvetitel'naia rabota*, 1969, p. 42.
17. Kenez, p. 77.
18. For Lunacharsky, see Fitzpatrick, *Commissariat of Enlightenment*, 1970, and O'Connor, *Politics of Soviet Culture*, 1980.
19. Fitzpatrick. op. cit., pp. 56–7.
20. *Kul'turno-prosvetitel'naia rabota*, 1969, p. 44.
21. Pethybridge, *Social Prelude to Stalinism*, 1974, pp. 152–3.
22. Pinalov, op. cit., pp. 119–121.
23. In SK 26 June 1986, p. 6.
24. Kabanov, *Ocherki kul'turno-prosvetitel'noi raboty*, 1955, p. 8.
25. Ibid., p. 9.

26. Ibid., p. 13.
27. Vishnevskaya *Galina*, 1986, p. 64.
28. *Problems of Communism*, no. 6, 1960, p. 11.
29. Quotation from Khrushchev, *SK*, 8 March 1963, p. 3.
30. *Klub*, no. 6 (June), 1953, p. 4; *SK*, various issues.
31. *Current Soviet Policies*, vol. 2, p. 61.
32. *SK*, 23 March 1961, p. 1.
33. Breslauer, *Khrushchev and Brezhnev*, p. 119; Hollander, *Soviet Political Indoctrination*, 1972, p. 161.
34. For the latter, see *Problems of Communism*, op. cit., p. 18.
35. See Unger, 'Soviet mass-political work', 1978, p. 557.
36. This view is based on reading *SK* and *Klub* for the period.
37. *Nekotorye tendentsii*, 1984, p. 57.
38. The ideological resolutions included several of direct relevance to cultural enlightenment: 'On the state of lecture propaganda and means to improve it' (27 February 1978); 'On measures to further improve cultural services to the rural population' (10 November 1977); 'On measures for the further development of amateur artistic creativity' (28 March 1978); and 'On the further improvement of ideological and political socialization work' (26 April 1979). *Ob ideologicheskoi rabote KPSS*, 1983, sections 2 and 3, contains all these resolutions and numerous others.
39. Ibid., p. 530.
40. Published in *Klub*, no. 16 (August), 1986, pp. 19–20. The 1985 resolution on clubs and sports facilities is published in *Pravda*, 16 June 1985, pp. 1–2.
41. *SK*, 24 July 1986, p. 1.
42. On youth centres: *Klub*, no. 17 (August), 1986, pp. 10–11. Interestingly, the announcement about these youth centres was preceded by an article about the new Petöfi Csarnok centre in Budapest, *Klub*, no. 13 (July), 1986, pp. 10–11. On leisure centres see, for example, *SK*, 12 October 1985, p. 1; 19 November 1985, p. 8; 5 June 1986, p. 1.
43. *SK*, 30 March 1989, p. 3.
44. *Ogonek*, no. 36 (September), 1987.
45. However, Jim Riordan's study of Soviet youth groups also leads him to conclude that 'it is not the elite (party and Komsomol) that has precipitated reform: it has merely acquiesced in a situation that had existed for several years and was rapidly getting out of control'. Riordan, 'Soviet youth', 1988, p. 570.
46. Barańczak, *Czytelnik Ubezwłasnowolniony*, 1983, 11.
47. *DKwPL*, op. cit., pp. 57–8; Mleczko, 'Casus domu kultury', 1984, p. 110; Wojciechowski, *Wychowanie dorosłych*, 1966, p. 514.
48. *DKwPL*, pp. 58–60.
49. *Słownik Polskich Towarzystw Naukowych*, 1978, p. 12–3; Wandycz, Lands of Partitioned Poland, 1974, p. 130.
50. *DKwPL*, pp. 60–73.
51. *Podstawy Działalnosci Kulturalno-Oswiatowej*, 1985, p. 175.
52. For a good description of the atmosphere of enthusiasm, see *Kultura i Ty*, no. 2, 1980, p. 56.
53. Gladysz, *Oświata, Kultura*, 1981, p. 135.

54. Kaczocha, *Rozważania nad Modelem Kultury*, 1981, pp. 39–41.
55. Kargul, *Z Teoretycznych Problemów Pracy Kulturalno- Oświatowej*, 1986, p. 56.
56. Ibid.; Gładysz, op. cit., p. 136.
57. Tóth, *A lengyel népföiskolák*, 1986, p. 13.
58. Zeromski, *Opowieści Entuziastow*, 1960, pp. 238–57; Aleksander and Aleksander, 'Uczestnictwo załogi pracowniczej w działalności domu kultury', 1977: 53 and interview information in Poznań, March 1986; on self-management, see Jankowski, *Problemy i Perspektywy*, 1987, p. 40.
59. Kargul, op. cit., pp. 56–7, based on the Commission's house bulletin.
60. Wiecki, *Funkcja Spoleczna i Organizacja Domów Kultury*, 1979, pp. 11–12; Gładysz, op. cit., p. 13.
61. Kargul, op. cit., p. 56.
62. *DKwPL*, p. 140.
63. On cultural policy in general during this period, see George Gömöri, 'The cultural intelligentsia: the writers' in Lane and Kolankiewicz (eds) *Social Groups in Polish Society*, 1973.
64. Kargul, op. cit., p. 59.
65. Wojciechowski, *Z Dziejów Oświaty Dorosłych*, 1984, p. 98; *Podstawy*, op. cit., p. 177.
66. Kargul, op. cit., p. 59.
67. The conference proceedings and resolution are published as *O Upowszechnienie Kultury*, op. cit.
68. Ibid. and Klanowski, *Organizacja i Metody Działalnosci Kulturalno-Oświatowej*, 1974, p. 13.
69. For detailed figures, see Wiecki, op. cit., p. 18.
70. For a positive assessment of the club movement, see Mleczko (ed.), *Placówki Wielokierunkowej Działalnosci Kulturalnej*, 1982, pp. 48–54. Paul Lewis believes that the impact of the new clubs was more superficial. See Lane and Kolankiewicz (ed.), *Social Groups*, 1973, p. 83.
71. See *Słownik*, op. cit.; *Inspiracje*, no. 10, 1986, p. 2.
72. Ibid. The author is head of the house of culture department at the ministry of culture.
73. Curry and Johnson, *Media and Intra-Elite Communication in Poland*, 1980, p. 3.
74. *Kultura i Ty*, no. 1–2, 1964, p. 33.
75. *Kultura i Ty*, no. 1, 1968, pp. 5–6.
76. *Kultura i Ty*, no. 1–2, 1964, p. 34.
77. Kaczocha, op. cit., pp. 104–5.
78. *Kultura i Ty*, no. 1, 1968, p. 10.
79. Klanowski, op. cit., p. 167. *Kultura i Ty*, no. 5, 1968, pp. 5, 6; ibid., no. 11, 1968, pp. 7, 4; ibid., no. 5, 1968, p. 7.
80. *RFE*, Polish SR no. 13, 1971, p. 9.
81. *Kultura i Ty*, no. 2, 1973, p. 7.
82. Kaczocha, op. cit., p. 102.
83. *Kultura i Ty*, no. 12, 1971, p. 5.
84. *Kultura i Ty*, no. 7–8, 1975, p. 8.
85. *Kul'turno-prosvetitel'naia rabota v PNR*, 1978, p. 3.

86. Ministerstwo Kultury i Sztuki, *O Dalszy Rozwój*, 1977.
87. Kargul, op. cit., p. 20.
88. Meloch, *Nasz Klub*, 1976, p. 8. My translations.
89. See Curry, op. cit.; Kargul, op. cit., part I, section 2.
90. Barańczak, op. cit., p. 15.
91. *Kultura i Ty*, no. 3, 1983, p. 9.
92. *Poland: the State of the Republic* 1981, pp. 163, 69; McGregor, 'Polish public opinion', 1984, pp. 21–3.
93. See, for example, the many articles on the subject in *Uncensored Poland*, especially no. 5, 28 February 1985, p. 35.
94. A report of their meeting was published in *Kultura i Ty* in no. 10. 1980, pp. 7–8.
95. *Kultura. Oceny i Propozycje*, 1981.
96. Raina, *Poland 1981*, 1984, pp. 235, 248–9.
97. *Kultura i Ty*, no. 2, 1981, p. 7.
98. Raina, op. cit., pp. 353–5.
99. Tóth, *A lengyel*, op. cit., p. 16.
100. *Kultura i Ty*, no. 3, 1981, p. 14.
101. *Inspiracje*, no. 2, 1987, p. 16. *Inspiracje* replaced *Kultura i Ty*.
102. *Uncensored Poland*, no. 18, 1984, p. 11.
103. *RFE* Polish SR no. 3 1985.
104. Interview information and Narodowa Rada Kultury, 'Raport o Stanie Kultury', 1985, appendix.
105. *Inspiracje*, no. 11, 1986, p. 7; Barańczak, op. cit., p. 17.
106. *Inspiracje*, no. 10, 1986, p. 2.
107. *Népmüvelés*, no. 11, 1974, p. 9.
108. Półturzycki, *Rozwój Oświaty*, 1981, p. 269.
109. *Information Hungary*, 1968, p. 578.
110. Półturzycki, op. cit., p. 269; *Information Hungary*, p. 578.
111. Ibid., pp. 578–9; Szigeti Tóth *Fél évszazad*, 1984, pp. 75–6.
112. Tökés, *Béla Kun*, 1967, pp. 19–21; *Ismeretterjesztés*, 1986, p. 5.
113. Półturzycki, p. 270.
114. Fitzpatrick, *Commissariat*, op. cit., p. 141.
115. Półturzycki, p. 271; *Information Hungary*, p. 579.
116. Szigeti, op. cit., pp. 72–8.
117. Téth, *A lengyel*, op. cit.; Gati, *Hungary and the Soviet Bloc*, 1986, p. 59. Hegedüs, *Élet*, 1985.
118. Lang, *Az 1970-es, 1980-es évek szociográfiai táborai*, 1984, p. 5.
119. For this period see Szigeti, op. cit., pp. 107–18; *Tanulmányok a magyar népi demokrácia*, 1985, pp. 272–3; *Information Hungary*, pp. 579–80; *Szocialista Közmüvelödés*, 1978, p. 333.
120. Váli, *Rift and Revolt*, 1961, p. 246.
121. Much of the following draws on the account given by Jenö Széll, the director of the Folk Culture Institute and – according to his own later testimony – an opponent of the prevailing government policy, in an unpublished interview with Sándor Lontai.
122. Széll, p. 9 and Lontai, p. 79.
123. Széll, p. 13.

124. Ibid., p. 16.
125. Ibid., p. 3.
126. Beke and Koncz, 'Müvelödési otthonok', 1985, p. 14.
127. 'Theses of the IIIrd Congress of House of Culture Directors', *Népmüvelés*, no. 4, 1972, p. 2 and Köpeczi, *A magyar kultúra*, 1977, p. 193.
128. Ibid., p. 190.
129. *Tanulmányok*, op. cit., p. 152; Lontai, p. 3.
130. Köpeczi, p. 192.
131. *Népmüvelés*, no. 1. 1954, p. 2.
132. Ibid., p. 6.
133. Lontai, p. 78.
134. Ibid.
135. Köpeczi, p. 192.
136. Lomax, *Hungary 1956*, 1976, p. 33; Váli, op. cit., p. 229.
137. Lomax, p. 179.
138. Ibid., p. 93.
139. 'Nyilt levél'.
140. *Szocialista Közmüvelödés*, op, cit., p. 345.
141. *Népmüvelés*, no. 1 (September), 1957, p. 1.
142. *Szocialista Közmüvelödés*, p. 346.
143. *Népmüvelés*, no. 6, 1967, p. 14.
144. *RFE* BR no. 19, 6 November 1968.
145. See, for example, no. 8, 1966 pp. 3–5; no. 1, 1968, pp. 3–5; no. 5, 1968, pp. 3–5. See also *RFE* Hungarian SR, 31 January 1967, p. 2 (on cultural autonomy) and BR no. 13, 11 July 1968 (on NEM and culture).
146. See, for example, *Népmüvelés*, no. 8, 1969, p. 5 and *Népmüvelés*, no. 9, 1970, p. 6.
147. The law is published in *Népmüvelés*, no. 12, 1976.
148. Interviews at NI, April 1986; see *IBAE* June 1985, pp. 32–4; Láng, op. cit.; *RFE* Hungarian SR no. 12, 8 November 1985 for the contradictory official reactions to these experiments.
149. Tóth, *A lengyel*, op, cit., pp. 16, 21.
150. *IBAE*, June 1985, p. 48; Katus and Tóth (eds), *On adult education*, 1985.
151. *Kölcsey....munkaterve*, 1987, p. [1]; *Ismeretterjesztö nagyrendezvények*, (1982).
152. *IBAE*, June 1985, p. 31.
153. Speeches from this conference are reprinted in *Országos Közmüvelödési tanáczkozás*, 1985.
154. Ibid., p. 8.
155. Ibid., p. 29.
156. *Magyarország müvelödési viszonyai*, 1984, p. 283.
157. *Országos*, op. cit., p. 12.

Chapter 3: Changing content – changing goals?

1. Várhelyi, *Az összehasonlító andragógia*, 1979, p. 120; Khachaturian, *Puti povysheniia effektivnosti*, 1977, p. 64; *SK*, 30 March, 1989, p. 3.
2. *Klub*, no. 1, 1952, p. 1.

3. Miłosz, *Captive Mind*, 1980, pp. 197–9.
4. Starr, *Red and Hot*, 1983, pp. 216–18. For a fictional evocation of period, and the issues raised by the hijacking of folk art and the fate of jazz, see Milan Kundera's *The Joke*, 1984, parts 2 and 4.
5. See Chapter Six for an assessment of real participation levels.
6. *Podstawy*, 1985, p. 250 (in the context of mass festivals).
7. *Klub*, no. 2, 1986, pp. 18–19.
8. *Klub*, no. 5 (March), 1986, p. 1.
9. *Sbornik rukovodiashchikh materialov*, 1983, p. 34.
10. *Ateisticheskaia rabota*, 1985, p. 65.
11. Powell, *Antireligious Propaganda in the Soviet Union*, 1975, p. 111 and observation in Novaia Usman' (Voronezhskaia *oblast'*), 1981.
12. Lane, *Rites of Rulers*, 1981, pp. 54–5.
13. *Ład*, 9 April 1989, p. 4.
14. However, see *RFE* BR no. 219, 27 October 1976.
15. *Kultura i Ty*, no. 1, 1968, pp. 5–6.
16. Miścicki, *Społeczny Aspekt Działalnosci Domów Kultury*, 1969, part, IV.
17. *Trud*, 31 January 1985, p. 3.
18. Interview information, London, 1985. See the ministry of culture 'Instruction concerning the pre-registration of concert, circus and other programmes' and the 'Model statute for amateur discos', passed by the USSR ministry of culture in agreement with the VTsSPS and the Komsomol CC, 13 August 1980 in *Sbornik*, op. cit., pp. 133, 172.
19. *Khudozhestvennaia kul'tura SSSR*, 1984, p. 124.
20. *Klub*, no. 3, 1953, p. 10.
21. *Sbornik* p. 30–3; the other resolutions are published in part or full in the same collection.
22. *Metodicheskim tsentram RSFSR – 50 let*, 1981, p. [8].
23. *Voprosi partiinogo*, 1973, p. 88.
24. *Sbornik*, p. 115.
25. *Metodicheskim tsentram*, p. [10]; information from personal acquaintances who participated on these Hungarian and Polish tours.
26. Aleksander, *Oddziaływanie kulturalne dużego miasta na region*, 1985, pp. 112–16.
27. *SK*, 17 October 1964, p. 3.
28. Ibid., 1 December 1984, p. 3, 'Diskoteka: krizis zhanra': a detailed historical survey of the 'problem'.
29. *Sbornik*, p. 25; ibid., p. 133.
30. Ibid., p. 25.
31. *Klub*, no. 14, 1987, p. 5.
32. *Sbornik*, p. 26.
33. *Klub*, no. 11, 1987, p. 3.
34. Népmüvelés, no. 6, 1956, p. 3.
35. Vészi, 1975, p. 7.
36. *Klub*, no. 23, 1985, p. 8.
37. Published in *Kul'turno-prosvetitel'naia rabota*, no. 7, 1988, pp. 7–10.
38. See Chapter Two.
39. Personal observation, Voronezh, 1981 and Leningrad, 1987.

40. On leisure centres, see, for example, *SK*, 19 November 1985, p. 8 and 19 August 1986, p. 3.
41. *Klub*, no. 13, 1987, p. 11.
42. *Klub*, no. 8, 1956.
43. Reprinted in *Közmuvelodési ismeretek*, (1978), p. 12.
44. *Kul'turno-prosvetitel'naia rabota: opyt...*, (1986), p. 28.
45. Interviews and observation, 1985–7.
46. *Nekotorye tendentsii*, op. cit., p. 50.
47. Kapeliush et al., *Uchrezhdeniia kul'tury v nebol'shom gorode*, 1985, pp. 74–5.
48. 'Be(le)menjünk-e', op. cit., p. 24.
49. *Nekotorye tendentsii*, op. cit., p. 51.
50. Ibid., p. 32.
51. *Ismeretterjeszto nagyrendezvények*, 1982, p. 34.
52. House of culture programmes.
53. *Ismeretterjesztés*, 1986, p. 23.
54. *Nekotorye tendentsii*, pp. 74–5.
55. *Rocznik*, 1980, p. 432.
56. *Kul'turno-prosvetitel'naia rabota*, no. 7, 1972, p. 432.
57. *Klub*, no. 16, 1986, pp. 19–20; ibid., no. 14, 1987; *Glasnost*, nos. 16–18, January 1989, p. 68.
58. House of culture programmes; Moscow United Cultural-Enlightenment Methodological Centre, *Dosug i moi dom*, (1987).
59. Palace of Culture of Communication Workers' programme 'Kollektsiia sluzhit liudiam'.
60. *Glasnost*, nos, 16–18, January 1989, p. 67.
61. *Klub*, no. 14, 1987, p. 8.
62. Ibid., no. 3, 1986, p. 3.
63. Ibid., no. 14, 1987, p. 4.
64. Figures calculated by A. White from Moscow Popular Front Information Centre, *Samodeiatel'nye obshchestvennye organizatsii SSSR*, part I [Slavic republics, Moldavia, Central Asia], 1988 [actually 1989].
65. *Deiatel'nost' po interesam*, 1987, p. 13; *Kul'turno-prosvetitel'naia rabota*, no. 3, 1989, p. 16.
66. Interview information in Novosibirsk, July 1989, from Vadim Lugov (Institut istorii SO AN SSSR) and Vsevolod Lytkin (Charity); *Samodeiatel'nye obshchestvennye organizatsii SSSR*, Part 1, op. cit., pp. 49–50 on Leningrad Centre. The final sentence of this paragraph is based on information garnered from individual entries in this work.
67. *RFE* Polish SR no. 1, 11 January 1989, p. 20; ibid., no. 5, 23 March 1989, pp. 21–5; *Wprost* (Poznan), 9 April 1989, p. 15.
68. *Index on Censorship*, no. 4, 1986, pp. 5–6.
69. *East European Reporter*, vol. 2, no. 3 (1987), pp. 37–8.
70. *RFE* Hungarian SR, no. 2, 8 February 1989, pp. 8–9.
71. *Labour Focus on Eastern Europe*, vol. 10, no. 3, (no. 1, 1989), p. 5, interview with Boris Kagalitsky.
72. See *RFE* BR no. 228, 18 November 1988 'Independent movements in Eastern Europe' and BR no. 100, 13 June 1989 'An annotated survey of

independent associations in Eastern Europe' for brief descriptions of known groups in Hungary, Poland and the Baltic republics and *Samodeiatel'nye obshchestvennye organizatsii SSSR*, Part 1, op. cit.

73. *Labour Focus*, vol. 9, no. 3 (November 1987), p. 5.
74. Published in *Detente*, no. 11 (1988), pp. 20–1.
75. On the conference and its aftermath see *Labour Focus*, op. cit., p. 9; see also Kagalitsky, p. 349; *Labour Focus* vol. 10, no. 3, (no. 1, 1989), p. 15.
76. Calculated by A. White from *Samodeiatel'nye obshchestvennye organizatsii SSSR*, Part 1, op. cit.
77. Ibid; *Labour Focus*, vol. 10, no. 3, (no. 1, 1989), pp. 4–8; *Detente*, no. 14, 1989, pp. 3–8.
78. 'Tipovoe polozhenie o klubnykh uchrezhdeniakh' in *Kul'turnoprosvetitel'naia rabota*, no. 7, 1988, p. 8.
79. The *Ogonek* article, 'Proshchanie s Bazarovym', 6 September 1987 (no. 36), about the August 1987 conference of unofficial associations interestingly, in this context, spelled out the great age range of those participating.
80. A good recent account of the different strands of youth culture is by Jim Riordan, 'Soviet youth: pioneers of change', 1988.
81. *Deiatel'nost'*, op. cit., p. 15.
82. Ibid., p. 16.
83. Ibid., p. 15.
84. VTsSPS, *O sereznykh nedostatkakh*, (1986).
85. *SK*, 5 August 1986, p. 3.
86. Interviews, Leningrad 1988; Davydov and Matveev, *Klub na predpriatii*, 1983; Kliushnikov and Matveev, *Leningradskoe pravlenie VOS*, 1986, Kulicheva, *Organizatsiia kul'turno-prosvetitel'noi raboty*, 1985.
87. A distinction is not always made between pensioners (who may be in later middle age) and elderly people, although the titles of some clubs imply one or the other. Hungarian clubs are nearly always for 'pensioners'.
88. See Chapter 5, note 27.
89. *Kul'turno-prosvetitel'naia rabota sredi zhenshchin*, 1955, p. 5; Khasbulamova, *Lektsionnaia propaganda*, 1984. For a similar account of gender-role reinforcing women's entertainment, organized by the *zhensovety* (women's councils) see Browning, *Women and Politics in the USSR*, 1987, pp. 101–2.
90. *Kul'turno-prosvetitel'naia rabota sredi zhenshchin*, op. cit., pp. 6–22.
91. Zygulski, *Przemiany Kultury*, 1982, p. 158, q.v. p. 131. Efforts to socialize the new industrial workers into urban life were generally inadequate: see Kolankiewicz, 'The Polish Industrial Manual Working Class' in Lane and Kolankiewicz (eds), op. cit., p. 95.
92. *DKwPL*, op. cit., p. 45.
93. See, for example, Tóth, *Mozgalom*, 1980, p. 118.
94. 'Be(le)menjünk-e', 1985, p. 24.

Chapter Four: Policy and practice 1: party and state

1. Hill and Frank, *Communist Party of the Soviet Union*, 1987, p. 49.
2. Kargul, 1986, pp. 56–7.

3. See, for example, *Klub*, no. 1, 1951, p. 4; no. 3 (March), 1951, p. 10.
4. *Kul'turno-prosvetitel'naia rabota*, no. 7 (July), 1972, p. 6.
5. *Klubny rabotnik segodnia i zavtra*, 1981, p. 8.
6. *SK*, 24 October 1985, p. 3.
7. See Chapter Five.
8. For more on the ZSL, see below.
9. Klanowski, op. cit., p.197.
10. Jankowski (1977), op. cit., p. 131.
11. The list is printed in *Labour Focus*, vol. 4, no. 4–6, p. 55 and reprinted in Holmes, *Politics in the Communist World*, 1986, pp. 138–9.
12. Pinalov, 1983, p. 158.
13. Information from a former house of culture director and lecturer at the Moscow Institute of Culture, May 1987.
14. *SK*, 4 May 1976, p. 2.
15. Jankowski, 1977, p. 80.
16. Ibid., pp. 131–2.
17. *SK*, 6 February 1971, p. 2.
18. *Sotsiologicheskie issledovania*, no. 2, 1984, p. 121.
19. *DKwPL*, op. cit., p. 285.
20. Cf. party membership among the general population (excluding officials), in 1,000s:

	1983	1984
PZPR	2,185.7	2,117.3
candidates	41.7	51.9
ZSL	470.9	481.9
SD	100.9	105.6

(Data from *Rocznik Statystyczny* 1984, p. 29 and 1985, p. 30.)
21. Hough and Fainsod, *How the Soviet Union is Governed*, 1979, p. 421; *Szocialista közmüvelödés*, 1978, chapter 7.
22. *Wstęp do Metodyki*, 1982, p. 34–5.
23. *Szocialista Közmüvelödés*, pp. 497–501.
24. Jankowski, 1977, op. cit., p. 80.
25. *SK*, 14 September 1985, p. 3.
26. Ibid., 19 September 1985, p. 2.
27. *Voprosy partiinogo rukovodstva*, 1973, p. 15.
28. Interview information, Leningrad Institute of Culture, April 1987.
29. Information from a lecture at the VOS Palace of Culture, Moscow, May 1987.
30. *Népmüvelés*, no. 10, 1971, p. 7.
31. Jankowski, op. cit., p. 85.
32. Report of János Molnár's speech to the National Cultural Policy Conference, *Népmüvelés*, no. 2, 1984, p. 9.
33. *Klub*, no. 15 (August) 1987, p. 14.
34. *SK* 12 June 1986, p. 2; the other article was 10 June 1986, p. 2. Q.v. Hammer 'Inside the ministry of culture', 1980 for a detailed account of the structure and workings of the ministry (with however very little reference to cultural enlightenment: Hammer concentrates his attention on theatre).
35. *SK*, 24 July 1986, p. 1.

36. *SK*, 30 March 1989, p. 3.
37. *SK*, 24 July 1986, p. 1.
38. *SK*, 6 September 1986; 27 November 1986; 2 December 1986.
39. *Literaturnaia gazeta* 5 June 1985, p. 10.
40. *SK*, 18 April 1963, p. 4.
41. Summarized in *Sovety narodnykh deputatov*, no. 7, 1985, p. 26.
42. *Upravlenie* at the *oblast'* level, *otdel* at *raion* level.
43. *Klub*, no. 13, 1987, p. 27; no. 15, 1987, p. 14.
44. Ibid., p. 15.
45. Ibid., p. 14.
46. Interview information form E. Kunina, director of the All-Russian Scientific and Methodological Centre of Popular Creativity and Cultural Enlightenment, Moscow, May 1987.
47. Ibid.
48. *SK*, 30 March 1989, p. 3.
49. Exact dates are unclear.
50. Jankowski, op. cit., pp. 51–4.
51. *DKwPL*, op. cit., p. 52.
52. Katus, op. cit., pp. 157–63.
53. *Népművelés*, no. 8, 1966, p. 4.
54. See 'Be(le)menjünk', op. cit., p. 24.
55. See *RFE* Hungarian SR no. 31, 26 September 1977, p. 2.
56. *Budapesti Népművelö*, no. 3, 1986, pp. 2–3.
57. Interview information, Leningrad, May 1987.
58. Népművelés, no. 9, 1970, p. 4.
59. *RFE* Hungarian SR no. 19, 5 December 1988, pp. 3–6; *RFE* Polish SR no. 3, 6 February 1989, p. 21.
60. According to an HNF official in Debrecen in July 1987, the priority is to revitalize *village* cultural life in particular.
61. *Budapesti Népművelö*, no. 1, 1985, p. 24.

Chapter Five: Policy and practice 2: house of culture staff and the public

1. *Klub*, no. 14, 1987, p. 5, 'Prikazano liubit''.
2. Ibid., pp. 4–5, 10–12.
3. Ibid., p. 5.
4. *Népművelés*, no. 11, 1976, p. 9.
5. Ibid., p. 8.
6. See, for example, complaints in *Klub*, no 1, 1959, p. 17; this assertion is also made on the basis of interview information.
7. These people were in general selected for me by the institutes of culture or cultural centres – in which case I usually had a 'minder'; I also interviewed friends of friends in all countries and visited some cultural-enlightenment institutions without giving warning or going through official channels.
8. *SK*, 8 October 1964, p. 1.
9. *Klub*, no. 23 (December), 1985, p. 9.
10. *SK*, 19 November 1985, p. 6.
11. *SK*, 5 August 1987, p. 3.

12. Krasil'nikov, 1982, p. 71.
13. *Népmüvelés*, no. 8, 1978, p. 8.
14. *Országos... tanácskozás*, 1985, p. 44.
15. *Inspiracje*, no. 4, 1987, p. 28.
16. Interview information, March 1986.
17. Jankowski, *Dom Kultury*, 1977, pp. 108–116.
18. *Problema motivatsii uchastnikov*, (1983) p. 12.
19. *Nekotorye tendentsii*, 1984, p. 6.
20. *Sovershenstvovanie podgotovki kadrov*, 1983, pp. 42–7.
21. *Klub*, no. 11, 1987, p. 23.
22. *Klubny rabotnik*, 1981, pp. 67–72.
23. *Pravda*, 13 June 1985, p. 3.
24. *Népmüvelés*, no. 9, 1985, p. 28; *Inspiracje*, no, 4, 1987, p. 3; ibid., no. 1, 1987, p. 12.
25. B.Gołębiowski et al. 'Kluby kultury na wsi' in *Kadra dla kultury*, Warsaw, quoted in Mleczko (ed.) *Placówki*, 1982, p. 123.
26. Mleczko, op. cit., p. 122.
27. For example, *Klubny rabotnik*, p. 101; *Itogi vsesoiuznoi perepisi...1970*, Vol. VI, Tables 18–33 (Raspredelenie zhenshchin...po zaniatiam), pp. 168–243; *Inspiracje*, no. 12, 1986, p. 2 and no. 3, 1987, p. 7; my own count of contributors to specialist journals; interview information. In certain Central Asian collective farms there has been since the early 1960s a deputy chairperson with responsibility for cultural enlightenment. This is invariably a woman, chosen to serve as an example to local women of how to lead an emancipated, non-religious and socially active life. See *SK*, 29 May 1962, p. 2 and 26 November 1985.
28. Shishkan, *Sotsial'no-ekonomicheskie problemy*, 1980, Table 10, p. 73.
29. *Narodnoe obrazovanie*, (1971), p. 32.
30. *Voprosy ekonomiki*, 1979, p. 110 and *Klubny rabotnik*, p. 103.
31. *Népmüvelés*, no. 6, 1976.
32. *Aktual'nye problemy podgotovki kadrov*, 1986, p. 33; *Pravda Vostoka*, 5 January 1986, p. 3. See also Susan Bridger, *Women in the Soviet Countryside*, 1987, pp. 74–5.
33. *Wstęp*, 1982, p. 138.
34. Barghoorn and Remington, *Politics in the USSR*, 3rd ed., 1986, p. 134.
35. After transferring to the HNF in 1982, Pozsgay was able to impart energy and status to what had been an organisation of marginal importance. In the process, the cultural-enlightenment role of the HNF was also enlarged.
36. *Népmüvelés*, no. 12, 1976, p. 8.
37. Strąk (comp.), *Kultura*, 1984, p. 166.
38. *Népmüvelés* no. 9, 1981, p. 8.
39. Jankowski, *Problemy*, 1987, esp. pp. 40–1.
40. *Nekotorye tendentsii*, op. cit., p. 58.
41. See Stephen White's work on propaganda listed in bibliography and the *Statistical Yearbook*, (Budapest), *Rocznik Statystyczny*, (Warsaw), and *Narodnoe obrazovanie, nauka i kul'tura v SSSR*, (Moscow).
42. See e.g. *Klub*, no. 1, 1955, p. 1; no. 1, 1956, p. 1.
43. Interview, April 1987.

44. Chapter Six discusses the merits of the more academic or political research.
45. *Klubny rabotnik*, p. 56.
46. Ionkus, *Metody sotsiologicheskogo issledovaniia*, 1981, p. 3.
47. For example, in *A Kölcsey... munkaterve*, 1987, pp. 78–80.
48. *SK*, no. 3, 1965, pp. 14–15.
49. *Voprosi teorii i istorii*, 1977, p. 98; personal observation.
50. *Ismeretterjesztö nagyrendezvények*, 1982, p. 85.
51. Jankowski, 1977, op. cit., p. 65.
52. *SK*, 14 September 1985, p. 3.
53. Ionkus, op. cit., p. 4.
54. *Dosug i moi dom*, op. cit.
55. For this methodology see, for example, *Klub*, no. 5, 1986, p. 3 *re* Tadzhikistan; Ivanova, *Rabota kul'turno- prosvetitel'nykh uchrezhedenii*, 1986, p. 6. *re* middle-aged and elderly people.
56. *Voprosy teorii*, op. cit., p. 98.
57. Ibid., p. 25.
58. *Klub*, no. 12, 1986, pp. 16–17.
59. *Voprosy teorii*, pp. 22–4.

Chapter Six: The effectiveness of cultural enlightenment

1. *Klub*, no. 5, 1962, p. 1.
2. Russian title: *Otsenka ideologicheskoi, politiko-vospitatel'noi raboty v regionakh*.
3. Ibid.
4. *DKwPL*, 1985, pp. 353, 342, 348.
5. See, for example, *Klub*, no. 15, 1986, p. 3.
6. Powell, *Antireligious Propaganda*, 1975, p. 99.
7. *SK*, 12 October 1985, p. 6.
8. Jankiewicz, 'Analiza rozwoju placówek kulturalnych', p. 18.
9. *Voprosy ekonomiki i upravleniia*, 1978, pp. 43–4.
10. VNII Sistemnykh Issledovanii, Paper 4, 1984, p. 64.
11. *SK*, 5 September 1985, p. 2.
12. *Klub*, no. 3, 1987, p. 3.
13. As published in *Narodnoe khoziaistvo* and *Narodnoe obrazovnie, nauka i kul'tura*, various years.
14. *SK*, 30 March 1989, p. 3.
15. *Roczniki*, various years. The Kielce research was published as Przecławska, Anna (ed.), *Funkcjonowanie Wiejskich Placówek Upowszechniania Kultury w Warunkach Przeobrażeń Wsi Rolniczej*, Warsaw, 1974; see comments on these findings, together with discussion of absence of research in the latter 1970s and likely level of participation in Mleczko (ed.) *Placówki*, 1982, pp. 73–4.
16. Kargul, *Z Teoretycznych Problemów*, 1986, p. 35.
17. *DKwPL*, op. cit., p. 339.
18. Ibid., p. 351.
19. Compare the *Statistical Yearbooks* and *Magyarország Müvelödeési Viszonyai*, 1984.

20. *Népmüvelés*, no. 9, 1976, pp. 9–10.
21. Kargul, op. cit., pp. 86–7.
22. Tóth, *Increasing State Care*, 1983, p. 9.
23. *Népmüvelés*, no. 10, 1956, pp. 1–3.
24. See, for example, *Klub*, no. 6, 1962, pp. 2–3.
25. See Unger, 'Soviet mass-political work', 1978; and *Klub*, e.g. no. 11, 1961, p. 2.
26. *SK*, 25 March 1989, p. 5.
27. *Nekotorye tendentsii*, 1984, p. 13.
28. *Klub*, no. 5, 1986, p. 14.
29. Kapeliush et al., *Uchrezhdeniia kul'tury*, 1985, p. 80.
30. Kargul, op. cit., p. 87; *Inspiracje*, no. 10, 1986, p. 3; Kaczocha, *Rozważania nad Modelem Kultury*, 1981, p. 125.
31. Miścicki, *Spoteczny Aspekt Działalnosci Domów Kultury*, 1969, p. 39.
32. Kargul, op. cit., p. 91.
33. Ibid., p. 94.
34. Żygulski (ed.) *Przemiany Kultury*, 1982, p. 143.
35. Kerekes et al., *A müvelödési otthonok*, 1973, p. 6. The authors included both typically middle- and working-class residential areas in their survey.
36. Ibid., p. 3.
37. Ibid., pp. 21, 42.
38. *Népmüvelés*, no. 9, 1976, p. 9.
39. Heinrich, *Hungary*, 1986, p. 124.
40. *Budapesti Népmüvelö*, no. 3–4, 1984, p. 6.
41. Böhm and Kolosi (eds), *Structure and Stratification*, 1978, p. 266.
42. Tyszka, *Rodziny Robotnicze*, 1977; Kargul, op. cit.
43. *Voprosy ekonomiki*, op. cit., pp. 36–7.
44. Kerekes, op. cit., p. 28.
45. *Klub*, no. 19, 1987, p. 9.
46. Interview information.
47. Khachaturian, *Puti povysheniia*, 1977, p. 90; *Klubny rabotnik*, 1981, p. 107.
48. *Klub*, no. 11, 1987, p. 22–4.
49. Aleksander, *Oddzialywanie Kulturalne*, 1985, pp. 27–32.
50. Miścicki, op. cit., p. 20.
51. *RFE Hungarian SR* no. 19, 5 December 1989, p. 5.
52. *Ty prishel v klub*, 1980, p. 133.
53. *Klub i sovremennost'*, 1985, p. 72.
54. Khachaturian, op. cit., p. 73.
55. *Kul'turno-prosvetitel'naia rabota*, no. 3, 1989, p. 18.
56. Kapeliush, op. cit., p. 72.
57. *Népmüvelés*, no. 1, 1985, p. 24.
58. *Kul'turno-prosvetitel'naia rabota*, no. 7, 1988, p. 7 (editorial commentary on the new statute).
59. *SK*, 21 August 1986, p. 3.
60. *SK*, 13 April 1989, p. 1.
61. Miller (ed.), *Politics, Work and Daily Life*, 1987, p. 133.
62. *Kultura i Ty*, no. 2, 1981, p. 8.

Chapter Seven: Conclusions: the death of Communist cultural enlightenment?

1. See, for example, 'Be(le)menjünk', 1985, p. 24; Mleczko (ed.), op. cit., p. 134.
2. See, for example, the 1988 draft statute on clubs in *Kul'turno-prosvetitel'naia rabota*, no. 7, 1988, pp. 7–8.
3. See Jacques Rupnik, 'Totalitarianism revisited' in Keane (ed.), *Civil Society and the State*, 1988.
4. *Kul'turno-prosvetitel'naia rabota*, no. 3, 1989, p. 18.
5. Fehér et al., *Dictatorship over Needs*, 1983, p. 195.
6. See, for example, the end of Chapter Two for Hungarian policy in the mid-1980s.

Bibliography

Aktual'nye problemy podgotovki kadrov kul'trabotnikov i ikh zakrepleniia na mestakh raboty (Current issues concerning the training and job placement of cultural workers), Cheliabinsk, 1986.

Aleksander, A. and T., 'Uczestnictwo Zalogi Pracowniczej w Dzialalnosci Domu Kultury. Na Przykladzie Badan Domu Kultury Zwiazku Zawodowego Kolejarzy w Nowym Saczu' (Personnel participation in houses of culture: a case study of the Railwaymen's House of Culture in Nowy Sącz), *Pedagogika Pracy Kulturnalno-Oświatowej* (Pedagogy of Cultural Enlightenment), no. 2., Katowice, 1977.

Aleksander, T., *Oddzialywanie Kulturalne Duzego Miasta na Region* (The cultural influence of a large town on the surrounding area), Warsaw, 1985.

Arnol'dov, A. I., *Sotsialisticheskaia kul'tura: teoriia i zhizn'* (Socialist culture: theory and life), Moscow, 1984.

Ateisticheskaia rabota v klube (Atheist work in the club), Moscow, 1985.

Az Ujkerti Altalános Muvelodési Központ Közmüvelodési egységének középtávú terve 1985–1990 (Medium-term plan, 1985–1990: Újkert General Cultural Centre cultural- enlightenment units) Debrecen, 1985.

Barańczak, S. *Czytelnik ubezwlasnowolniony* (The reader deprived of a sane person's rights), Paris: Libella, 1983.

Barghoorn, F. C. and Remington, T. F., *Politics in the USSR* (3rd edn), Boston: Little, Brown and Co., 1986.

Beke, P. 'Köz-müvelödés' ('Public' cultural enlightenment), *Ifjusági Szemle* (Young People's Review), 1985, no. 6.

Beke, P. and Koncz, G., 'Müvelödési otthonok: gondok, lehetöségek' (Houses of culture: problems and possibilities), *Magyar Épitömüvészet* (Hungarian Architecture), 1985, no. 4.

Beke, P. and Varga, I. (eds), *Muvelodési otthoni tevekénység – müvelödési otthoni hálózat: segédlet a tételes fogalmazáshoz* (Towards a theory of house of culture activity and organization) Budapest, 1981.

'Be(le)menjünk-e a nyitott házba?' (Should we go along with, or into, the open house?), *Mozgó Világ* (World in Motion), 1985, no. 7.

Berton-Hogge, R. 'Maisons de la culture en masse', *Problèmes politiques et sociaux* 315 (Série URSS 51), Paris, 1977.

Beszámoló a Kölcsey Muvelodési Központ munkájáról különös tekintettel városi tevékenységére, valamint az Általános Müvelödési Központ müködésének tapasztalatairól a lakótelepek kulturális életének szervezéseben, további feladatok (Introduction to some aspects of the local work of the Kölcsey Cultural Centre and the experience of the General Cultural Centre in organizing cultural life on housing estates, with tasks for the future) (Typescript) Debrecen, 1987.

Bialer, S. (ed.), *The Domestic Context of Soviet Foreign Policy*, London: Croom Helm, 1981.

Böhm, A, and Kolosi, T. (eds), *Studies of Social Structure*, Budapest, 1978.

——*Structure and Stratification in Hungary*, Budapest, 1982.

Bol' shaia Sovetskaia Entsiklopedia (Great Soviet Encyclopedia), Moscow, 1973.

Bornstein, M., Gitelman, Z., and Zimmerman, W. (eds), *East-West Relations and the Future of Eastern Europe: Politics and Economics*, London: Allen and Unwin, 1981.

Breslauer, George W., *Khrushchev and Brezhnev as Leaders. Building Authority in Soviet Politics*, London: Allen and Unwin, 1982.

Brezhnev, L. I. *O kommunisticheskoi vospitanii trudiashchikhsia. Rechi i stat' i* (On the population's socialization into Communist values. Speeches and articles), vol. 1 (2nd, revised edn) Moscow, 1975.

Bridger, S., *Women in the Soviet Countryside. Women's Roles in Rural Development in the Soviet Union*, Cambridge University Press, 1987.

Brooks, J., *When Russian Learned to Read: Literacy and Popular Literature, 1861–1917*, Princeton, New Jersey: Princeton University Press, 1985.

Brown, A. (ed.), *Political Culture and Communist Studies*, London: Macmillan, 1984.

Brown, A. and Gray, J. (eds), *Political Culture and Political Change in Communist States*, (2nd edn) London: Macmillan, 1979.

Browning, G. K., *Women and Politics in the USSR. Consciousness Raising and Soviet Women's Groups*, Brighton: Wheatsheaf, 1987.

Budapesti Népmüvelö (Budapest cultural-enlightenment worker), various issues.

Burlatsky, F. M., *Lenin, gosudarstvo, politika* (Lenin, state, politics), Moscow, 1970.

Chelovek, svobodnoe vremia i profsoiuzy (Man, free time and trade unions), Moscow, 1980.

Chislennost' i sostav naseleniia po dannym Vsesoiusnoi perepisi naseleniia 1979 goda (Size and composition of the population according to the All-Union Census of 1979), Moscow, 1984.

Culture in People's Poland Warsaw, 1966.

Current Digest of the Soviet Press Columbus, Ohio: AAASS.

Current Soviet Policies New York: Columbia University Press, 1962; following years: Columbus, Ohio: AAASS.

Curry, J. L. and Johnson, A. R., *The Media and Intra-Elite Communication in Poland*, Santa Monica: RAND, 1980.

Czajka, S. A., *Z Problemów Teorii i Metodologii Uczestnictwa w Kulturze* (Some theoretical and methodological issues concerning cultural diffusion), Warsaw, 1985.

Czerwinski, M., 'Spojrzenie na działalność kulturalna związków zawodowych do 1980 roku' (A glance at the cultural activity of trade unions before 1980) in *Warunki i Cele Rozwoju Kultury w Polsce Ludowej* (Conditions and goals of cultural development in People's Poland), Warsaw, 1981, pp. 67–84.

Davydov, E. A. and Matveev, L. A., *Klub na predpriiatii. Opyt proizvodstvennogo ob' 'edineniia 'Kontakt' leningradskogo pravleniia VOS* (The club at the factory. The experience of the production association 'Contact' of the Leningrad organization of VOS), Moscow, 1983.

Dawisha K. and Hanson, P. (eds), *Soviet-East European Dilemmas: Coercion, Competition and Consent*, London: Heinemann, 1981.

Deiatel'nost' po interesam v sfere dosuga (Hobby clubs and leisure time), Moscow, 1987.

Detente, Leeds, various issues.

Domy Kultury w Polsce Ludowej (Houses of culture in People's Poland), Wrocław, 1985.

Dosug v Moskve (Leisure in Moscow), various issues.

Dupré, L., *Marx's Social Critique of Culture*, New Haven: Yale University Press, 1983.

Dzhibladze, Z. I., *Otsenka ideologicheskoi, politiko- vospitatel'noi raboty v regionakh* (The evaluation of ideological and political socialization work in the localities), Tbilisi, 1986.

Dzieje Pewnego Domu (One house's history), Kłodzko: Powiat House of Culture, 1957.

East European Reporter, London, various issues.

Evans, A. B., 'The decline of Developed Socialism? Some recent trends in Soviet ideology', *Soviet Studies*, vol. 38, no. 1, 1986.

Fehér, F., Heller, A. and Márkus, G., *Dictatorship over Needs*, Oxford: Blackwell, 1983.

Fitzpatrick, S., *The Commissariat of the Enlightenment: Soviet Organization of Education and the Arts under Lunacharsky, October 1917–21*, Cambridge, Cambridge University Press, 1970.

——(ed.) *Cultural Revolution in Russia, 1928–1931*, Bloomington: Indiana University Press, 1978.

Francz, V. and Koczokné Boruzs, J., *Munkatársak, barátok, családok, lakótársak önművelő körei* (Independent adult education clubs of colleagues, friends, families and neighbours), Debrecen, 1983.

Gati, C. *Hungary and the Soviet Bloc*, Durham, USA: Duke University Press, 1986.

Genkin, D. M., *Kul'turno-prosvetitel'naia rabota v stranakh sotsialisticheskogo sodruzhestva* (Cultural enlightenment in the countries of the socialist commonwealth), Leningrad, 1984.

Gilison, J. M., *The Soviet Image of Utopia*, Baltimore: Johns Hopkins University Press, 1975.

Gładysz, A., *Oświata, Kultura, Nauka w Latach 1947–1959. Węzłowe Problemy Polityczne* (Education, culture and scholarship 1947–1959. Key political problems), Warsaw, 1981.

Glasnost, English-language edition, New York, various issues.

Goldfarb, J. C., *On cultural freedom: an exploration of public life in Poland*

and America, University of Chicago, 1982.

Gorbachev, M. S., *Perestroika*, London: Collins, 1987.

Gorzka, G., 'Proletarian Culture in Practice – Workers' Clubs in the Period from 1917–1921'. Paper presented to the IIIrd World Conference for Soviet and East European Studies, Washington D.C. 1985.

——*Arbeiterkultur in der Sowjetunion am Beispiel der Industriearbeiter-Klubs 1917–1929. Beitrag zur sowjetischen Kulturgeschichte*, Kassel, 1988.

Grushin, B., *Svobodnoe vremia, Velichina, Struktura, Problemy, Perspektivy* (Free time. Size, structure, issues and prospects for the future), Moscow, 1966.

——*Svobodoe vremia – aktual'nye problemy* (Free time – current issues), Moscow, 1967.

——'Tvorcheskii potentsial svobodnogo vremeni' (The creative potential of free time), *Kommunist*, no. 2, 1980.

Hammer, D. P., 'Inside the ministry of culture: cultural policy in the Soviet Union' in G. B. Smith (ed.), *Public Policy and Administration in the Soviet Union*, New York: Praeger, 1980.

Hankiss, E., '"Második társadalom?"' (Second society?), *Valóság* (Reality) Budapest, vol. 27, 1984, no. 11.

Hegedüs, A. *Élet egy eszme árnyékában* (Life in the shade of a single idea), Vienna: Zoltán Zsille, 1985.

Heinrich, H.-G., *Hungary: Politics, Economics and Society*, London: Pinter, 1986.

Heller, A. (ed.), *Lukács Revalued*, Oxford: Blackwell, 1983.

Hill, R. J. and Frank, P., *The Soviet Communist Party*, (3rd edn), London: Allen and Unwin, 1986.

Hollander, G. D., *Soviet Political Indoctrination: Developments in Mass Media and Propaganda since Stalin*, New York: Praeger, 1972.

Holmes, L., *Politics in the Communist World*, Oxford University Press, 1986.

Hough, J. and Fainsod, M., *How the Soviet Union is Governed*, Harvard University Press, 1979.

Hutchison, R. and Forrester, S., *Arts Centres in the United Kingdom*. (Policy Studies Institute Research Report, no. 668.) London: PSI, 1987.

Hyman, H., *Political Socialization*, Glencoe, Illinois: The Free Press, 1959.

Index on Censorship, London, Writers and Scholars International, various issues.

Information bulletin on adult education, Budapest, Cultural-Enlightenment Institute.

Information Hungary, Oxford: Pergamon, 1968.

Inspiracje (Inspirations), Warsaw, various issues.

Instytucje i Placówki Kulturalno-Wychowawcze (Cultural-enlightenment institutions), Warsaw, 1979.

Ionkus, A. P., *Metody sotsiologicheskogo issledovaniia v oblasti kul'turno-prosvetitel'noi raboty* (Methods of sociological investigation in cultural enlightenment), Moscow, 1981.

Ismeretterjesztés '80–'90 (Knowledge diffusion '80–'90) Budapest, 1986.

Ismeretterjesztő nagyrendezvények a Kölcseyben (Large-scale knowledge

diffusion programmes in the Kölcsey Cultural Centre (Debrecen)),
Budapest, 1982.

Itogi vsesoiuznoi perepisi naseleniia 1970–ogo goda (Results of the 1970
All-Union census), vol. 6., Moscow, 1973.

Ivanova, N. I., *Rabota kul'turno-prosvetitel'nykh uchrezhdenii s vozrastnymi
gruppami naseleniia* (The work of cultural- enlightenment institutions with
older age groups), Moscow, 1973.

Jankiewicz, T., 'Analiza rozwoju placówek kulturalnych w PRL' (An analysis
of the development of cultural institutions in People's Poland) (Praca
kontrolna (assessed essay) no. 1, Panstwowe Zaoczne Studium Oswiaty i
Kultury Doroslych (State extra-mural course in adult education and
culture), course: Polityka kulturalna PRL), 1985.

Jankowski, D., *Dom Kultury*, Warsaw, 1977.

——*Projektowanie Dzialalanosci Kulturalno-Oswiatowej*
(Cultural-enlightenment planning), Warsaw, 1979.

——*Problemy i Perspektywy Samorzadnosci Kulturalnej* (Problems and
prospects for self-management in culture), Warsaw, 1987.

Jaworska, H., *Klub Osrodkiem Życia Kulturalnego* (The club as centre of
cultural life), Warsaw, 1983.

Kabanov, P. I., *Ocherki kul'turno-prosvetitel'noi raboty v SSSR v
poslevoennye gody, 1946–1953* (Studies of Soviet cultural enlightenment
in the post-war years, 1946–1953), Moscow, 1955.

Kaczocha, W., *Rozważania nad Modelem Kultury Socjalistycznej w Polsce*
(Reflections on a model of socialist culture in Poland), Warsaw, 1981.

Kagalitsky, B., *The Thinking Reed. Intellectuals and the Soviet State from
1917 to the Present*, London: Verso, 1988.

Kapeliush, I. S., Sazonov, V. V. and Fedotova, L. N., *Uchrezhdeniia kul'tury
v nebol'shom gorode i naselenie* (Cultural institutions in a small town and
the local population), Moscow, 1985.

Káposztás, F., Koncz, G. and Monigl, I., *A kulturális szféra tervezése*
(Planning in the sphere of culture), Budapest, 1974.

Karaev, R., *Ob opyte organizatsii obshchestva 'Znanie' Turkmenskoi SSR po
propagande znanii sredi zhenshchin mestnoi natsional'nosti. (V
pomoshch' lektoru)* (On the experience of Turkmen branches of the Znanie
Society in educational work among women of the indigenous local
nationality (A lecturer's aid.)), Tashkent, 1984.

Kargul J., *Z Teoretycznych Problemów Pracy Kulturalno- Oswiatowej* (On
theoretical problems of cultural enlightenment), Warsaw, 1986.

Katus, J. and Tóth, J. (eds), *On Adult Education and Public Information in
Hungary and the Netherlands*, Papers of the 1984 Hungarian-Dutch
symposium on adult education and public information, Budapest, 1985.

Keane, J. (ed.), *Civil Society and the State*, London: Verso, 1988.

Kenez, P., *The Birth of the Propaganda State: Soviet Methods of Mass
Mobilization 1917–1929*, Cambridge University Press, 1986.

Kerekes, G., Roland, F. and Sántha, P., *A muvelodés otthonok látogatóinak
összetétele* (The composition of house of culture users), Budapest, 1973.

Khachaturian, A. P., *Puti povysheniia effektivnosti pedagogicheskogo
vozdeistviia klubnogo rabotnika na auditorii* (Methods of improving the

effectiveness of club workers' educational work among their visitors),
Candidate of education dissertation, Leningrad State Institute of Culture,
1977.

Khasbulamova, O. A., *Lektsionnaia propaganda v zhenskom trudovom
kollektive. Iz opyta raboty Ivanovskoi oblastnoi organizatsii ob-a 'Znanie'.
(V pomoshch' lektoru)* (Lecture propaganda in women's labour collectives.
Based on the experience of the Ivanovo branch of the Znanie Society. (A
lecturer's aid)), Moscow, 1984.

Khudozhestvennaia kul'tura SSSR. Lingvo-stranovedcheskii slovar' (The arts
in the USSR. An encyclopedia) compiled by T. N. Cherniavskaia,
Moscow, 1984.

Klanowski, T., *Organizacja i Metody Działalności Kulturalno- Oświatowej*
(Organization and methods of cultural enlightenment), Poznań, 1974.

Kliushnikov, E. V. and Matveev, L. A., *Leningradskoe pravlenie VOS* (The
Leningrad Branch of VOS), Moscow, 1986.

Kloskowska, A., *Z Istorii i Socjologii Kultury* (On the history and sociology
of culture), Warsaw, 1969.

Klub, Moscow, various issues, 1951–63.

Klub i khudozhestvennaia samodeiatel'nost' (The club and amateur arts),
Moscow, various issues, 1964–87.

Klub i sovremennost'. Problemy i perspektivy razvitiia sovetskogo kluba (The
club and the present day. Issues and prospects for the development of the
Soviet club), Moscow, Papers of the NII kul'tury, no. 138, 1985.

Klubny rabotnik segodnia i zavtra. Professiogramma klubnogo rabotnika
(The club worker today and tomorrow. A club worker's job description)
(Papers of the NII kul'tury, no. 104.), Moscow, 1981.

Kmita, J., *O Kulturze Symbolicznej* (On symbolic culture), Warsaw, 1982.

*A Kölcsey Ferenc megyei városi Művelődési Központ és Ifjúsági Ház
munkaterve 1987* (Debrecen Cultural Centre Yearly Plan, 1987).

Köpeczi, B., *A magyar kultúra harminc éve (1945–1975)* (30 years of
Hungarian culture (1945–1975)), Budapest, 1977.

Közművelődési ismeretek. (Alapfok). Olvasókönyv (Facts about cultural
enlightenment. (Elementary) A reader), Budapest, 1978.

KPSS v resoliutsiiakh i resheniiakh s''ezdov, konferentsii i plenumov TsK
(KPSS congress, conference and CC plenum resolutions and decisions)
(3rd edn), Moscow, 1959–1965, vol. 8.

Krasil'nikov, I. D., *Osnovy teorii kul'turno-prosvetitel'noi raboty* (Bases for a
theory of cultural enlightenment), Moscow, 1982.

Kudrina, T. A., *Kul'tura sovremennoi derevni* (Culture in the countryside
today), Moscow, 1980.

Kulicheva, N., *Organizatsiia kul'turno-prosvetitel'noi raboty v klubakh i
domakh kul'tury VOS* (The organization of cultural enlightenment in clubs
and houses of culture belonging to VOS), Moscow, 1985.

Kultura i Ty, (Culture and You), Warsaw, various issues.

Kultura. Oceny i Propozycje (Culture. Assessments and suggestions), (4
unnumbered volumes, 3 by various staff of the Instytut kultury in Warsaw,
one containing the 'Theses' of the Krakow 'Kuznica' group), Warsaw,
1981.

De-Stalinization and the house of culture

Kultura Powiatu Kłodzkiego w Latach 1962–1966 (Culture in the Kłodzko Powiat, 1962–1966), Kłodzko, 1967.
Kul'turnoe stroitel'stvo v Smolenskoi oblasti (Cultural development in the Smolensk oblast'), part 2, Smolensk, 1987.
Kul'turno-massovaia rabota profsoiuzov. Sbornik ofitsial'nykh materialov (Trade union cultural enlightenment. A collection of official materials), Moscow, 1982.
Kul'turno-prosvetitel'naia rabota (Cultural enlightenment), Moscow monthly journal, various issues.
Kul'turno-prosvetitel'naia rabota (Cultural enlightenment), Moscow, 1969.
Kul'turno-prosvetitel'naia rabota: Opyt, Problemy, Perspsektivy, (Cultural enlightenment: experience, issues and prospects), Moscow, 1986.
Kul'turno-prosvetitel'naia rabota sredi zhenshchin. (V pomoshch' sel'skomu klubnomu rabotniku) (Cultural enlightenment among women (A village club worker's aid)), Penza, 1955.
Kul'turno-prosvetitel'naia rabota v PNR (Cultural enlightenment in People's Poland), Moscow, 1978.
Kul'turno-prosvetitel'naia rabota v sisteme ideologicheskoi deiatel'nosti KPSS (Cultural enlightenment in the KPSS system of ideological work), Leningrad, 1984.
Kundera, M., *The Joke*, Harmondsworth: Penguin, 1984.
Labour Focus on Eastern Europe, Oxford.
Ład, Warsaw, various issues.
Lane, C., *The Rites of Rulers: Ritual in Industrial Society – the Soviet Case*, Cambridge University Press, 1981.
Lane, D. and Kolankiewicz, G. (eds), *Social Groups in Polish Society*, London: Macmillan, 1973.
Lang, K. and Nyilas, G. (eds), *Az 1970-es 1980-es évek szociografiai táborai* (Sociographic camps of the 1970s and 1980s), Budapest, 1984.
László, E., *The Communist Ideology in Hungary*, Dordrecht: D. Reidel, 1966.
Lee, D. C., 'Voluntary teachers in Soviet adult education: their recruitment, training and performance', *Soviet Education Study Bulletin*, (Bulletin of the Study Group on Soviet Education), vol. 5, no. 2 (Autumn 1987).
Literaturnaia gazeta, Moscow, various issues.
Lomax, B., *Hungary 1956*, London: Allison and Busby, 1976.
Lontai, S., *A Népmuvészeti Intézet története (1951–1957)* (History of the NI, 1951–1957), Budapest, 1985; typescript.
McGregor, J. P., 'Polish public opinion in a time of crisis', *Comparative Politics*, vol. 17, no. 1, October 1984.
Magyarország Müvelödési Viszonyai, 1960–1982 (Hungarian cultural relations, 1960–1982), Budapest, 1984.
Mason, D. S., *Public Opinion and Political Change in Poland, 1980–1982*, Cambridge: Cambridge University Press, 1985.
Materialy po kul'turno-prosvetitel'noi rabote. Sbornik (Documents on cultural enlightenment: a collection), Moscow, 1959.
Materialy po razvitiu obshchestvennykh nachal v organakh i uchrezhdeniiakh kul'tury (Materials on the development of voluntary principles in cultural organs and institutions), Iaroslavl', 1963.

184

Meloch, K., *Nasz Klub* (Our Club) (FSZMP sejmik wiejskich dzialaczy kultury (conference of rural cultural activists), 1976: one of 6 brochures)

Metodicheskim tsentram RSFSR – 50 let (The 50th anniversary of methodological centres in the RSFSR), Moscow, 1981.

Meyer, A., 'The functions of ideology in the Soviet political system', *Soviet Studies*, vol. 17, no. 3, 1966.

Mickiewicz, E., *Soviet Political Schools: The Communist Party Adult Instruction System*, New Haven: Yale University Press, 1967.

Millar, J. R., (ed.), *Politics, Work and Daily Life in the USSR: A Survey of Former Soviet Citizens*, Cambridge: Cambridge University Press, 1987.

Milosz, C., *The Captive Mind*, Harmondsworth: Penguin, 1980.

Ministry of culture and art, Warsaw, *O Dalszy Rozwój Aktywnego Uczestnictwa Ludzi Pracy i ich Rodzin w Kulturze. Materialy Pomocnicze do Planowania Działalnosci Kulturalno- Wychowawczej w Latach 1977–1978* (On increasing the active participation of working people and their families in culture. Aids for planning cultural enlightenment in 1977–8), Warsaw, 1977.

Miscicki, W., *Spoleczny Aspekt Dzialalnosci Domów Kultury* (The social aspect of house of culture activity), Warsaw, 1969.

Mleczko, F. W., 'Casus Domu Kultury' (The case of the house of culture), *Kultura i spoleczenstwo* (Culture and Society), no. 4, 1984.

——(ed.), *Placówki Wielokierunkowej Dzialalnosci Kulturalnej: Ich Funkcje i Dynamika Rozwoju* (Multi-functional cultural institutions: their functions and dynamics of growth), Warsaw, 1982.

Morton, M., *The Arts and the Soviet Child: the Esthetic Education of Children in the USSR*, New York: Free Press, 1972.

Moscow City Soviet Cultural Department and United Scientific-Methodological Centre [for Cultural Enlightenment], *Anketa 'Dosug i moi dom'* (Questionnaire: leisure and my home), Moscow, 1987.

Moscow Popular Front Information Centre, *Samodeiatel'nye obshchestvennye organizatsii SSSR* (Independent social organizations of the USSR) Part 1, Moscow, 1988 [actually February 1989].

Moskoff, W., *Labour and Leisure in the Soviet Union*, London: Macmillan, 1984.

Narodnoe khoziaistvo SSSR (USSR economy), Moscow, various years.

Narodnoe obrazovanie, nauka i kul'tura v SSSR. Statisticheskii sbornik (Education, scholarship and culture in the USSR. A statistical handbook), Moscow, 1971 and 1977.

Narodowa Rada Kultury, *Raport o Stanie Kultury w Polsce* (Report on the state of culture in Poland), Warsaw, 1985. (Handwritten copy.)

Nekotorye tendentsii kul'turno-prosvetitel'noi deiatel'nosti (Some trends in cultural enlightenment), Moscow: Papers of NII kul'tury, no. 131, 1984.

Niżnik, J., *Spoleczne Przeslanki Projektowania Dzialalnosci Kulturalnej* (Social preconditions for cultural planning), Warsaw, 1983.

Nogee, J. L. (ed.), *Soviet Politics: Russia after Brezhnev*. New York: Praeger, 1985.

Nyilt levél (Open letter), of the NI Revolutionary Committee, 20 November 1956.

Ob ideologicheskoi rabote KPSS: Sbornik dokumentov (On the ideological work of the KPSS: a collection of documents), (2nd edn), Moscow, 1983.

Obostrenie ideologicheskoi bor'by (The intensification of the ideological struggle), Moscow, 1982.

O'Connor, T. E., *The Politics of Soviet culture: Anatolii Lunacharskii* (Studies in the Fine Arts: The Avante-Garde, no. 42), Ann Arbor, Michigan: UMI Research Press, 1980.

Országos közmüvelödési tanácskozás, 1984, (National Cultural-Enlightenment Conference), Budapest, 1985.

Osnovnye poniatiia teorii kul'turno-prosvetitel'noi raboty. Materialy dlia obsuzhdeniia na koord. sovete MK SSSR (Basic concepts of cultural enlightenment: Materials for consideration by the co-ordinating council of the USSR Ministry of Culture), Leningrad, 1981.

O Upowszechnienie Kultury i Oswiaty. Materialy Krajowej Narady Działaczy Kulturalno-Oswiatowych w dn. 18–19 Grudnia 1958 r. (On cultural and educational diffusion. Documents from the National Conference of Cultural-Enlightenment Activists, 18–19 December 1958), Warsaw, 1959.

Pal'vanova, B. P., *Emantsipantsia musul'manki. Opyt raskreposhcheniia zhenshchin sovetskogo Vostoka* (The emancipation of the Moslem woman. Women's liberation in the Soviet East), Moscow, 1982.

Párbeszéd Debrecenben. Kutatók, oktatók, gyakorlók a müvelödési otthonokról (Debrecen debate. Researchers, teachers and practitioners on houses of culture), Debrecen, 1980.

Pesti Müsor, various issues.

Pethybridge, R., *The Social Prelude to Stalinism*, London: Macmillan, 1974.

1 [Pierwsza] Ogólnopolska Partijna Konferencja Ideologiczna-Teoretyczna (1st Polish conference on party ideology and theory), Warsaw, 1982.

Pinalov, S. A., Cherniavsky, G. I. and Vinogradov, A. P., *Istoriia kul'turno-prosvetitel'noi raboty v SSSR* (The history of cultural enlightenment in the USSR), Kiev, 1983.

Plan Pracy Warszawskiego Ośrodku Kultury na 1986 rok Warsaw Cultural Centre 1986 Plan.

Podstawy Działalnosci Kulturalno-Oświatowej (Foundations of culture enlightenment), Warsaw, 1985.

Poland: the State of the Republic. Reports by the Experience and Future Discussion Group (D. i P.), Warsaw, (ed. Michael Vale.), London, 1981.

Półturzycki, F., *Rozwój Oświaty Dorosłych w Państwach Socjalistycznych* (The development of adult education in socialist states), Warsaw, 1981.

Popławski, F. *Polskie Uniwersytety Ludowe* (Polish people's universities), Warsaw, 1985.

Pospielovsky, D. V., *A History of Marxist-Leninist Atheism and Soviet Anti-Religious Policies. Volume 1: A History of Soviet Atheism in Theory and Practice, and the Believer*, London: Macmillan, 1988.

Powell, D. E., *Antireligious Propaganda in the Soviet Union: a Study of Mass Persuasion*, Cambridge, Mass: MIT, 1975.

Problema motivatsii uchastnikov samodeiatel'nykh khudozhestvennykh kollektivov. (Sotsial'no-psikhologicheskiie issledovaniia funktsii khudozhestvennoi samodeiatel'nosti) (The issue of motivation among participants in amateur arts collectives. Socio-psychological studies of the functions of amateur arts), USSR ministry of culture/Lenin Library, Information Centre for Culture and Art, information bulletin, no. 3, series IV, April 1983. (Typescript).

Problems of Communism, vol. 9 (1960), no. 6, 'The Soviet Union en route to Utopia: a progress report'.

Raina, P. (ed.), *Poland 1981. Towards Social Renewal*, London: Allen and Unwin, 1985.

Ransel, D. L. (ed.), *The Family in Imperial Russia. New Lines of Historical Research*, Urbana: University of Illinois, 1978.

Riordan, J., 'Soviet youth: pioneers of change', *Soviet Studies*, vol. 40, no. 4, (October), 1988.

Rocznik Statystyczny (Statistical Yearbook) Warsaw, various years.

Runikhina, A. P., *Nash sovet kul'tury*, (Our culture council), Moscow, 1965.

Sbornik rukovodiashchikh materialov i normativnykh dokumentov po kul'turno-prosvetitel'noi rabote (A collection of laws and regulations about cultural enlightenment), Moscow, 1983.

Shishkan, N. M., *Trud zhenshchin v usloviiakh razvitogo sotsializma* (Female labour under developed socialism), Kishinev, 1976.

——*Sotsial'no-ekonomicheskie problemy zhenskogo truda* (Socio-economic issues concerning female labour), Moscow, 1980.

Shlapentokh, V., 'Bi-level concept of Soviet mentality and the quality of Soviet sociological data', Unpublished paper, 1983/4.

Słownik Polskich Towarzystw Naukowych, vol. 1 (Dictionary of Polish scholarly societies), Wroclaw, 1978.

Smolskaia, E. P., *'Massovaia kul'tura': Razvlechenie ili politika?* ('Mass culture': entertainment or politics?), Moscow, 1986.

Sopuch, K. *Uczestnictwo Mieszkańców Ziemi Kościerskich w Kulturze* (Cultural participation among inhabitants of Kashubia), Wrocław, 1987.

Sovershenstvovanie podgotovki kadrov kul'turno-prosvetitel'noi raboty (Improving the training of cultural-enlightenment cadres), Leningrad, 1983.

Sovety narodnykh deputatov (Soviets of people's deputies), Moscow, various issues.

Stalin, J. V., *The Essential Stalin: Major Theoretical Writings 1905–1952* (ed. Bruce Franklin), London, Croom Helm, 1973.

Starr, F. S., *Red and Hot: the Fate of Jazz in the Soviet Union, 1917–1980* Oxford University Press, 1983.

Statistical Handbook (English-language edition of *Statisztikai évkönyv*), Budapest, various years.

Strąk, Michał, *Bronię Drugiego Układu* (Defending the second system), Warsaw, 1983.

——(compiler), *Kultura*, Warsaw, 1984.

Strumilin, S. G., 'Mysli o griadushchem' (Thoughts on the future), *Oktiabr'* no, 3, 1960.

Szczepanski, J., *Polish Society*, New York: Random House, 1970.

Széll, J., (director of the Népmüvészeti Intézet): interview by Sándor Lontai. (Typescript).

Szigeti Tóth, J. (ed.), *Fél évszázad két évtizede. 1930–1950* (Two decades of

De-Stalinization and the house of culture

half a century), Budapest, 1984.
Szoboszlai, G. (ed.), *Politics and Political Science in Hungary*, Budapest, 1982.
Szocialista közmüvelödés. A Marxista-leninista Esti Egyetem tankönyve (Socialist cultural enlightenment. The Evening University of Marxism-Leninism textbook), Budapest, 1978.
Tanulmányok a magyar népi demokrácia negyven évérol (Studies on Hungarian popular democracy from 1940), Budapest, 1985.
Taras, R., *Ideology in a Communist State*, Cambridge: Cambridge University Press, 1986.
Taubman, W., *Governing Soviet Cities: Bureaucratic Politics and Urban Development in the USSR*, New York: Praeger, 1973.
Teague, E., *Solidarity and the Soviet Worker. The Impact of the Polish Events of 1980 on Soviet Internal Politics*, London: Croom Helm, 1988.
Tokés, R. L., *Béla Kun and the Hungarian Soviet Republic*, New York: Praeger, 1967.
Tóth, J., *Mozgalom – müvelödés – ismeret* (Movement – artistic activity – knowledge), Budapest, 1980.
——*Increasing State Care – Increasing Social Independent Activity*, Budapest, 1983.
——*A lengyel népfoiskolák* (Polish people's colleges), Budapest, 1986. (Typescript).
——*Some aspects of the experience obtained during the new stage of the initiatives in Hungarian adult education*, Budapest, 1986. (Typescript).
Tucker, R. C., *The Soviet Political Mind*, New York: Norton, 1971.
——(ed.), *Stalinism. Essays in Historical Interpretation*, New York: Norton, 1977.
Ty prishel v klub, (You have come to the club), Leningrad, 1980.
Tyszka, A., *Rodziny Robotnicze w Polsce* (Working-class families in Poland), Warsaw, 1977.
Unger, A. L., 'Soviet mass-political work in residential areas', *Soviet Studies*, vol. 30, no. 2, 1978.
Uncensored Poland (London), various issues.
Váli, F., *Rift and Revolt in Hungary*, Cambridge, Mass., 1961.
Várhelyi, I., 'Az összehasonlító andragógia elméleti problémai' (Theoretical problems of comparative andragogy), Ph.D. dissertation, Debrecen, 1979.
Vészi, J. et al., *A müvelödési otthoni tevékenység távlati koncepciója (1976–1980) (Tervtanulmány)* (House of culture activity in the long term: a working draft), Budapest, 1975.
Vishnevskaya, G., *Galina*, London: Sceptre, 1986.
Vitányi, I., *Obshchestvo, kul'tura, sotsiologia* (Society, culture, sociology), Moscow, 1984: translation of *Társadalom, Kultúra, Szociológia*, Budapest, 1981.
VNII Sistemnykh Issledovanii, Collected papers no. 4, Moscow, 1984.
Völgyes, I., (ed.) *Political Socialization in Eastern Europe: A Comparative Framework*, New York: Praeger, 1975.
Voprosy ekonomiki i upravleniia kul'turnym obsluzhivaniiem naseleniia. Materialy nauchnoi konferentsii (Economic and managerial aspects of

cultural services for the population. Papers of an academic conference [in Tomsk, March 1978]), Moscow, 1979.

Voprosy partiinogo rukovodstva uchrezhdeniiami kul'tury i iskusstva (Questions of party direction of cultural and arts institutions), Cheliabinsk *obkom* KPSS, Cheliabinsk, 1973.

Voprosy teorii i istorii kul'turno-prosvetitel'noi raboty (Questions in the theory and history of cultural-enlightenment work), Moscow, 1977.

VTsSPS (Secretariat), *O ser'eznykh nedostatkakh v rabote klubnykh uchrezhdenii profsoiuzov v Omske* (On serious shortcomings in the work of trade union clubs in Omsk), Resolution, 28 February 1986.

Wandycz, P. S., *The Lands of Partitioned Poland 1795–1918* Seattle and London: University of Washington Press, 1974.

White, A., 'Optimists and Oblomovs in Gorbachev's house of culture', *Soviet Union/Union Soviétique*, vol. 14, no. 2, 1987.

White, S., 'The effectiveness of political propaganda in the USSR', *Soviet Studies*, vol. 32, no. 3, 1980.

——'Political socialisation in the USSR: A study in failure?', *Studies in Comparative Communism*, vol. 10, pp. 328–42, 1977.

——*Political Culture and Soviet Politics*, London: Macmillan, 1979.

——'Propagating communist values in the USSR', *Problems of Communism*, vol. 34, no. 6. 1985.

White, S. and Pravda, A. (eds), *Ideology and Soviet Politics*, London: Macmillan, 1988.

Wiecki, W., *Funkcja Społeczna i Organizacja Domów Kultury* (The Social Function and Organization of Houses of Culture), Warsaw, 1979.

Williams, R., *Culture*, London: Fontana, 1981.

Wojciechowski, K., *Wychowanie Dorosłych* (Adult education), Wrocław, 1966.

——(ed.) *Z Dziejów Oświaty Dorosłych w Polsce* (From the history of adult education in Poland), Warsaw, 1984.

Wprost Poznan, various issues.

Wstęp do Metodyki Działalnosci Kulturalno-Oświatowej (Introduction to the methodology of cultural enlightenment), Poznań, 1982.

Zaslavsky, V. *The Neo-Stalinist State: Class, Ethnicity and Consensus in Soviet Society*, New York: M. E. Sharpe, 1982.

Z Dnia na Dzién (From day to day), Warsaw, 1983.

Zeromski, T. (ed.), *Opowieści Entuziastów. Wspomnienia Milośników Teatru. Muzyki i Tańca* (Enthusiasts' tales. Reminiscences of amateur actors, musicians and dancers), Warsaw, 1960.

Ziegler, C. E., *Environmental Policy in the USSR*, Amherst: University of Massachusetts, 1987.

Zygulski, K. (ed.), *Przemiany Kultury Klasy Robotniczej w Polsce* (Changes in working class culture in Poland), Wroclaw, 1982.

Index

Note In this index (P) after an entry denotes Poland, and (H) Hungary.

Abalkin, S. I. 22
Abaúj 70
access to culture 26–7, 46, 53
activists 38–9, 126–7
Aczél, G. 57, 80, 104
adult education 2, 31, 37, 40, 45, 49,
    57, 60, 68, 82, 83, 139
advertising 145
advice session 82, 93
aesthetic education 75; *see also*
    socialization
agriculture 38–9, 52
Akademgorodok (Novosibirsk) 86
alcoholics 66, 71, 93–4
Alexander II 31
All-Russian Methodological Centre
    for Popular Creativity and
    Cultural Enlightenment 75; *see*
    also methodological centres
All-Union Review of Amateur Arts
    1983-5 41, 82
Alma Ata *oblast'* 103
Altai *krai* 78
amateur arts 70–76
amateur associations and hobby
    clubs 2, 42, 77–8, 81–9
amateur technical work 70, 79–81
anti-religious and atheist propaganda
    37, 71–3, 113
anti-semitism 51
Arts Studies Research Centre
    (USSR) 129

Assembly of Russian Factory
    Workers 32
atheist propaganda, *see* anti-religious
    propaganda
attendance, *see* effectiveness

Babits, M. 58
Baranya county 143
Barghoorn, F. C. 124
Bártok, B. 58
Bártok Society 60
Belinsky, V. 33
Belorussia 36
Birmingham 73
Boros, S. 118
Brezhnev 18–19, 21, 39
Brzostowski, P. K. 45
Budapest 58, 65, 67, 70, 83, 127,
    138, 143, 145
Budapest Association for Public
    Education 57

C Major Lady 37
Captive Mind 48
Catholic Church (P) 45–6, 49–50
Catholic Intellectuals' Clubs (P) 4
censorship 73–74
centralized club systems 40
Central Asia 106
Centre for Creative Initiative 86
Champion 71
Charity Society, *See* Miloserdie

Cheliabinsk 103
Chernobyl' 80
children 94, 136–7, 140–2
churches (H) 57–60
clubs, *see* cultural-enlightenment institutions
Club for Social Initiatives 89
collective farms 2, 91–2, 101
commissariat of enlightenment 34
Communist party, *see* KPSS, MSZMP, PZPR, leading role
community development 93–4
community houses 45
commuters 139
computers 67, 80–1, 95
Congress of People's Deputies 19
counselling, *see* advice
cottage reading rooms 34
CPSU, *see* KPSS
culture: definitions 17–19
culture and sports complex 40
cultural associations (H) 66
cultural diffusion, *see* access to culture
cultural enlightenment: conferences (H) **(1953)** 61, **(1984)** 66, 118, 124; definitions 1, 6, 26–9; principles 1–2; study of 5; laws and directives (USSR) **(1929 and 1930)** 35, **(1944)** 36, **(1960: on propaganda)** 38, **(1980)** 74, 77, **(1981)** 76, **(1982)** 41, 77, **(1983)** 28, **(1985)** 26, 29, 42, 83, 105, 136, 147, **(1986)** 42–3, 84, 90, 115, **(1987)** 79, **(1988)** 78, 89, 148; (P) **(1968–9)** 51, **(1977–8)** 52, **(1983)** 55, **(1984)** 55, 121, 124–5; (H) **(1968)** 64, **(1974)** 65, **(1976)** 65, 124, **(1983)** 66
cultural-enlightenment institutions: directors 116–18; numbers 34, 36, 38, 49; staff 97–101, 118–23, 148
cultural levels 18–19, 129
cultural revolution (P) 19
Cyrankiewicz, J. 47
Czechoslovakia 64, 76

DIY 42

Darvas, J. 61
Debrecen 60, 66–7, 70, 82, 123, 127
Del'ta 86
Demichev, P. N. 42, 105
Democratic Party (P), *see* SD
Devils 90
directors, *see* cultural-enlightenment institutions
disabled people 91, 139
discothèques 40, 72, 76–8
dissent and opposition 22, 44, 53
Dnepropetrovsk 128
DOSAAF 113
Dostoevsky, F. M. 90
Dushanbe 72
Dzhibladze, Z. I. 134

effectiveness of cultural-enlightenment 4–5, 15–17, 48, 54, 61, 65, 81, Chapter 6
elderly people and pensioners 91, 139–40, 142
election campaigns 46, 101
El'tsin, B. N. 89, 104
Engels, F. 17
entertainment 78–9
ethnic relations 75
Evaluation of Ideological and Political Socialization Work in the Localities 134
Experience and the Future 53

families 66, 93–4
Far East 40
finance 51–3, 78, 66–7, 83, 148–9
fire brigades 45
Fitzpatrick, S. 18
folk culture 60, 65, 67, 70
free time, *see* leisure time
free universities, *see* adult education
Fund for Cultural Development (P) 55

Galileo Circle 57
Gierek, E. 2, 19, 52, 56, 73, 110, 153
Golubtsova, T. V. 84
Gomułka, W. 49, 56, 153

Gorbachev, M. S. 13, 19, 42, 135
Gor'ky *oblast'* 137
Górzow 138
Great Hungarian Plain 57–8
Grushin, B. A. 23

HNF 65, 67, 82, 112, 125
Hajdú county 143
Hajdúböszrömény, 67, 84
Hankiss, E. 14
Higher Trade Union School of
  Culture, Leningrad 127
hobby clubs, *see* amateur
  associations
Hollander, G. D. 10
house of culture, *see*
  cultural-enlightenment institutions
housewives 139
housing cooperatives 2
human factor, *see* participation
Hungarian Association of
  Cultural-Enlightenment Workers
  (MNE) 113, 148
Hungarian National Congress for
  Education Outside the School 58
Hungarian Society for Natural
  History 57
Hungarian Soviet Republic, *see*
  Republic of Councils

Iadov, V. A. 129
Iakovlev, A. 42
Iaroslavl' 32
ideological struggle 24–5, 37, 75,
  112
ideology 3, 9–17, 19, 41, 51, 56, 67,
  76, 108–9, 116, 123
Illyés, G. 87
informal organizations 4, 43–4, 81,
  112
Inspiracje 118
intelligentsia 23, 31–4, 38, 41, 62,
  67, 113, 120–1, 127, 139, 141–4
international women's day 63
Ivanovo *oblast'* 92

Jankowski, D. 100, 104, 109–10
Jaruzelski, W. 56

jazz 70, 78

KGB 74
KISZ 64, 67, 111–12, 147; *see also*
  youth culture
KPSS: conferences, 19th 88–9;
  congresses, 20th 38, 24th and 25th
  40, 27th 135; programme (**1961**)
  24
Kádár, J. 63
Kargul, J. 13–14, 142
Kashubia 141
Kazakhstan 106
Kecskemét 87
Kharchev, A. 120
Khar'kov 28, 149
Khrennikov, T. N. 71
Khrushchev, N. S. 13, 20, 24, 38, 49
Kielce *województwo* 137
Kiev 36
Kirgizia 106
Kloskowska, A. 18, 139
Klub 35, 139
Kmita, J. 18
Knowledge Society, *see* Znanie
Kodály, Z. 58
Kogan, L. N. 23
Komsomol 28, 41, 48, 86, 101, 105,
  112, 129; *see also* young people
  and students
Konin 141
Köpeczi, B. 67
Köznevelés 87
Kraków 141, 146
Krupskaia, N. K. 32, 36
Kuznica 54

labour training and productivity 75,
  79–80
Lakitelek 87
language teaching 66–7
Latvia 23
Lavrovians 31
leading role of Communist party
  4–5, 25, 50, 74
Legnica 93, 110
leisure centres 43, 79
Leisure in Moscow 145

'Leisure' organization 128
Lenin, V. I. 17–19, 25, 33–4, 36, 67, 74
Leningrad and Leningrad *oblast'* 35, 70, 80. 84, 116, 120, 127–8, 145
Leszak, S. 87
Leszno, 100, 104, 109, 119, 128
Ligachev, E. 42, 89
literacy 34–5, 46, 58
Lithuania 90, 117
Łódź 134
Lublin 134, 138
Lukács, G. 12
Lunacharsky, A. V. 34, 36

MNE, *see* Hungarian Association of Cultural-Enlightenment Workers
MSZMP CC cultural policy directive, **1958** 62, 104
McAuley, Mary 16
Main Commission for Cultural Affairs (P) 47
Main Political Adminstration 3
management committees, *see* public management committees
Mari ASSR 107
Marx, K. 12, 17, 20, 37
Medvedev, V. 42
Memorial 86
methodological centres 108, 127–8, 151
Mickiewicz, E. 16
Millenium of Poland 50
Miloserdie 41, 86
Miłosz, C, 48, 76
Miscicki, W. 147
Miskolc 62
Mlynář, Z. 13
Módra, L. 143
Morawski, J. 49
Moricz, Z. 58
Moskoff, W. 71
Moscow 41, 70, 84, 89, 119, 141, 145
Moscow Popular Front 85
Mozart, W. A. 72

NI 60, 62, 110, 121

Nagy, Imre 13, 61
narodny dom, see people's house
National Board for Free Education 60
National Cultural Council (H) 66, (P) 55
nationalism 46, 63, 65, 74, 110, 112
Nazis 36
NEP 19, 35
Népmüvelés 61–2
Népszabadság 87
nomenklatura 85, 89, 97, 100, 112
Novaia Kakhovka 107–8
Novosibirsk 86
Nowe Miasto Lubawskie 47

Ochab, E. 48
October Revolution **(1917)** 34, 74
Okudzhava, B. 81
Omsk 90
open house 65, 94
organic work 45
Orthodox Church (Russian) 32
outreach work 76

PZPR, Central Committee propaganda department 52; 9th congress 54; 'Ideological Manifesto' **(1948)** 47
paid services, *see* finance
Pamiat' 86, 89, 132
Panina, S. V. 32
parents of small children 139
participation, active: 26, 63, 89, 123–9
party, *see* KPSS, MSZMP, PZPR, leading role
party guidance Chapter 4
party school for cultural-enlightenment workers (P) 48
Pavlovian psychology 18
Peasant Self-Help 47
peasants 139, 142
pensioners, *see* elderly
Penza 92
people's colleges 4, 47, 59–60, 62–3, 68, 110, 112
people's house 32–4, 104

People's Unity Front (P) 109
people's universities, *see* adult
    education
peredvizhniki 32
Perm' 32, 80
Petöfi Club 4, 62, 88
planning in cultural-enlightenment
    institutions 114–17
planners 21
Polish-Soviet Friendship Society 55
Polish Students' Union 112
political culture 6, 15–20
Pomerania 47
Pope John Paul II 54
popular music 39, 41, 78
populists, Hungarian 57–60, 65;
    Russian 31
poverty 142, 149
Poznań 49, 70, 73, 116, 128
Pozsgay, I. 66, 110, 125
principle of last priority, *see* residual
    principle
'privatization' of leisure 39–40, 44,
    81
Prognosis for Cultural Development
    (P) 53
Proletarian Culture (*Proletkul't*) 34
Prosvita 45
Pskov *oblast'* 145
public councils, *see* public
    management committees
public management committees 38,
    98, 118, 124–6

Rajk, L. 60
Rákosi, M. 61–2
rationality 24
regional cultural societies 50, 112
reading clubs 57
Remington, T. F. 124
residual principle 21, 106
Revai, J. 60–1
Riga 41
rites and festivals, socialist 2, 10, 12,
    37, 40, 72
rock music 28
Rossattraktsion 43, 79
RSFSR 23, 40, 76, 89, 98, 122–3,
    144
Rural Youth Union 50, 55, 140
Russian cultural diffusion, *see*
    Sovietization
Russian Empire 31–4

SD 101
samizdat 77
sejm 54
self-management *see* participation,
    public management committees
'A sentence on tyranny' 87
Shishkan, N. 121
Shlapentokh, V. 11
Siberia 40
Silesia 142
Smallholders' party 88
Smolensk *oblast'* 137
social policy and problems 68, 90–4
socialization 1–2, 5–6, 10, 16, 27–8,
    Ch. 3, 108, Ch. 6; political/decline
    of political 4, 5, 59–61, 65, 68–70,
    89.
socialist brigades (H) 67, 80
sociography/sociographical camps
    59, 64–5, 110
Sokol (P) 45
soldiers 136
Solidarity 54–5
Soviet Cultural Fund 42
'Soviet way of life' 75
sovietization 60, 73, 91, 110
Spasenie 86
staff, *see* cultural-enlightenment
    institutions
Stalin, J. V. 17–18, 34
Starr, J. F. 78
Staszic, S. 45
statistics 135–6
Striganov, V. N. 98
students, *see* young people
survey research 5, 40–1, 44, 58,
    81–2, 98, 102, 104, 110, 120, 122,
    127–9
Sverdlovsk 104

Tadzhikistan 72, 106, 129, 137
Tallin 41

tánchÃ¡z 65
Taras, R. 11
Tashkent 123
teachers 58, 142
Tbilisi 134
Tczew 100
TIT 62, 113, 127
Tiumen' *oblast'* 74
Tiutikov, L. N. 105
TKKS 113
Togliatti 106
Tomsk 22
Tomsky, M. P. 35
TÃ³th, J. 139
trade unions, *see especially* 111
Triodin, V. E. 141
TTIT 61
Turkmenistan 106
Tver' 32
TWP 113, 127
Tyszka, A. 141

Ukraine 98
Union of Siberians 86
United Peasant Party, *see* ZSL
unofficial clubs, *see* informal
    organizations
urbanization 50
Uzbekistan 129

VAAP 74
videos 67
village study camps, *see*
    sociographical camps

Vilna 115
Virgin Lands 38, 139
VitÃ¡nyi, I. 17â€“18, 29
Vladimir 129
VÃ¶lgyes, I. 97
volunteers, *see* activists
VOOPiK 113
Voronezh 77
Voroshilovgrad 103, 128
VOS 91
Vysotsky, V. 81

Warsaw 10, 70, 83, 86
Western cultural influences 22,
    24â€“5, 37, 41, 50, 57, 64, 70, 74,
    77, 119
White, Stephen 10, 16
women 23, 91â€“2, 117, 121â€“2, 140
workers 62, 139, 141â€“4
working week 20â€“1, 23
Writers' Union (H) 62, 87
WrocÅ‚aw 50

young people and students 43, 52,
    63â€“4, 90, 111â€“12, 140â€“3

Zdnia na dzieÅ„ 99, 116
Zakharov, V. G. 40, 105
Zaslavsky, V. 16
zemstvo 32
Znanie Society 37, 113, 127
ZSL 100â€“1
ZSP see Polish Students' Union

For Product Safety Concerns and Information please contact our EU
representative GPSR@taylorandfrancis.com
Taylor & Francis Verlag GmbH, Kaufingerstraße 24, 80331 München, Germany